Fodor's InFocus

NASHVILLE

Welcome to Nashville

Heralded as the Music City and the world's country-music capital, Nashville also shines as a leading center of higher education, appropriately known as the Athens of the South. The city's prospered from both labels, emerging as one of the South's most vibrant regions. From sprawling East Nashville to the more compact Gulch, you'll find plenty to savor in the diverse neighborhoods, from honky-tonks and dives to food havens and live music venues. As you plan your upcoming travels to Nashville, please let us know when we need to make updates by writing to us at editors@fodors.com.

TOP REASONS TO GO

★ **The Music:** From street corners to music halls, the city oozes every type of music.

★ **The Food**: James Beard–nominated chefs rub elbows with barbecue masters and everyone in between.

★ **The History:** Civil War battles, Suffragettes, and Civil Rights activists have all made their mark.

★ **The Art:** There's everything from galleries and museums to outdoor art and a print shop.

Contents

MAPS

EXPERIENCE
NASHVILLE

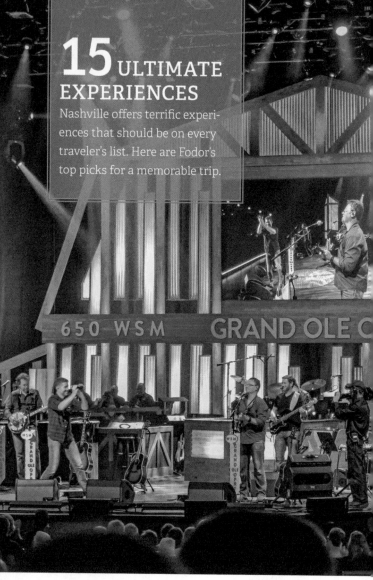

15 ULTIMATE EXPERIENCES

Nashville offers terrific experiences that should be on every traveler's list. Here are Fodor's top picks for a memorable trip.

1 Hear Live Music at the Grand Ole Opry and Ryman Auditorium

Listen to live bluegrass and country music at the iconic Grand Ole Opry or catch a show at one of the best venues in the country (and where the Opry first began)—the Ryman Auditorium. *(Ch. 3, 13)*

2 Visit a Brewery or Distillery

Grab a pint of local beer from Bearded Iris Brewing or a shot of Tennessee whiskey from Corsair Distillery. If you have the extra time, make the drive to Jack Daniel's Distillery in Lynchburg. *(Ch. 5, 14)*

3 Stroll through Cheekwood

Tucked away in a residential neighborhood, this art-and-garden-lover's haven has expansive gardens and a historic mansion that houses rotating and permanent collections. *(Ch. 14)*

4 Walk Down Honky Tonk Highway at Night

Lower Broadway is a lively four-block stretch of live country music, shops, celebrity-owned bars and restaurants, and, honky-tonks, including Robert's Western World and Tootsie's Orchid Lounge. *(Ch. 3)*

5 Join a Walking Tour

Having a difficult time choosing where to go? Get some local intel by joining a walking tour focused on showing off the best street art, food, or history the city has to offer.

6 Learn about American Music's Roots

Dive into the history of Music City with a visit to the National Museum of African American Music, the Country Music Hall of Fame and Museum, and the Musicians Hall of Fame and Museum. *(Ch. 3)*

7 Shop 'til You Drop

If you're looking for souvenirs, head to the Nashville Farmers' Market for locally made goods or visit locally owned shops in 12South like imogene + willie and Draper James. *(Ch. 5, 9)*

8 Kayak the Cumberland River

Be rewarded with amazing skyline views while exploring Nashville from a different vantage point by kayaking down the Cumberland River. *(Ch. 2)*

9 Attend a Sports Game

Nashville has four professional teams—NFL's Tennessee Titans, NHL's Nashville Predators, MLS's Nashville Soccer Club, and MiLB's Nashville Sounds—so there's always a game to watch. *(Ch. 3, 5, 11, 12)*

10 Create Your Own Goo Goo Cluster

America's first combination candy bar, the Goo Goo Cluster, was invented in Nashville in 1912. Visit the shop to learn its history and make your own ooey-gooey candy bar. *(Ch. 3)*

11 Visit Centennial Park's Parthenon

This 132-acre oasis is home to the only exact replica of the Greek Parthenon, a testimony to Nashville's "Athens of the South" nickname. It has an art museum and a 42-foot-tall Athena statue. *(Ch. 7)*

12 Nashville's Civil Rights History

Visit the Witness Walls at Public Square Park, the John Lewis–dedicated mural, Fisk University, and Nashville Public Library's Civil Rights Room to learn about the city's history. *(Ch. 3, 5)*

13 The Pedestrian-only Bridge

This bridge crosses the Cumberland River connecting Downtown to East Nashville. Its iconic look and location offer one of the best views of the city and the perfect photo op. *(Ch. 3)*

14 Eat Hot Chicken

No trip to Nashville is complete without a taste of hot chicken. The options are endless, from the place that started it all, Prince's Hot Chicken Shack, to the trendy hot spot Hattie B's.

15 Visit The Gibson Garage or Carter Vintage

Carter Vintage Guitars is a leader in vintage and collectible guitars. The Gibson Garage is a great place to try out a guitar, take a lesson, and learn about Gibson's history. *(Ch. 4)*

WHAT'S WHERE

1 Downtown and SoBro. Lower Broadway is a must for first-timers.

2 The Gulch. Once a rail yard, this ritzy area has rooftop bars, music venues, and dining.

3 Germantown and Marathon Village. Notable restaurants and the Tennessee State Museum.

4 Sylvan Park and The Nations. Come here for shopping, dining, and green spaces.

5 Midtown, West End, Music Row, and Edgehill. Close to attractions with lots of local shops and Music Row.

6 Hillsboro Village and Belmont. Home to university students and the historic Belcourt Theatre.

7 12South. A walkable neighborhood with cafés, restaurants, and shops.

8 Melrose and Berry Hill. Eclectic neighborhoods with recording studios and the antiques-laden 8th Avenue.

9 Wedgewood-Houston. High-end restaurants and craft distilleries mingle with railroad tracks and warehouses.

10 East Nashville. Several smaller neighborhoods offering excellent dining and nightlife.

11 Opryland and Music Valley. Home to the Grand Ole Opry and country music-themed attractions.

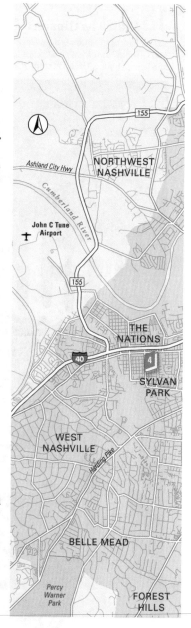

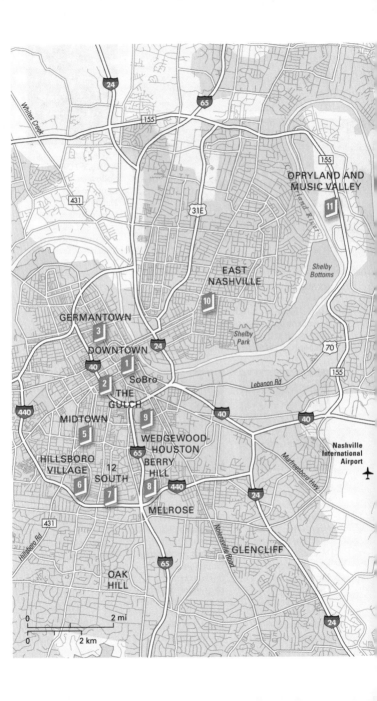

Best Places for Live Music

RYMAN AUDITORIUM

The historic Ryman Auditorium, also known as the "Mother Church of Country Music," is one of the best places to hear a wide range of musical artists. Grab tickets to one of the almost-nightly shows or take a tour. *(Ch. 3)*

BROADWAY HONKY-TONKS

Follow the neon lights to find Nashville's lively honky-tonks that line Lower Broadway. Start at Robert's Western World for a Recession Special—a fried bologna sandwich, chips, and a PBR for $6—and hear live country classics. Then work your way down to end the night at Tootsie's Orchid Lounge, where the crowd gets a little more rowdy.

THE ELECTRIC JANE

The Electric Jane is a modern and swanky take on a supper club, offering up a mystical dinner and a show. Come on Saturday, when you can experience a themed drag brunch. *(Ch. 7)*

MUSIC FESTIVALS

The city's dedication to music extends to festivals and events like CMA Fest, Tin Pan South, Musicians Corner, and Americana Music Festival. Outside the city, there's Franklin's Pilgrimage Music and Cultural Festival and Bonnaroo in Manchester.

THE LISTENING ROOM CAFE

A perfect spot for feeling connected to the people behind the songs, acoustic performances range from up-and-coming songwriters to number-one hit songwriters during the week. Weekends host local Tennessee bands. *(Ch. 3)*

The Bluebird Cafe

THE BLUEBIRD CAFE
Located in Green Hills, this quintessential listening room hosts intimate music sessions that are a rite of passage for any serious songwriter. Be sure to line up early to secure a spot. *(Ch. 8)*

SKULL'S RAINBOW ROOM
Nestled in the historic Printer's Alley district, Skull's Rainbow Room offers up award-winning fine dining, signature craft cocktails, nightly live jazz, and late-night burlesque (Thursday, Friday, and Saturday). *(Ch. 3)*

EXIT/IN
Midtown's Exit/In, where the Red Hot Chili Peppers once had Thanksgiving dinner after a late-night set, offers an eclectic mixture of punk, rock, and hip-hop performances for those looking for a country alternative. *(Ch. 7)*

3RD & LINDSLEY
This neighborhood bar and grill showcases a variety of music, including rock, country, and Americana, as well as regular acts such as The Time Jumpers, a Western swing band that plays every Monday night. *(Ch. 3)*

THE STATION INN
At this music listening room in The Gulch, music lovers can enjoy the best bluegrass, Americana, classic country, and roots music every night of the week. Every Sunday, come experience the free Bluegrass Jam—if you're a player, bring an instrument and join in. *(Ch. 4)*

History in Nashville

ANDREW JACKSON'S HERMITAGE
The historic home of President Andrew Jackson includes gardens and farmland. Consider a walking tour like In Their Footsteps, which highlights the lives of the enslaved and their stories. *(Ch. 14)*

HISTORIC RCA STUDIO B
Visit the historic spot on Music Row known as the birthplace of the "Nashville Sound," where artists like Dolly Parton, Chet Atkins, and Elvis recorded classic hits. *(Ch. 7)*

TENNESSEE STATE MUSEUM
Adjacent to the Capitol Building, this museum displays Tennessee's heritage with exhibits highlighting the role of African American soldiers in the Civil War, an 18th-century print shop, and a look at the state's natural history. *(Ch. 5)*

CIVIL WAR SITES
One of the Civil War's bloodiest battles took place in Franklin. Visit the Carnton estate, Carter House, or Lotz House, each with a unique story to tell, or take a tour with Franklin Walking Tours. *(Ch. 14)*

CIVIL RIGHTS ROOM
Explore the Nashville Public Library's collection about the city's civil rights movement including the nonviolent protest that helped it become the first Southern city to desegregate public services. *(Ch. 3)*

BELMONT MANSION
The largest house built in Tennessee before the Civil War is also one of the few 1850s-era homes still standing in Nashville. Visit to learn about the people—both free and enslaved—who occupied it. *(Ch. 8)*

National Museum of African American Music

NATIONAL MUSEUM OF AFRICAN AMERICAN MUSIC

This is the only museum of its kind dedicated to preserving and celebrating the history of Black music in America, with interactive exhibits like a psychedelic disco dance lesson chamber and a rap battle studio. *(Ch. 3)*

19TH AMENDMENT RATIFICATION

In 1920, Tennessee became the 36th and final state needed to ratify the 19th Amendment, with the final vote being cast in Nashville. Stop by the Women's Rights Pioneers Monument in Centennial Park or the Hermitage Hotel—the War of the Roses headquarters. *(Ch. 3, 7)*

BICENTENNIAL CAPITOL MALL STATE PARK

A simple stroll in the shadow of the Capitol gives visitors a taste of Tennessee's history, geography, culture, and musical heritage. Grab some snacks at the Nashville Farmers' Market next door for a picnic in the park. *(Ch. 3)*

FISK UNIVERSITY

Nashville's oldest university is also one of the first to offer a liberal arts education to people of color. Its students were instrumental in many of the city's sit-in demonstrations. Check out the extensive art collection in the Carl Van Vechten Art Gallery or visit Jubilee Hall to see a floor-to-ceiling portrait of the original Jubilee Singers. *(Ch. 5)*

What to Eat and Drink

BISCUITS

Whether served with homemade jam, gravy, or pimento cheese, fluffy flaky biscuits are a Southern staple. Get your fix at one of the Biscuit Love locations or at Monell's.

FRITO PIE

Despite its name, Frito pies aren't actual pies. It's a delicious mess of chili, cheese, corn chips, and other varying toppings. Grab one from Dino's, East Nashville's oldest dive bar, or from Redheaded Stranger, where the Frito pie comes in an actual Fritos bag.

HOT CHICKEN

Originating at Prince's Hot Chicken Shack, this iconic dish can be found all over the city, including the trendy favorite Hattie B's. It can be spotted by its dark crust made from a cayenne pepper paste and is often accompanied by white bread and pickles.

MEAT AND THREE

The cafeteria-style "meat and three" tradition originated in Nashville and it's still an integral part of the city's food scene. Spots like Elliston Place Soda Shop and Swett's Restaurant offer the traditional Southern option with the choice of one meat and three comfort food sides.

TENNESSEE WHISKEY

There's no shortage of whiskey in Nashville, but a trip to the city wouldn't be complete without trying Tennessee whiskey. Take a tasting tour at Corsair Distillery, make the drive to Jack Daniel's Distillery in Lynchburg, or create your own whiskey flight at Embers Ski Lodge in 12South, where they have the city's largest selection of whiskey.

SWEETS AND TREATS

If you're on the hunt for baked desserts, check out Five Daughters Bakery and their Hundred Layer Donut, or pick up a dozen cookies at The Christie Cookie Company. Stop by Olive & Sinclair Chocolate Company for small-batch chocolate, or create your own chocolate bar at Goo Goo Chocolate Company.

Nashville has five Edley's Bar-B-Que locations.

BARBECUE

Typically cooked "low and slow," Nashville barbecue is an eclectic mixture of flavors. The city is full of great barbeque joints, like Martin's Bar-B-Que Joint and Edley's Bar-B-Que, each putting their own spin on it.

FRIED CATFISH

Breaded and fried catfish is a classic Southern dish that can be found at places like Paula Deen's Family Kitchen or Monell's, but we suggest you take it a step further with hot fish at Bolton's Famous Hot Chicken and Fish.

BRUNCH

Nashville's brunch scene ranges from upscale dining to Southern comfort food. You won't go hungry at spots like Adele's, Milk & Honey, or White Limozeen, an all-pink rooftop bar and restaurant atop the Graduate Nashville.

Nashville Today

Tourism is one of Nashville's most lucrative industries, but that doesn't mean you have to spend a ton of money to have a great time. Here's where the locals go for fun at no cost.

FIRSTBANK FIRST SATURDAY ART CRAWL

On the first Saturday of every month, art galleries throughout Downtown open their doors to the public from 5 to 8 pm. Art lovers can browse galleries presenting the work of local and world-renowned artists. By getting your parking ticket validated at CHAUVET Arts, attendees can park for $10 at the 5th Avenue of the Arts Garage.

LIVE MUSIC AT THE FRIST

On occasional Thursday evenings, you can lounge in The Frist's café while listening to live music. Admission to the café is free, though food and drinks are not.

BIG BAND DANCES IN METRO PARKS

Summer months bring lots of activities to Nashville's parks, and Big Band Dances is one of them. They take place on Saturday nights, and attendees are encouraged to bring blankets and lawn chairs, as well as a few bucks for food-truck goodies, since part of the concession proceeds help sponsor the event. If you're not the most confident about your moves, group dance lessons are offered from 6:30 to 7 pm, shortly before the dance begins.

WARNER PARK NATURE CENTER EVENTS

If you want to get down and dirty and learn about birds, insects, and trees, consider attending one of the Nature Center's free summer events. There's a lot to choose from, but some standouts include Explore with a Naturalist, where naturalists help park visitors discover, observe, and connect with nature; and Bird Banding, where you can observe federally licensed bird banders collect information for the park's Monitoring Avian Productivity and Survivorship research program.

JAZZ ON THE CUMBERLAND

From May until October, this concert series is held monthly on Sundays in Cumberland Park from 5:30 to 8 pm. The concert itself is free, but drivers must pay $10 to park in nearby lots. Food trucks and other concessions are also on hand, though no alcoholic beverages are allowed.

FOURTH OF JULY IN NASHVILLE

Nashville is a great place to celebrate Independence Day, and there's no better place to be than the Let Freedom Sing!

Music City July 4th Celebration. Downtown events typically begin at noon with a string of free concerts, culminating with a Nashville Symphony performance that's synchronized with one of the country's largest fireworks displays.

PREDATORS' PRACTICE SESSIONS

If you're a sports fan on a budget, you can still snag an opportunity to see some live action on the ice: the Nashville Predators' practice sessions at Centennial Sportsplex and Ford Ice Center are open to the public. Dates vary but are posted on their website as they become available.

OKTOBERFEST IN NASHVILLE

This German street fair and fall festival includes a dachshund derby, a 5K Bier Run, a beer slide, and live German music, all set in Nashville's Germantown neighborhood, just north of Downtown. Admission to the four-day event is free and offers free and kid-friendly activities throughout, though VIP tickets are available. VIP access includes beer and whiskey tastings, an all-you-can-eat buffet, and private (air-conditioned) bathrooms.

ARRINGTON VINEYARDS

If you've got a little gas to burn, consider visiting Arrington Vineyards, a 75-acre winery approximately 30 miles south of the city. Parking and admission are free, and visitors are encouraged to bring along blankets, chairs, and food to enjoy with Arrington's world-class wines. (You can also have food delivered to you by Simply Living Life, which has a special catering menu for vineyard guests.) Wine tastings, small concessions, and private events are also available for a fee.

KIDSVILLE

Every Saturday between 10:30 and 11:30 am, musicians, storytellers, and educators host a free event for children at the Parthenon in Centennial Park. Events include live music (of course), interactive games, as well as fitness, literacy, and nutrition programs. If you're looking for other free kid-friendly outings, several parks and museums—including The Frist and Fort Nashborough Interpretive Center—are free for kids.

Free Things to Do

NASHVILLE: SCENES FROM THE NEW AMERICAN SOUTH BY ANN PATCHETT AND HEIDI ROSS

Written by best-selling author Ann Patchett with photography by Heidi Ross, this novel challenges everything you think you know about the South. This is not about Nashville's past but its explosive present. Tip: Get a (possibly signed) copy at Parnassus Books, Patchett's independent bookstore in Green Hills.

MURDER & MAYHEM IN NASHVILLE BY BRIAN ALLISON

For a tale with more grit, crack open Allison's look into the colorful history of a section of the city called Smoky Row, the site of mysterious and macabre activity in the 1930s.

STRONG INSIDE: PERRY WALLACE AND THE COLLISION OF RACE AND SPORTS IN THE SOUTH BY ANDREW MARANISS

This is the true story of Perry Wallace, a Vanderbilt University student who was the first black Southeastern Conference basketball player, and his experiences, struggles, and triumphs in the 1960s.

LORRAINE: THE GIRL WHO SANG THE STORM AWAY BY KETCH SECOR

Secor, founder of bluegrass band Old Crow Medicine Show, wrote this story of a girl growing up with her grandfather in Tennessee, for whom music provides both comfort and identity. It's beautifully illustrated by famous Nashville artist Higgins Bond. All that's missing is a soundtrack.

MARCH BY JOHN LEWIS, ANDREW AYDIN, AND NATE POWELL

This graphic novel trilogy is a vivid firsthand account of John Lewis's lifelong dedication to civil and human rights. The last part of Book One and the first part of Book Two particularly focus on Lewis's time in Nashville and his involvement in the civil rights movement with lunch counter sit-ins.

COOKBOOKS

For authentic Southern recipes you can take home, peruse cookbooks by Nashville's notable country stars, including Tammy Wynette (*The Tammy Wynette Southern Cookbook*) and Dolly Parton (*Dolly's Dixie Fixin's Cookbook*). Still hungry? Check out Caroline Randall Williams' cookbook *Soul Food Love*, which she co-wrote with her mother, author Alice Randall.

A WORD ON WORDS

Nashville Public Television's Emmy Award–winning reboot, filmed in Nashville, features famous authors discussing their prestigious works at local spots in three-minute segments—but it's more fun than it sounds. Think Celeste Ng in firefighter gear discussing her novel *Little Fires Everywhere* and Margaret Atwood (author of *The Handmaid's Tale*) discussing her 2015 novel *The Heart Goes Last* from a local jail.

THE THING CALLED LOVE

This 1993 film follows songwriter Miranda Presley (Samantha Mathis) as she leaves New York to seek stardom in Nashville. There's marriage and mayhem and guitars and drunken brawls … everything you need to get in the country spirit. Much of the film is set in the iconic Bluebird Cafe, where so many country stars got their start. It also stars River Phoenix and Sandra Bullock.

HEARTWORN HIGHWAYS

This two-part documentary from 1976 follows iconic singer-songwriters like Guy Clark and Steve Young during their rise to fame. Its sequel, *Heartworn Highways Revisited*, picks up 40 years in the future and features modern artists like Jonny Fritz and Langhorne Slim as they pursue the same dream as their predecessors.

WALK THE LINE

This biopic follows Johnny Cash (Joaquin Phoenix), beginning as a young boy on the family farm and through his journey to break into the music scene and finding the love of his life, singer June Carter (Reese Witherspoon). Watch before your visit to the Johnny Cash Museum.

FOR THE LOVE OF MUSIC: THE STORY OF NASHVILLE

From the Fisk Jubilee Singers to the Grand Ole Opry to Kings of Leon, this one-hour documentary tells the story of Nashville through the eyes of the musicians, songwriters, producers, and artists who make this city what it is today.

ELVIS COUNTRY (I'M 10,000 YEARS OLD)

Elvis may be synonymous with Memphis, but it was at Nashville's Historic RCA Studio B that he recorded more than 200 songs, including "Are You Lonesome Tonight?," "Stuck on You," and "Little Sister." It was also here during one of his "marathon sessions" that he recorded 30+ songs in just five days, most of which were on the *Elvis Country (I'm 10,000 Years Old)* album.

Nashville Today

THE NEXT NEIGHBORHOODS

The area southeast of Lower Broadway, now known as South Bank, is the city's latest rapidly changing neighborhood. It includes the Schermerhorn Symphony Center, Ascend Amphitheater, and Four Seasons, as well as the forthcoming multi-use Peabody Union structure.

Situated between Midtown and Downtown, Nashville Yards is an upcoming 19-acre mixed-use development that includes the Grand Hyatt Nashville; the newly renovated Union Station Nashville Yards hotel; numerous food, beverage, and shopping options; a 4,500-capacity live music and event venue; and 7 acres of open spaces.

GAME-CHANGING NEW TITANS STADIUM

The Tennessee Titans will be getting a brand-new stadium, expected to be completed by 2026 or 2027. Nestled on the east bank of the Cumberland River, the $2.1 billion stadium and grounds will feature a 62,000-seat stadium with a translucent dome, making it a contender for future Super Bowls and other big events.

MAJOR AIRPORT MAKEOVER

Over the past couple years, Nashville International Airport (BNA) has seen major renovations aimed at meeting the growth of the city and the travel needs of visitors. The changes include three six-story terminal garages, an on-site hotel, a very spacious grand lobby, expanded ticketing and baggage areas, additional security screening areas, a new concourse and gates, and more. Visitors and locals alike can get a taste of Nashville before or after their trip with local favorites like The Pharmacy Burger Parlor, Tennessee Brew Works, Bongo Java, 400 Degrees Hot Chicken, Draper James, and Parnassus Books.

THE FUTURE OF TPAC

Tennessee Performing Arts Center (TPAC) is moving forward with a new performance home after nearly 50 years. With the new and larger home, TPAC will be able to expand programming with world-renowned artists, Broadway productions, and ballet, opera, and dramatic theater performances, while also continuing to grow its nationally recognized arts education programs that serve students and teachers across the state. While the new location has yet to be determined, a possibility is the east bank of the Cumberland River.

TRAVEL SMART

Updated by
Ashley Hubbard

POPULATION:
1,294,000

LANGUAGE:
English

$ CURRENCY:
U.S. dollar

AREA CODE:
615

⚠ EMERGENCIES:
911

🚗 DRIVING:
On the right

⚡ ELECTRICITY:
120-240 v/60 cycles;
plugs have two or
three rectangular
prongs

⏱ TIME:
Central Standard
Time (1 hour behind
New York)

🌐 WEBSITES:
www.visitmusiccity.
com

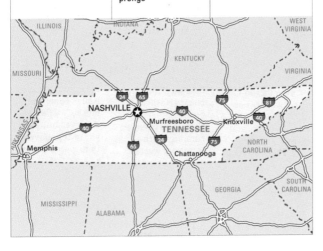

Know Before You Go

Nashville is a desirable destination for foodies, music enthusiasts, and culture seekers. Take the guesswork out of packing and planning for your next trip to the Music City with these insider tips on what to expect, what to bring, and what to avoid.

TO RENT (A CAR) OR NOT TO RENT (A CAR)

Some of the best things to see and do in Nashville are outside of Downtown, but the logistics of getting to them can be tricky or pricey if you don't have a car, as public transportation is limited and the city is too spread out. Rideshares are helpful but can become rather expensive if you use them to get everywhere you want to go. It's best to plan out your day-to-day activities for your trip and weigh the cost of a rental and parking versus the cost of rideshares. If you plan to primarily stay Downtown, you can likely skip the car rental.

HOTEL PRICING

Nashville doesn't really have a "low season" when it comes to hotel prices anymore. Nashville is big on event-based tourism, embracing large events like the NFL Draft, music festivals, and the Music City Grand Prix. These events only increase hotel demand (and prices), so consider researching and booking your hotel before your flight.

GETTING AROUND

The Cumberland River horizontally bisects Nashville's central city. Numbered avenues, running north–south, are west of and parallel to the river; numbered streets are east of the river and parallel to it as well. Traffic in Nashville can get congested quickly, especially when there are big events going on. Give yourself plenty of time to get somewhere during rush hour and try to avoid switching neighborhoods between 4 and 6 pm on weekdays.

NO OPEN CONTAINERS

For a place that's known for its nightlife and getting a little rowdy (at least Downtown), there are still some things you should know before you start a honky-tonk crawl. It's important to remember that open containers are allowed in the street. Open containers are also prohibited on unenclosed operating party vehicles. There is one small exception: alcohol can be carried openly on a short stretch of 5th Avenue, between the Country Music Hall of Fame and Music City Center. However, unless you're at a convention, there's really no specific benefit to this.

PLAN YOUR PARKING

Parking can become overcrowded and overpriced, but it doesn't have to be. Consider planning a bit before you head Downtown. Music City Center is home to Downtown's largest covered parking garage with fairly reasonable rates and 24-hour security. For a guaranteed budget-friendly option, the Nashville Public Library Garage is a $10 flat rate after 6 pm, on weekends, and for special events. Barring an event at Nissan Stadium, there is limited free street parking at the base of the John Siegenthaler Pedestrian Bridge.

KEEP CALM IF YOU SPOT A CELEBRITY

Numerous celebrities (not just country music stars) call Nashville home, and it's a point of pride that the locals (and visitors) don't disturb them. Nashville and the surrounding areas—especially Franklin and Leiper's Fork—are home to A-listers like Justin Timberlake and Jessica Biel, Dolly Parton, Jack White, Nicole Kidman and Keith Urban, and Steven Tyler. So don't be too shocked if you run into them while you're out and about—just keep calm and carry on.

RESPECT HOT CHICKEN SPICE LEVELS

Hot chicken is synonymous with Nashville. The spicy dish pops up on menus across the city now, but it has a long history in Nashville's Black community. It was originally created by the Prince family (of Prince's Hot Chicken Shack) decades ago. Whether you can make it to try the spot that started it all or not, one thing you should do is trust that this is not your standard hot-wing-level spice. Most places have levels of heat, and when it says "hot," it absolutely means hot.

SWEET TEA MEANS SWEET

Sweet tea is the South's quintessential drink. The tea is sweet—really sweet—down here. As in if you order tea, expect to get sugar with a side of tea. If you like plain iced tea, specify by ordering "unsweetened tea." If you want sweet tea but not on a Southern level, order a "half and half" to reduce the sweetness.

CHECK THE WEATHER

Nashville is lucky to get to experience all four seasons. The bad news? Sometimes all four seasons happen in one day. It's a common saying that "If you don't like the weather, wait a few minutes and it will change." When packing for your trip or even heading out for the day, check the forecast and adjust accordingly.

DON'T BE AFRAID TO GET OUTDOORS

Nashville may be known for its music and its food, but it also has fantastic green spaces. Pack a picnic and head to Bicentennial Capitol Mall State Park or Centennial Park, put on those walking shoes, or rent a bike to explore the greenways. Just don't forget the sunscreen and a bottle of water, especially during the summer months!

Getting Here and Around

Air

More than 80 cities fly nonstop into Nashville International Airport (BNA). Nashville is serviced by Air Canada, Alaska, Allegiant, American, Avelo, British Airways, Contour, Delta, Flair, Frontier, JetBlue, Silver, Southwest, Spirit, Sun Country, United, and WestJet.

AIRPORT

Nashville International Airport (BNA) is 8 miles east of Downtown. It takes at least 15 minutes to travel between Downtown and the airport, but it can take longer during rush hour.

AIRPORT TRANSFERS

All transportation options listed depart from the Ground Transportation Center on Level 1 of Terminal Garage 2. Rideshare apps and taxis are the most commonly used transportation into the city from the airport. For taxis, the meter starts at $9 and the rate is $2.50 per mile. There is a flat rate of $30 to Downtown and the Gaylord Opryland Resort area. Several limo and courtesy car services are available as well and pick up in the same area. Some of the larger hotels, especially those located in Music Valley, offer shuttle services to and from the airport. Graduate Nashville is one of the few hotels near Downtown that offers an airport shuttle.

Bicycle

There are more than 30 BCycle stations throughout the city (⊕ *nashville.bcycle.com*). Just set up an account on your smartphone, unlock any bike for $2, and ride as long as you want for $0.10 per minute. Membership rates are also available for longer stays. For another biking option, you can rent a bicycle from Green Fleet Bikes in Germantown or Shelby Ave. Bicycle Company in East Nashville (⊕ *www.greenfleet-bikes.com*).

Bus

While Megabus and Greyhound have routes to Nashville, most visitors fly in or drive.

Car

Nashville is, geographically speaking, in a perfect position. Approximately 40% of the U.S. population lives within 600 miles of Nashville, making it a pretty accessible destination by car.

It's one of only a handful of cities in the country where three interstates connect; I–65 connects with Louisville, Indianapolis, and Chicago to the north and Birmingham, Montgomery, and Mobile to the south. The city is bisected by I–40, an east-west highway that passes through Asheville, Memphis, Little Rock, and Oklahoma City. Finally, I–24 crosses the city, connecting travelers from St. Louis, Chattanooga, and Atlanta.

CAR RENTALS

All major auto rental agencies can be found in town and at the airport. On average, you can expect rental cars in Nashville to cost approximately $40 per day. This fluctuates depending on the type of vehicle, the rental car company, and events happening in the city. It can sometimes be less expensive to rent from a location other than the airport, but you'll have to factor in the cost of getting to and from the airport.

GASOLINE

In general, gas prices in Nashville are at or below the national average. Gas stations are not difficult to find.

PARKING

Downtown parking can be a challenge during major events, but it's easy enough with a little planning. The easiest and safest option is to utilize one of the many parking garages. Some can be rather expensive, but there are several budget-friendly options as well. Metro Nashville owns and operates two public parking garages—Church Street Plaza Garage (attached to the library) and Public Square Garage (attached to the courthouse). Rates range from $3 to $20 during the day. Event parking ranges from $10 to $15. If there is not a scheduled event, night and weekend parking after 6 pm ranges from $5 to $10.

For street parking, it is imperative to read posted signage before parking. In recent years, the city has started implementing new parking meters; rates are $2.25 per hour in most of Downtown with a two-hour time limit.

Most Downtown hotels have their own paid parking garages. Few restaurants Downtown have their own parking.

Ⓜ Public Transport

WeGo (previously known as Metropolitan Transit Authority, or MTA) is Nashville's bus service, and the bright purple buses can easily be spotted.

Getting Here and Around

Buses run from 5 am to midnight, depending on the route. An all-day bus pass costs $4 for adults, $2 for ages 19 and younger, and $2 for senior citizens. Download the app (QuickTicket by WeGo) to see the full schedule and purchase tickets. WeGo provides hourly service between the airport and Downtown seven days a week; one-way fares cost $2. For information on getting to and around each neighborhood covered in our guide, refer to the Neighborhood Snapshot at the beginning of each chapter.

While it's possible to use the bus system in Nashville, it's not incredibly tourist-friendly and is primarily used by locals.

Ride-Sharing

Lyft and Uber are both active in Nashville. Just download the app and request a ride. Aside from driving yourself, ride shares are the most common way to get around the city. Fun fact: The Nashville International Airport was the first airport in the country to allow ride-sharing services to operate on the property.

Scooter

There are many different companies operating electric scooters in the city, with Lime being the first to arrive on the scene. Most of the scooters are found on the streets around Downtown; they're a viable option for short trips in a limited area, but be careful with the excessive amount of car and foot traffic.

In general, scooters cost $1 to unlock and 15 cents per minute riding. Riders must be 18 years old and hold a valid driver's license. In certain areas of Downtown (primarily Lower Broad), riding scooters on the sidewalk is prohibited.

Taxi

While taxi companies are available in Nashville, it's not a common way to get around the city. They are typically something you call and schedule ahead of time, rather than flag down on the street.

Cabs are usually available at the airport. Nashville features a flat-fee—$30—service triangle between the airport, Downtown, and Gaylord Opryland Resort and Convention Center.

Essentials

🏃 Activities

Music isn't the only thing Nashville residents are passionate about; sports and outdoor recreation are a large part of Nashville's culture. Nashville is home to four professional sports teams and several NCAA Division I programs. The city also has a number of parks just waiting to be explored with numerous hiking and biking trails. And, while Nashville may be nowhere near the coast, the city's residents still know how to have fun on the water with kayaking and stand-up paddleboarding opportunities.

GREEN SPACES

For those who prefer to stay on dry land, Nashville is home to a number of great city and state parks. Without even leaving the city, visitors can check out Bicentennial Capitol Mall State Park in Germantown and Centennial Park in West End. Just a short drive away, some of the other local favorites include Radnor Lake State Park for its lake views and abundant wildlife and the Edwin and Percy Warner Parks for their excellent hiking and historical landmarks.

If you have plenty of extra time and want to take a side trip, the Great Smoky Mountains National Park is a 3- to 4-hour drive east, while Mammoth Cave National Park in Kentucky is about 1½ hours north of Music City.

PROFESSIONAL SPORTS

Baseball: Even in Music City, you can enjoy America's favorite pastime—baseball! From April to September, come out to the ball field at First Horizon Park in Germantown to watch the Nashville Sounds, an AAA Affiliate of the Milwaukee Brewers.

Football: When the air starts to cool down, that means it's football time in Tennessee. Experience the thrill of a home game at Nissan Stadium (just across the John Seigenthaler Pedestrian Bridge from Lower Broad) as the Tennessee Titans play host against other NFL teams.

Hockey: If there's one thing Nashville has proven it's that they are a hockey town—or "Smashville," as Predators fans like to call it. The Nashville Predators will have you on the edge of your seat from the very moment the puck drops in Bridgestone Arena. Catch a home game from October to April and then hit the honky-tonks right outside the arena to celebrate the win!

Soccer: The most recent addition to Nashville's roster of professional sports is Nashville's Major League Soccer team, Nashville SC. Not far from Downtown, Nashville SC

Essentials

plays at its brand-new facility, GEODIS Park, in the Wedgewood-Houston neighborhood.

WATER SPORTS

Experience Nashville from a different perspective—on the water. The city is divided by the Cumberland River, and there are plenty of other rivers and lakes in the greater Nashville area where you can take advantage of guided tours and equipment rentals for kayaking, stand-up paddle boarding, and canoeing.

In Nashville, River Queen Voyages and Cumberland Kayak offer tours and rentals on the Cumberland River from May through September.

Downtown Nashville has much to offer in the way of history, music, entertainment, dining, and specialty shopping. In East Nashville, across the river from Downtown, small shops and galleries are popping up among the restored Victorian houses. Micro-neighborhoods with shopping, dining, and new living spaces are developing all over the city, including 12South and The Gulch.

To get a more complete feeling for the city, you'll want to explore the area beyond Downtown, too. Among the offerings are historic plantations, a variety of museums covering everything from art to cars to science, and the Grand Ole Opry.

🍴 Dining

Nashville diners enjoy lingering over their meals, partaking in good food and good conversation. There's a wealth of contemporary, ethnic, and experimental eateries from which to choose, as well as traditional Southern favorites, including a number of barbecue joints as good as any you'll find in Memphis. Many restaurants have opened second locations just south of Nashville in Franklin. Farm-to-table, chef's gardens, and food trucks are among the most recent influences on the local dining scene, offering new takes on the classics. More eateries are also opening in developing areas such as The Gulch, Midtown, and 12South areas.

MEALS AND MEALTIMES

Some popular restaurants serve both lunch and dinner, though many close in between meal services. Nashville has a pretty late nightlife, especially on the weekends when things are open a few hours longer than weekdays. For late-night dining, Downtown restaurants stay open anywhere from midnight to 2 am. Outside of Downtown, you can expect kitchens to close by 10 pm.

PAYING

Most restaurants take credit cards, but some smaller places do not. More and more establishments are going cashless, so it's worth asking before you order or when you make a reservation. Waiters expect a 20% tip at high-end restaurants; some add an automatic gratuity for groups of six or more.

PRICES

⇨ *Restaurant prices are the average cost of a main course at dinner or, if dinner is not served, at lunch. Restaurant reviews have been shortened. For full information, visit Fodors.com.*

What it Costs			
$	$$	$$$	$$$$
AT DINNER			
under $13	$13–$24	$25–$35	over $35

RESERVATIONS AND DRESS

Always make a reservation at upscale restaurants or casual restaurants in busy areas of town when you can. Smaller establishments, such as barbecue and hot chicken joints, don't take reservations. For popular spots like Hattie B's and Biscuit Love, expect a long line before you can enjoy your meal.

As unfair as it seems, the way you look can influence how you're treated—and where you're seated. Generally speaking, Nashville restaurants are mostly casual, but some higher-end restaurants require jackets and ties.

SMOKING

Smoking and vaping are banned in all restaurants and bars, with the exception of cigar, hookah, and vapor bars. However, many have outdoor patios and rooftop bars where smokers can light up.

⊕ Health and Safety

Especially Downtown, you'll notice a significant presence of police officers and security patrol cars. During the day, the streets are safe for pedestrians, but at night you should exercise reasonable caution, especially in poorly lit areas. Always lock your car and remove valuables that are visible through the windows.

🛜 Internet

Metro Public Wi-Fi offers free Wi-Fi in a number of facilities and outdoor spaces such as the Parthenon, Fort Negley, and West Riverfront Park. Metro Public Wi-Fi is listed under the network name "MetroPublicWiFi." Users are required to agree to the Public Internet

Essentials

Access Policy before being able to connect. Nashville Public Library also offers free Wi-Fi at all of its branches.

🛏 Lodging

The number of hotels in Nashville is growing at a pretty good clip, with new properties Downtown (drawn by the new Music City Center convention center), in the growing Midtown area, along West End, and near Vanderbilt. These areas will put you in the heart of things; or look for an option in the Opryland/Music Valley/Airport area if you plan to spend a lot of time at the Grand Ole Opry and neighboring venues. Luxury and boutique hotel options continue to expand, while mid-range and budget options are also a growing presence. CMA Fest week in mid-June is the busiest time, with rates increasing then and during the rest of the peak summer travel season; as Nashville's profile has increased the travel season has also expanded, bringing higher occupancy and room rates than one might expect.

FACILITIES

You can assume that all rooms have private baths, phones, TVs, and air-conditioning, unless otherwise indicated. Breakfast is noted as "Free Breakfast" when it is included in *all* rates; otherwise, "No Meals" means that no additional meals are included in the basic rates, even if they are offered at the lodging's restaurant.

PARKING

Parking in Nashville can be pricey, and hotel parking fees even more so. Independent garages may be slightly cheaper. Metered street parking is available but enforcement hours depend on if it's an old or new meter, which can get confusing, so pay attention to enforcement hours displayed on nearby signage. Metro operates two public parking facilities—the Church Street Plaza Garage connected to the main library and the Public Square Garage connected to the Metro Courthouse—that offer garage parking for anywhere from $3 to $20.

PRICES

⇨ *Prices are for a standard double room in high season. Hotel reviews have been shortened. For full information, visit Fodors.com.*

What it Costs			
$	$$	$$$	$$$$
FOR TWO PEOPLE			
under $300	$300–$449	$450–$600	over $600

RESERVATIONS

Always make a reservation in Nashville. Hotels often book up and rooms can be particularly hard to come by or expensive during high-traffic times, which includes anything from the annual CMA Fest to large one-time events like sporting events or major concerts.

🅨 Nightlife

Obviously there's a lot of music in Music City. The concentration of small crowded honky-tonks on Downtown's Lower Broadway is a good place to start (Tootsie's Orchid Lounge and Robert's Western World are always a good time!), and there are several big-name club brands (Hard Rock Cafe) for blues, rock, and country nearby. For clubs in all genres—but especially rock—head to venues in SoBro (south of Broadway), Elliston Place, and Marathon Village. For the trendiest clubs to see or be seen, The Gulch is presently the best bet. For a more low-key neighborhood experience, try one of the homegrown breweries in East Nashville that feature dynamite craft beers and local music on weekends.

🧳 Packing

Unless they're a genuine staple in your wardrobe, there's no need to pack your cowboy boots. They may look cute, but they're really not practical or comfortable. They take up way too much luggage space and are extremely hot during the summer months. When putting together your packing list, know that most people in the city tend to dress casually. However, if dressing up is more your style, you won't look out of place either. In general, outside of summer, pack layers as Nashville's weather can change day to day and even hour to hour.

🎭 Performing Arts

Downtown—the Tennessee Performing Arts Center, in particular—is the center for dance, opera, and theater performances by local and touring groups; the Schermerhorn Symphony Center stages orchestral and cabaret events.

👜 Shopping

Nashville's shopping climate has changed some in recent years, although there are still plenty of antique stores, boutiques for fashionable Western

Where Should I Stay?

	Vibe	Pros	Cons
Downtown and SoBro	Full of music venues, bars, museums, historic landmarks, and top restaurants.	If you're looking to party or hit up primarily tourist spots, this area is perfect.	Be prepared for more crowds—especially at night—and prices may be higher.
The Gulch	Boutiques and restaurants, Frist Art Museum, and The Station Inn.	Perfectly situated between Downtown and Midtown.	One of the city's most expensive areas.
German-town	This is a walkable residential neighborhood with plenty to do.	Lots of great din-ing and shopping to explore.	Short-term rentals or the German-town Inn.
Sylvan Park and the Nations	This is an easily walkable residen-tial area.	Breweries, coffee shops, and the Richland Park Farmer's Market.	Short-term rentals are the only option.
Midtown, West End, Music Row, and Edgehill	Home to Music Row and Vander-bilt University.	There are fewer crowds than Downtown.	Hotels can book up quickly with Vanderbilt events.
Hillsboro Village	This area between Vanderbilt and Belmont is high on charm.	Vintage shops, The Belcourt Theatre, coffee shops, and restaurants.	There are limited lodging options, and a car is a must.
12South	This mile-long strip is packed with local shops, bars, and restaurants.	12South is easily accessible via rideshare or taxi from the rest of the city.	Airbnb is the best option for short-term lodging.
Melrose and Berry Hill	A lively and young neighborhood while still quiet.	Unique restau-rants, bars, recording studios, and shops.	There are no traditional lodging options.
WeHo	A hub for art, culture, food, and drink.	Home to GEODIS Park and the Nashville SC.	Limited to short-term rentals, Soho House, or Placemakr.
East Nashville	Mostly residen-tial; full of coffee shops, restau-rants, and bars.	The Dive Motel, Urban Cowboy, and local spots listed on Airbnb.	You'll need a car or ride-share apps to get to other neighborhoods.

wear, and souvenir shops hawking country-music-inspired memorabilia. A number of ateliers have also opened, among them imogene + willie (known for artisanal blue jeans), and Hester & Cook (the people behind Kitchen Papers). For shopping, Downtown is a good place to start, but you'll find plenty of interesting shops along the city's edges, too, especially in East Nashville, Berry Hill, The Gulch, and 12South.

⊙ Visitor Information

Up-to-date information can be found on Nashville's tourism board website, ⊕ *www. visitmusiccity.com*. There are several local magazines, papers, and websites for an in-depth look at the city's culture. The Bitter Southerner (⊕ *bittersoutherner.com*) is a design-forward website, email newsletter, and podcast that celebrates the rich culture and history of the American South through stories about music, food, and cocktails, in addition to fascinating and forward-thinking people and organizations. *TimeOut Nashville* as well as the city's community station WXNA (101.5 FM) are great resources for things to do and see.

📅 When to Go

Nashville experiences all four seasons, with hot and muggy summers that can exceed 100°F, enjoyable springs and falls that feature warm days and cool nights, and mild winters with occasional freezes. Spring can bring quite a lot of pollen, allergy sufferers beware.

Low Season: While there isn't a true low season in regards to hotel prices, crowds tend to slow during the winter months, especially January and February. Winter can be cold, reaching temperatures below freezing, but there can be large swings in temperature as well.

Shoulder Season: Spring and fall are still busy but offer slightly smaller crowds compared to summer and great weather. September and October's calendar is full of events, but the large crowds from CMA Fest and 4th of July have dissipated.

High Season: Aside from August, which has a much slower month on the calendar, summer is Nashville's high season with large crowds, high prices, and hot temperatures.

Best Tours

BIKE TOURS

Green Fleet Bicycle Tours. This 2½-hour bike tour of Music City will have you cycling through the streets of Downtown and seeing neighborhoods like Germantown, Marathon Village, and beyond while experiencing Nashville's local history, art, and culture. Cost includes the use of a bike. ⊠ *Nashville* ☎ *615/870–8848* ⊕ *www.greenfleetbiketours. com* ⊠ *From $55 per person.*

BUS TOURS

Gray Line. Tours include driving tours of the city (Downtown, Music Row, etc.) and past stars' homes, walking tours, and visits to the Grand Ole Opry. Gray Line also runs the Music City Trolley Hop and shuttles between Opry Mills outlet mall and Downtown. ☎ *615/883–5555, 800/251– 1864* ⊕ *graylinetn.com.*

Music City Trolley Hop. This hop on, hop off trolley tour operated by Gray Line of Tennessee includes stops at major Nashville attractions. Ticket office is at the Hard Rock Cafe Downtown. ☎ *615/883–5555, 800/251–1864* ⊕ *graylinetn. com.*

NashTrash Tours. Traditional tours are great, but sometimes the best way to explore a new place is through laughter aboard a big pink bus. Nash-Trash Tours provides plenty of laughs in its tours of Music City, which showcase the city's sights, sounds, and significant spots through the eyes of two zany sisters. NashTrash offers three different tours, each tailored to different neighborhoods and themes. ⊠ *900 Rosa L. Parks Blvd., Germantown* ☎ *615/226–7300* ⊕ *nashtrash.com.*

The Redneck Comedy Bus Tour. Explore Music City on this two-hour fun-filled Nashville Redneck Tour. Don't forget your sense of humor! ⊠ *Nashville* ☎ *615/316–0014* ⊕ *www. theredneckbus.com* ⊠ *From $30 per person.*

BOAT TOURS

Cumberland Kayak. Whet your appetite for water adventures with Cumberland Kayak, conveniently located on the edge of East Nashville. Cumberland offers an array of kayaking options for people of all abilities, as well as hiking tours to local waterfalls. Plan ahead, as availability could depend on seasonal offerings, particularly during peak times like summer. ⊠ *2 Victory Ave., East Nashville* ☎ *615/800–7321* ⊕ *www. cumberlandkayakadventure. com* ⊠ *$45 for Nashville Skyline Paddle* ☉ *Closed Tues. and Wed. and Oct.–Apr.*

River Queen Voyages. If you're looking to get out on the Cumberland River, River Queen

Voyages is your one-stop shop for freshwater excursions. River Queen offers a variety of rentals, from single and tandem kayaks to "party pontoons" complete with a skilled captain. If you're feeling especially adventurous, try out the Nashville Scavenger Hunt, which adds a competitive element to your day on the water. Book ahead, especially during the summer. ⊠ *2 Victory Ave., East Nashville* ☎ *615/933–9778* ⊕ *riverqueenvoyages.com* ☒ *From $37* ⊙ *No tours Wed. Closed Nov.–Mar.*

SPECIAL-INTEREST TOURS

Grand Ole Opry Tours. Daytime, postshow, and VIP backstage tours of the Grand Ole Opry are offered February through October. ⊠ *2804 Opryland Dr., Nashville* ☎ *800/733–6779* ⊕ *www.opry.com.*

Nashville Pedal Tavern. This BYOB moving tavern (read: party bike) offers guests the option of a bar crawl, where they can hop off to take advantage of exclusive discounts, or they can bring their own alcohol (in plastic containers only), while the tavern provides cups, ice, and, of course, music. There are two routes: one that traverses Lower Broadway, the heart of Downtown's honky-tonk scene, and Midtown, which makes

stops on Music Row. Groups of at least six can opt for public tours with other groups, or reserve one (or several) trollies for private tours with family and friends. All guests must be 21 or older to ride. ⊠ *Nashville* ☎ *615/390–5038* ⊕ *www.nashvillepedaltavern.com* ☒ *From $49 per person (public tour).*

Opryland River Cruises. The *General Jackson,* Opryland's four-deck paddle-wheeler, has several two-hour cruises along the Cumberland River daily, including lunch and dinner cruises serving Southern cuisine, with a music review in the Victorian Theater. Tickets can be purchased either for the full experience or for the outer-deck sightseeing option.

Opryland's other boat is the *Music City Queen,* a 350-passenger paddle-wheel excursion boat used mainly for special events, including midday singer/songwriter cruises, evening comedy cruises, Country Christmas cruises, and a New Year's Eve cruise. ☎ *615/458–3900* ⊕ *generaljackson.com.*

WALKING TOURS

Franklin Walking Tours. About 20 miles south of Nashville, Franklin is full of history, architecture, food, and shopping. If you want to make the most of your time, sign up for the two-hour Franklin Charm tour, which details the town's

Best Tours

history, including the Civil War. There are also ghost tours, a female-focused tour, and a few other unique versions. Private tours are also available; most tours start at Landmark Booksellers on Main Street. ⊠ *Franklin* ☎ *615/604–7171* ⊕ *franklinwalkingtours.com* 🖅 *From $20 per person.*

Ghost City Tours. These macabre and spooky tour options include The Ghosts of Nashville Tour, Murder in Music City Ghost Tour, and Seeking Spirits Haunted Pub Crawl. ⊠ *Nashville* ☎ *855/999–9026* ⊕ *ghostcitytours.com/nashville/* 🖅 *From $25 per person.*

Photowalk Your Travel. Ever wanted someone to follow you around and take perfect Insta-worthy shots of you? This tour does just that. Leave Nashville with high-quality photos and plenty of suggestions for the best places to shop, eat, and drink around town. Options include the Nashville Insider Tour, a 12South mural tour, and options for couples and bachelorette parties. ⊠ *Nashville* ☎ *615/924–8997* ⊕ *photowalkyourtravel.com/nashville* 🖅 *From $75 per person.*

Underground Donut Tour. The Nashville Downtown Donut Tour begins at Parlor Doughnuts in SoBro and ends at Donut Distillery, with a couple stops in between, all while learning about Nashville. ⊠ *Nashville* ☎ *844/366–8848* ⊕ *www.undergrounddonuttour. com* 🖅 *From $45 per person.*

Walk Eat Nashville. This walking food tour offers options in East Nashville, Downtown, and 12South where you go behind the scenes at top-rated restaurants and try local favorites. ⊠ *Nashville* ☎ *615/587–6138* ⊕ *www.walkeatnashville.com* 🖅 *From $99 per person.*

Walkin' Nashville. Take the Music City Legends Tour for a look at the old Nashville from the days of Dolly Parton, Johnny Cash, and Loretta Lynn. The tour is packed full of history, fun trivia, and anecdotes while visiting destinations like Printers Alley and Tootsie's Orchid Lounge. Tours run on Fridays and Saturdays during the months of April through October. ⊠ *Nashville* ☎ *615/499–5159* ⊕ *www.walkinnashville. com* 🖅 *From $30 per person.*

Wander Nashville. Wander Nashville offers visitors a budget-friendly walking tour option. This two-hour tour leads groups Downtown past more than 200 points of interest and includes a personal listening device. ⊠ *Nashville* ☎ *205/892–5337* ⊕ *www.wandernashville. com* 🖅 *$10 per person.*

Great Itineraries

Nashville offers several fantastic neighborhoods to explore, plenty of history to brush up on, a wonderful nightlife scene, and enough food to keep you full.

NASHVILLE IN 3 DAYS

Nashville is perfectly built for a three-day itinerary that is full of the Music City essentials.

Day 1: Today is all about the music. Start at the Country Music Hall of Fame and Museum (CMHFM), learning all about the history of country music and the artists who made it what it is. Check out the Music City Walk of Fame in the park across the street before you head over to grab lunch at Hattie B's on Lower Broad (be prepared for a line). After lunch, head next door to the Ryman Auditorium for a self-guided tour. If you have time, consider a trip to the Historic RCA Studio B (you'll need to book this along with your ticket to CMHFM). Before you head out for an evening of honky-tonk hopping, take a quick walk over the John Seigenthaler Pedestrian Bridge to see how the city skyline looks all lit up at night.

Day 2: Your second day is about art, culture, and green spaces. Start the day off at Centennial Park and the Parthenon to find out why Nashville is known as the "Athens of the South."

Next, take the short drive over to 12South to pose in front of murals, shop at boutiques, and grab a bite to eat at Edley's Bar-B-Que. After lunch, drive over to Germantown, park the car, and find out why this historic neighborhood is one of the best places to explore. Drop into the Nashville Farmers' Market for local handmade goods and crafts and take a stroll through Bicentennial Capitol Mall State Park. Don't miss checking out the free Tennessee State Museum for a look at the Volunteer State's history. After all your shopping and walking, it's time to quench your thirst; stop by Corsair Distillery and Taproom for a tour and a taste of Tennessee whiskey before heading out to grab dinner, and hear live music at Skull's Rainbow Room (reservations can be made up to two weeks in advance).

Day 3: Take a step back at Andrew Jackson's Hermitage (timed tickets are necessary to tour the mansion) for a look at the seventh president's home as well as what life was like during the 19th century. After you spend the morning outside the city, head back to Lower Broad for lunch at Acme Feed and Seed (it's first come, first served), then take a stroll to appreciate the city outside of the neons. It's a short walk to the Nashville Public Library,

Great Itineraries

where you can visit the Civil Rights Room to learn more about Nashville's involvement in the civil rights movement. For a great last evening, head to Pinewood Social (reservations taken) for drinks, dinner, and bowling.

NASHVILLE IN 5 DAYS

Spend the first three days as outlined above.

Day 4: Time to get out of Nashville. Take a day trip south to the charming town of Franklin. Spend the morning exploring Downtown Franklin's shops before grabbing lunch at Frothy Monkey. After lunch, check out the historic Civil War sites in Franklin. To end your Franklin field trip, an evening picnic at Arrington Vineyards is the perfect way to relax.

Day 5: For your last day in Nashville, it's time for some more special Music City experiences. Start your day in The Gulch with breakfast at Biscuit Love, shopping, and mural hunting. Next, make the walk Downtown to tour Hatch Show Print (book your tickets in advance) and create your own keepsake poster. For lunch, head to Puckett's Grocery and Restaurant (reservations taken) for some Southern cooking before heading to The Goo Goo Chocolate Company to create your own dessert. For your last night, keep things more low-key but still quintessential Nashville by heading to The Listening Room Cafe (purchase your tickets in advance) or The Station Inn (seats are first come, first served).

On the Calendar

January

Antiques & Garden Show Nashville. Celebrating antiques, art, and horticulture, the Antiques & Garden Show is the longest-running and largest of its kind in the country. Proceeds from the event benefit Cheekwood. ⊕ *antiquesandgardenshow.com*

February

Dine Nashville: The Music City Way. For the month of February, Nashville's restaurants level things up, featuring collaborative chef experiences, a restaurant week, and discounts from food and beverage establishments across the city. ⊕ *www.visitmusiccity.com/dine-nashville*

March

Main Street Brewfest. On St. Patrick's Day weekend, come taste local, national, and international beers in Franklin amid live Celtic music. ⊕ *downtownfranklintn.com*

April

Nashville Fashion Week. Every April, Nashville Fashion Week hosts a citywide celebration featuring local, regional, and national industry professionals in a variety of events. ⊕ *www.nashvillefashionweek.com*

Tin Pan South Songwriters Festival. The world's largest songwriter festival presents established and up-and-coming songwriters at various venues around the city. ⊕ *www.tinpansouth.com*

May

Iroquois Steeplechase. Every spring since 1941, horses and riders have gathered at the 3-mile turf track at Percy Warner Park. Don't forget to wear your sundresses, suspenders, and big hats. ⊕ *www.iroquoissteeplechase.org*

Musicians Corner. This free concert series is held each summer in Centennial Park. ⊕ *www.musicianscornernashville.com*

The Tennessee Renaissance Festival. Every weekend in May, you can drive just outside of Franklin to watch a jousting match, toast someone in chain mail, and tour Castle Gwynn. ⊕ *www.tnrenfest.com*

June

CMA Fest. The world's longest-running country music festival features day and evening performances by a range of

On the Calendar

artists, including Tanya Tucker, Keith Urban, Eric Church, and Miranda Lambert. ⊕ *cmafest. com*

Nashville Pride Festival. This annual LGBTQIA+ festival is held in Bicentennial Capitol Mall State Park with hundreds of vendors, a dance tent, parades, and live performances. ⊕ *nashvillepride.org*

July

Let Freedom Sing! Music City July 4th. Nashville takes the 4th of July to new levels with one of the country's largest fireworks displays backed by the Nashville Symphony, free outdoor concerts (usually with big names!), and plenty of fun for the whole family. ⊕ *www. visitmusiccity.com/july4th*

Music City Hot Chicken Festival. Nashville's love of ultra-spicy chicken is the star of this free festival every Independence Day in East Park. Sample hot chicken from different establishments around town, wash it all down with local brews, and enjoy live music. ⊕ *www. hot-chicken.com*

August

Tomato Art Fest. Since 2003, the Tomato Art Fest has been paying homage to the power of the tomato as a "uniter, not a divider" through art. This quirky East Nashville two-day festival includes tomato costume contests, food trucks, vendors, entertainment, parades, and a 5K. ⊕ *www.tomatoartfest.com*

September

AmericanaFest. This festival brings together legendary artists, upcoming stars, industry professionals, and fans to enjoy panels, seminars, showcases, parties, the Annual Americana Honors and Awards Show, and more. ⊕ *americanamusic.org*

Pilgrimage Music and Cultural Festival. Franklin's newest festival is a two-day music fest that takes place on Harlinsdale Farm each September. It's young but growing in popularity. Past headliners have included Justin Timberlake, Zach Bryan, and Willie Nelson. ⊕ *pilgrimagefestival.com*

Nashville Film Festival. One of the country's oldest-running film festivals is an annual event showcasing international and local films in various formats. ⊕ *nashvillefilmfestival. org*

Nashville Shakespeare Festival. A summer tradition since 1988, these free ($10 suggested donation) Shakespeare performances are the perfect blend of nostalgia and contemporary relevance. Preshow entertainment includes local and regional talent, and food trucks are available on-site. ⊕ *www. nashvilleshakes.org*

October

Jubilee Day. On October 6, 1871, the Fisk Jubilee Singers departed Fisk University for a worldwide tour to raise funds and save the school from closing. Every October 6, the University observes Jubilee Day with a convocation, concert, and more. ⊕ *www.fisk.edu*

Oktoberfest. Nashville's Oktoberfest takes over 10 city blocks in Historic Germantown, offering a wide array of beers, bratwurst, and German food and craft vendors. This free family-friendly event includes a 5K, live music, and a dachshund derby. ⊕ *thenashvilleoktoberfest.com*

Pumpkinfest. Trick-or-treating, professional pumpkin carving, and a costume contest for every age. Revel in Tennessee's perfect fall weather with every incarnation of fried street food, live music, and a chili cook-off. ⊕ *williamsonheritage.org*

Southern Festival of Books. "A Celebration of the Written Word" is the goal of this three-day festival that brings book lovers of all types together for panels, book signings, performances, and vendors. ⊕ *sofestofbooks.org*

December

Dickens of a Christmas. Apple cider donuts, arts and crafts, and carolers in hoopskirts. This is middle Tennessee's largest outdoor Christmas festival, where Charles Dickens's characters come to life against a backdrop of Franklin's historic Victorian architecture. ⊕ *williamsonheritage.org*

ICE! Step into a winter wonderland carved by expert artisans at Gaylord Opryland. Explore the holiday ice sculptures, Christmas events, ice slides, and more. Each year sees a different holiday-centered theme. ⊕ *ice.gaylordhotels.com*

Music City Bowl. The Music City Bowl is a collegiate football game held at Nissan Stadium. In true Nashville fashion, the festivities typically include a free concert Downtown either the night before or after the game. ⊕ *www.musiccitybowl.com*

Contacts

✈ Air

CONTACTS Nashville International Airport (BNA). ✉ *1 Terminal Dr., Nashville* ☎ *615/275–1675* ⊕ *flynashville.com.*

🚲 Bicycle

CONTACTS BCycle. ✉ *Nashville* ⊕ *nashville.bcycle.com.* **Green Fleet Bikes.** ✉ *Nashville* ☎ *615/379–8687* ⊕ *www.greenfleetbikes.com.*

🚌 Bus

CONTACTS Greyhound. ✉ *709 Rep. John Lewis Way S, Nashville* ☎ *800/231–2222* ⊕ *www.greyhound.com.* **Megabus.** ✉ *Nashville* ☎ *877/462–6342* ⊕ *www.megabus.com.*

Ⓜ Public Transport

CONTACTS WeGo Public Transit. ✉ *400 Charlotte Ave., Nashville* ☎ *615/862–5950* ⊕ *www.wegotransit.com.*

📍 Visitor Information

CONTACTS Visit Music City. ✉ *Nashville* ☎ *800/657–6910* ⊕ *www.visitmusiccity.com.*

Chapter 3

DOWNTOWN AND SOBRO

Updated by
Chris Chamberlain

⊙ Sights	🍴 Restaurants	🛏 Hotels	🛍 Shopping	🍸 Nightlife
★★★★☆	★★★★★	★★★★★	★★★☆☆	★★★☆☆

NEIGHBORHOOD SNAPSHOT

TOP EXPERIENCES

■ **Live Music:** Downtown's numerous live music venues range from talented street-corner buskers to national acts playing stadiums and arenas—it's easy to see where the Music City nickname came from.

■ **Honky-tonks:** A Nashville trip isn't complete without a stop at a dimly-lit barroom for a longneck beer and some classic country music.

■ **Quality Dining:** Nashville's reputation as a creative center has expanded to talented chefs with fantastic restaurants.

■ **Music History:** Between the Ryman, the Country Music Hall of Fame and Museum, and the National Museum of African American Music, much of the country's music heritage is preserved here.

■ **Shopping:** Whether you're searching for boots to go out scootin' or some fine art as a souvenir, Downtown has great shopping.

PLANNING YOUR TIME

The concept of "weekend" has changed over the past few years, with visitors arriving earlier in the week and extending their stays into the middle of the following week, so pedestrian traffic is pretty much constant after noon when tourists roll out of their hotels and back onto Broadway. A morning walk around Downtown can be a relatively peaceful time to take in the sights, and some honky-tonks start their live music schedule before lunchtime. Newly installed parking meters accept credit card payments, a welcome development— but there's no longer free metered parking at any time of the day or week.

VIEWFINDER

■ Stand on the steps leading into the Fifth + Broadway complex (⊠ 5th Ave. N between Broadway and Commerce St.) for the best shot of the Ryman's famous facade; you'll quickly understand why it's called "The Mother Church of Country Music."

PAUSE HERE

■ For a unique viewpoint of Downtown and SoBro that includes views up and down the Cumberland River and the skyline looming above Broadway, walk about a third of the way across the John Seigenthaler Pedestrian Bridge (heading towards East Nashville); it's especially striking at night. And, if you need a break while out and about, Church Street Park is a delightful little pocket park that offers organized weekly programs for all ages.

For most of the 20th century, Downtown and the area south of Broadway (known as SoBro) were rarely spoken of together, as they were very different neighborhoods. Downtown has long been the commercial and entertainment center of the city, while SoBro was primarily industrial warehouses and the odd adult entertainment venue.

Fast-forward to today, and Downtown is home to most of the things that make Nashville one of the top tourist destinations in the country. The crown jewel of Downtown's entertainment is Lower Broadway, located right in the middle of Downtown. This stretch of road is called the Honky Tonk Highway, where live country and rock music pour out of nearly every window while beer flows out of every tap. While there is so much of Nashville to explore, spending a night on Broadway captures the essence of the city and is a great choice for short stays. Surrounding Broadway is a growing fine arts scene, with multiple galleries and plenty of restaurants cooking up Southern food. Just a few blocks away are world-class museums and the Nashville Symphony.

The opening of the Bridgestone Arena in 1996 led to a necessary loosening of building codes so that hotel and convention center amenities could be built to complement the venue. Residential growth led to the development of restaurants and bars south of Broadway, and now Downtown and SoBro are essentially one giant playground for adults, primarily tourists but some adventurous locals as well.

Downtown

Downtown Nashville basically encompasses the area from where I–40 crosses under Broadway to the Cumberland River, continuing north from Broadway to the area around the State Capitol Building. While there are still plenty of businesses headquartered in the neighborhood, the area has become much more residential and tourist-focused over the past two decades.

A park map that can help you find your way around the 19-acre Bicentennial Capitol Mall State Park can be picked up in the visitor center.

Sights

Bicentennial Capitol Mall State Park

PEDESTRIAN MALL | FAMILY | Built to celebrate Tennessee's bicentennial, this beautifully landscaped 19-acre park includes a 2,000-seat amphitheater, a scaled map of the state in granite, a World War II memorial, a wall etched with a time line of state events, and fountains representing each of Tennessee's rivers (you'll see both kids and adults splashing in them April–October). The park has a number of picnic tables and there are several dining options at the nearby Nashville Farmers' Market. ⊠ *600 James Robertson Pkwy., Downtown* ☎ *615/741–5280* ⊕ *tnstateparks.com/parks/info/bicentennial-mall* ⌦ *Free.*

CHAUVET Arts Nashville

ART GALLERY | Occupying multiple floors in two adjoining historic buildings, this vibrant gallery features artworks from local and regional artists to showcase the unique styles that characterize the South. Prices range from premium to affordable enough for tourists to pick up a fine art souvenir of their vacation in Nashville. The atmosphere is particularly lively during the monthly First Saturday Downtown Art Crawl where CHAUVET is an anchor destination of the route. ⊠ *215 Rep. John Lewis Way N, Downtown* ☎ *615/278–9086* ⊕ *www.chauvetarts.com* ☉ *Closed Sun.*

Church Street Park

CITY PARK | A small urban block originally earmarked for yet another Downtown skyscraper has been repurposed into a delightful little pocket park that offers organized arts, music, and fitness programs for children and adults throughout the week. ⊠ *600 Church St., Downtown* ☎ *615/862–8400* ⊕ *www.churchstreetpark.org.*

Civil Rights Room at the Nashville Public Library

LIBRARY | Nashville's role in the civil rights movement comes alive in this interactive display inside the library's main branch. Explore the ways Black Nashvillians protested segregation, challenged racist laws, and contributed to the nationwide fight for equality through the library's time lines, archival materials, and photos. ⊠ *615 Church St., 2nd fl., Downtown* ☎ *615/862—5782* ⊕ *library. nashville.org/research/collection/civil-rights-room.*

The Hermitage Hotel

HOTEL | Built in 1910, this Beaux Arts building has classic Italian and French Renaissance features that help create such a storied space, and you'll no doubt feel that greatness as you ascend the grand staircase into the magnificent lobby. From hosting guests like Babe Ruth and John F. Kennedy to playing a role in the ratification of the 19th Amendment, this building has seen it all. In 1920, all eyes were on Tennessee, as it was the last state with the power to ratify—or nullify—the 19th Amendment. Both supporters and those who opposed women's suffrage made their headquarters in the hotel while waiting to vote on the amendment's ratification in the nearby state capital. Fortunately, the pros won out by a single vote. You can learn about the War of the Roses at a small exhibit in the lobby. The Draper James–inspired Afternoon Tea on Friday, Saturday, and Sunday is worth your time, as is grabbing a drink or a bite to eat at the hotel's restaurant Drusie & Darr (check out those ceilings). We'd be remiss if we didn't suggest you check out the bathrooms. ⊠ *231 6th Ave. N, Downtown* ☎ *888/888–9414* ⊕ *www.thehermitagehotel.com.*

Musicians Hall of Fame and Museum

SPECIALTY MUSEUM | Located inside the Municipal Auditorium, the Musicians Hall of Fame is another powerful testament to the musical legacy of the city. You'll find special exhibits on the Grammy Awards, Motown, Stax Records, Muscle Shoals, and more—and, of course, some Nashville pioneers. Beyond big-name acts, you'll also learn about the lesser-known session musicians who played on some of the most popular recordings in history. ⊠ *401 Gay St., Downtown* ☎ *615/244–3263* ⊕ *www.musicianshalloffame.com* ⧠ *$28* ⊘ *Closed Sun.*

★ National Museum of African American Music

SPECIALTY MUSEUM | Showcasing the contributions of Black musicians to just about every genre of American music from the Civil War era to today, this important museum dedicates more than

Downtown

NORTH CAPITOL

Bicentennial Capitol Mall State Park

Victory Park

Legislative Plaza

Tennessee Tower Plaza

Sights

Bicentennial Capitol Mall State Park, **1**

CHAUVET Arts Nashville, **8**

Church Street Park, **10**

Civil Rights Room at the Nashville Public Library, **11**

The Hermitage Hotel, **6**

Musicians Hall of Fame and Museum, **3**

National Museum of African American Music, **13**

Printers Alley, **9**

Public Square Park, **4**

Riverfront Park, **5**

Ryman Auditorium and Museum, **12**

Tennessee State Capitol, **2**

Tinney Contemporary, **7**

Restaurants

Black Rabbit, **1**

Boqueria, **8**

Church & Union, **4**

Deacon's New South, **7**

Drusie & Darr by Jean-Georges, **5**

Fleet Street Pub, **2**

Puckett's Grocery and Restaurant, **6**

Sinatra Bar & Lounge, **3**

The Twelve Thirty Club, **9**

Quick Bites

Assembly Food Hall, **3**

D'Andrews Bakery & Cafe, **1**

Hattie B's, **4**

Mike's Ice Cream, **2**

Hotels

Bobby Hotel, **2**

Fairlane Hotel, **1**

The Hermitage Hotel, **4**

Holston House Nashville, **5**

Noelle, **3**

KEY
- Sights
- Restaurants
- Quick Bites
- Hotels

Cumberland River

Riverfront Park

41

Woodland Street

5

Public Square Park

4

Cumberland Park

Trans Way

Gay Street

2nd Avenue North

1st Avenue North

Jo. Johnston Avenue

3rd Ave. N.

2nd Avenue North

3rd Ave. N.

Gay Street

Gay Street

Charlotte Avenue

3rd Avenue North

4th Avenue North

5th Avenue North

Deaderick Street

Union Street North

2nd Avenue North

1st Avenue North

Riverfront Park

0   250 m
0   500 ft

DOWNTOWN

1

2
3   2

7

4   3

8

6   7

3rd Avenue North

4th Avenue North

Printers Alley

9

10

1

11

Commerce Street

2

2nd Avenue South

1st Ave. S.

6th Avenue North

5th Avenue North

3   8

12

Broadway

3rd Avenue South

4th Avenue South

5   4   9   13

5th Avenue South

Broadway

6th Ave. S.

SOBRO

Music City Walk of Fame Park

Demonbreun Street

Demonbreun Street

In the early 1900s, the area known as Printers Alley was home to 13 publishers and 10 printers, including Nashville's two largest newspapers.

50,000 square feet of exhibit space to showcasing the evolution of African American music and performers. Galleries display instruments and performance costumes from the world of spirituals, blues, jazz, gospel, R&B, and hip-hop. ⊠ *Fifth + Broadway, 510 Broadway, Downtown* ☎ *615/301–8724* ⊕ *www.nmaam.org* ⌨ *$26.95.*

Printers Alley

BUSINESS DISTRICT | If you don't know where to find it, you'll almost miss it. Printers Alley is a historic Nashville landmark reminiscent of a London side street that stretches between Church and Union Streets parallel to 3rd and 4th Avenues. It's full of watering holes, karaoke bars, and a jazz club, but you can have just as much fun chatting outside with the locals as you will entering any of its infamous haunts. The historic sign will let you know you've made it to the right place. ⊠ *Downtown* ✛ *Between Church and Union Sts., east of 4th Ave. N* ⊕ *nashvilledowntown.com/go/printers-alley* ⌨ *Free.*

Public Square Park

CITY PARK | Known for formerly hosting festivals like Live on the Green or Nashville Pride, Public Square is located in front of the courthouse. Featuring an expansive green space perfect for having a picnic or playing ball, statuesque elevator towers that can be climbed for an expansive view, and fountains that children play in during warmer months, it's a lovely place to take a break from the hubbub of Downtown. ⊠ *Union St. at 3rd Ave. N, Downtown* ☎ *615/743–3090* ⊕ *nashvilledowntown.com/go/public-square-park* ⌨ *Free.*

A Brief History of Printers Alley

When it comes to Nashville nightlife, the Honky Tonk Highway on Lower Broadway gets the lion's share of attention, but it's not the only Downtown street designated for good times. Located between Union and Church streets, just 2½ blocks north of Lower Broad, Printers Alley was Nashville's printing and publishing hub in the first half of the 20th century; by the 1940s, the printing presses were replaced with saloons, burlesque shows, and Prohibition-era speakeasies. Nightclubs showcased diverse acts from Boots Randolph, Chet Atkins, Waylon Jennings, Barbara Mandrell, Dottie West, and Hank Williams to The Supremes and Jimi Hendrix.

Today, you can still find plenty of music in Printers Alley, along with several boutique hotels. Bourbon Street Blues and Boogie Bar upholds the alley's legacy of live jazz music, and Skull's Rainbow Room serves great food in addition to hosting burlesque performances. Karaoke is also a stronghold of Printers Alley culture, and Ms. Kelli's Karaoke Bar is a great spot to sing and dance.

Riverfront Park

CITY PARK | Though considerably smaller than the Mississippi, the Cumberland River has been as important to Nashville as the Mississippi has been to Memphis. This welcoming green enclave on its banks has an expansive view of the river and Nissan Stadium, where the Tennessee Titans play. The park serves as a popular venue for free summer concerts, block parties, and the annual New Year's Eve and 4th of July celebrations (Nashville boasts the largest fireworks display in the South). It's also home to Fort Nashborough Interpretive Center, which was home to the city's first European settlers in the later 1700s. ✉ *100 1st Ave. N, Downtown* ☎ *615/743–3090* ⊕ *nashvilledowntown.com/go/riverfront-park* ✍ *Free.*

★ Ryman Auditorium and Museum

PERFORMANCE VENUE | A country music shrine, the Ryman Auditorium and Museum was home to the Grand Ole Opry from 1943 to 1974 and is listed on the National Register of Historic Places. The auditorium seats 2,000 for live performances of classical, jazz, pop, gospel, and, of course, country. Self-guided tours include photo ops on the legendary stage and a stroll through the museum, with its photographs and memorabilia of past Ryman Auditorium performances. Visitors can also take a backstage tour of the dressing rooms and even record their own version of a legendary

Visitors can take guided and self-guided tours of the Tennessee State Capitol, first opened in 1859.

song at the in-house recording studio. ✉ *116 Rep. John Lewis Way N, Downtown* ☎ *615/889–3060* ⊕ *www.ryman.com* ✉ *$29.95.*

Tennessee State Capitol

GOVERNMENT BUILDING | The State Capitol was designed by noted Philadelphia architect William Strickland (1788–1854), who was so impressed with his Greek Revival creation that he requested—and received—entombment behind one of the building's walls. On the grounds you'll also find the graves of the 11th U.S. president, James K. Polk, and his wife. ✉ *600 Charlotte Ave., Downtown* ☎ *615/741–2692* ⊕ *www.tn.gov* ✉ *Free* ⊗ *Closed weekends.*

Tinney Contemporary

ART GALLERY | Helmed by owner Susan Tinney, Tinney Contemporary displays contemporary paintings, photography, drawings, and beyond in a stylish space on 5th Avenue. The gallery offers full-service art consultation, from purchasing to installation, and participates in the First Saturday Downtown Art Crawl on the first Saturday of each month. ✉ *237 Rep. John Lewis Way N, 1st fl., Downtown* ☎ *615/255–7816* ⊕ *www.tinneycontemporary.com* ⊗ *Closed Sun. and Mon.*

🍴 Restaurants

Black Rabbit

$$$ | AMERICAN | Housed in a historic building from the 1890s over a tunnel where Al Capone legendarily smuggled booze from boats on the Cumberland River to Printers Alley nightclubs, Black Rabbit comes by its speakeasy vibe honestly. Exposed brick walls, tall ceilings, and the original hardwood floors maintain the Roaring '20s ambience, as do jumpin' jazz performers that play there frequently on weekends. **Known for:** wood-fired cuisine prepared in an open kitchen; live entertainment that has been known to spill out into the adjoining alley; creative and affordable cocktail program. $ *Average main: $25* ⊠ *218 3rd Ave. N, Downtown* ☎ *615/891–2380* ⊕ *www.blackrabbittn.com* ☉ *Closed Sun.*

Boqueria

$$ | SPANISH | Located right across the street from the Ryman Auditorium, Boqueria is an ideal spot for a preshow meal made up of flavorful Spanish tapas that emerge quickly from the kitchen as soon as they are ready. You might not receive your plates in the order you requested them, but everything comes together to create a cohesive meal; favorite dishes include traditional Spanish staples such as *patatas bravas* (Spanish fried potatoes), grilled octopus, and paella, or diners can opt for a choice between two prix fixe menus that offer culinary tours through Spain. **Known for:** lively atmosphere as diners share small plates; traditional preparations of Spanish tapas; decadent brunch with free-flowing beverages. $ *Average main: $13* ⊠ *Fifth + Broadway, 5005 Broadway, Downtown* ☎ *615/245–7160* ⊕ *boqueriarestaurant.com.*

Church & Union

$$$ | ECLECTIC | First-time visitors to Church & Union can't help but look up immediately upon entering the massive dining space, their eyes drawn skyward by the dramatic hand-lettered mural that covers the entire ceiling with all 11,450 words of Sun Tzu's *The Art of War*. The kitchen staff wins most of the battles with their playful and inventive takes on New American cuisine, pairing international inspirations with regional ingredients and local specialties to create an intriguing menu of hearty dishes. **Known for:** lively atmosphere, especially on weekends; unexpected twists on traditional dishes; dramatic interior design. $ *Average main: $35* ⊠ *201 4th Ave. N, Suite 101, Downtown* ☎ *615/864–0977* ⊕ *churchandunionnashville.com.*

Deacon's New South

$$$$ | STEAK HOUSE | Occupying the ground floor of the Life & Casualty Tower, once the tallest skyscraper in the South, Deacon's is a decidedly modern tenant of the venerable building. Offering a traditional steak-house menu with Southern twists, Deacon's dry ages full tenderloins and rib eye racks of beef in a custom aging room visible at the back of the main dining room. **Known for:** dry-aged prime beef; modern interpretations of classic Southern dishes; Gulf Coast–inspired seafood offerings. $ *Average main:*

$50 ✉ 401 Church St., Downtown ☎ 615/994–1994 ⊕ deacons-newsouth.com ⊘ No lunch.

★ Drusie & Darr by Jean-Georges

$$$$ | AMERICAN | Internationally acclaimed chef Jean-Georges Vongerichten brings his thoughtful approach to regional cuisine to The Hermitage Hotel's architecturally interesting flagship restaurant. Classy but not stuffy, the kitchen serves three meals a day to hotel guests and smart Downtown denizens who know that a meal here is a surprisingly affordable indulgence—the delightful wood-fired pizzas benefit from fresh produce toppings, and the seasonal menu features the freshest and most exciting local vegetables uniquely prepared alongside premium seafood and meats. **Known for:** wood-fired pizzas; creative vegetable-based main dishes and sides; delightfully decadent flourishes like caviar on the egg toast appetizer. Ⓢ Average main: $38 ✉ 231 6th Ave. N, Downtown ☎ 615/345–7116 ⊕ www.thehermitagehotel.com.

Fleet Street Pub

$$ | BRITISH | The closest thing that Nashville has to an authentic British pub, this subterranean tavern serves as a "third space" to many different constituencies. Soccer fans know they will be able to watch big matches on the telly, while other patrons prefer to pass quieter times enjoying a pint on a comfy sofa while reading a book or playing a board game with a friend. **Known for:** legit fish-and-chips that would make Gordon Ramsay proud; wide variety of British beers and Scotch whiskies; home to soccer fans, especially Arsenal supporters. Ⓢ Average main: $14 ✉ 207 Printers Alley, Suite 101, Downtown ☎ 615/200–0782 ⊕ www.fleetstreetpub.com.

Puckett's Grocery and Restaurant

$$ | AMERICAN | If you're walking Downtown near 5th and Church, you'll probably pick up the aromas from Puckett's before you see it: Puckett's is an in-town version of the popular Leiper's Fork Puckett's, a Tennessee eatery and music venue. Here you'll find new twists on Southern favorites, including barbecue sliders and "redneck burritos" of pulled pork, baked beans, and slaw, as well as salads. **Known for:** down-home country food; live music; daily specials. Ⓢ Average main: $19 ✉ 500 Church St., Downtown ☎ 615/770—2772 ⊕ puckettsgro.com.

Sinatra Bar & Lounge

$$$$ | ITALIAN | Manhattan meets Palm Springs at this homage to Ol' Blue Eyes; the walls are covered with photographs of Frank Sinatra with his famous pals and artwork painted by the legendary singer, some of it sourced directly from the Sinatra family. The main upstairs dining space looks into the kitchen, where the staff creates a classic chophouse menu and some of Sinatra's personal favorite pasta and classic Italian dishes. **Known for:** old-school Italian cuisine prepared using premium ingredients; "My Way" customizable martini menu; rare artwork and photographs adorning the walls. $ *Average main: $46* ✉ *222 4th Ave. N, Downtown* ☎ *615/866–2224* ⊕ *www.sinatranashville.com* ⊗ *No lunch Sun.–Thurs.*

Downtown's 🎫
Must-See Murals

■ Legends Corner ✉ 428 Broadway

■ Good Trouble ✉ 5th Ave. N at Commerce St.

■ Revive ✉ 144 5th Ave. N

■ Get Your Tickets! ✉ 401 Gay St.

The Twelve Thirty Club

$$$$ | **AMERICAN** | Native Tennessean Justin Timberlake is an investor in this top-floor supper club, which harkens back to the day when dinner and a show were a regular option in Music City. Guests dine in opulent velvet and leather booths, enjoying a classic steak-house menu while small combos entertain during the dinner hour. **Known for:** a throwback to the heyday of Nashville dinner theater shows; extensive and interesting list of wines; dramatic architecture and interior design. $ *Average main: $49* ✉ *Fifth + Broadway, 550 Broadway, Downtown* ☎ *629/236–0001* ⊕ *thetwelvethirtyclub.com.*

☕ Coffee and Quick Bites

Assembly Food Hall

$ | **ECLECTIC** | More than your average food court, Assembly Food Hall offers more than 30 restaurants and bars spread across two levels in two wings. Many of the restaurant stalls are outposts of favorite local establishments like Prince's Hot Chicken and Pharmacy Burger, offering limited menus of their "greatest hits." With bars and live music stages on each level, the atmosphere is always lively. **Known for:** wide variety of dining options across different cusines; live music for mealtime entertainment; smaller outposts of local restaurant favorites. $ *Average main: $12* ✉ *Fifth + Broadway, 5055 Broadway, Downtown* ☎ *615/800–5395* ⊕ *www.assemblyfoodhall.com.*

D'Andrew's Bakery & Cafe

$ | **CAFÉ** | Breakfast and lunch sandwiches made using housebaked bread, braised meats, gourmet aioli, and premium produce are the most popular items at this airy and amiable café, but the pastry case just inside the front door is the real showstopper. Get there early for the best selection of flaky croissants, delectable cookies and muffins, colorful macarons, and other baked goods.

Known for: flaky laminated pastries that take three days to make; fantastic breakfast sandwiches; splurge-worthy baked goods like a Double Chocolate Dulcey cookie and brioche donuts. ⑤ *Average main: $11* ⊠ *555 Church St., Downtown* ☎ *615/375–4934* ⊕ *dandrewsbakery.com.*

★ Hattie B's

$$ | SOUTHERN | Look no further than Hattie B's Lower Broadway location to get your Nashville hot chicken fix. Customers pick their level of heat (from no-heat "Southern" to "Shut the Cluck Up!!!"), chicken (bones or no bones, dark meat, white meat, or wings), and sides (pimento mac and cheese to black-eyed pea salad), and delicious platters are delivered to your table. **Known for:** Nashville hot chicken; heat levels known to make grown men cry; multiple locations around the city. ⑤ *Average main: $15* ⊠ *5069 Broadway Pl., Suite 103, Downtown* ☎ *615/576–8700* ⊕ *www.hattieb.com.*

Mike's Ice Cream

$ | AMERICAN | FAMILY | A downtown Nashville staple for many years, Mike's reminds you of a classic 1950s soda parlor, complete with vintage murals. Featuring classics like perfectly dipped cones and tall sundaes covered in chocolate, it's a great way to end a day walking around Downtown. **Known for:** hand-dipped ice cream; extravagant sundaes; old-fashioned sodas. ⑤ *Average main: $7* ⊠ *129 2nd Ave. N, Downtown* ☎ *615/742—6453* ⊕ *mikesicecream. com.*

 Hotels

Bobby Hotel

$$ | HOTEL | Named after a fictional fun-loving world traveler, Bobby is designed to appeal to the wanderlust of guests with decor accented by global souvenirs, premium room amenities, and a variety of dining options. **Pros:** great location near Printers Alley; changing artwork curated by Tinney Contemporary; multiple in-house dining options. **Cons:** converted office building floor layout can be confusing; rooftop bar occasionally gets crowded on weekends, leading to slower service; no complimentary breakfast plan. ⑤ *Rooms from: $400* ⊠ *230 4th Ave. N, Downtown* ☎ *615/782–7100* ⊕ *bobbyhotel.com* ⇱ *144 rooms* ⦿*l No Meals.*

Fairlane Hotel

$ | HOTEL | Just a stone's throw away from the iconic Batman building and three blocks from the hustle and bustle of the honky-tonks sits this boutique hotel resplendent with '70s retro-modern flair befitting its past history as a bank building. **Pros:** attractive redesign of former bank building; outdoor restaurant patio offers

Downtown views from above; often offers room packages with bonus perks. **Cons:** fewer rooms than most Downtown hotels; main restaurant only open for dinner; no self-parking option. $ *Rooms from: $269 ⌆ 401 Union St., Downtown ☎ 615/988–8511 ⊕ www.fairlanehotel.com ⇗ 81 rooms* ⦿ *No Meals.*

★ The Hermitage Hotel

$$$ | HOTEL | This is a quintessential Nashville experience for both guests and all Nashville travelers alike. **Pros:** great location (especially for taking in performances at TPAC); lots of character; lovely bathrooms and large rooms. **Cons:** small elevators; surrounding area can feel a bit deserted after hours; can get crowded with theater traffic. $ *Rooms from: $549 ⌆ 231 6th Ave. N, Downtown ☎ 615/244–3121, 888/888–9414 ⊕ www.thehermitagehotel.com ⇗ 122 rooms* ⦿ *No Meals.*

Holston House Nashville

$$ | HOTEL | Art deco style lives on in the decor of the lobby of this 1920s building housing a boutique hotel which also offers luxury rooms and a popular rooftop pool. **Pros:** luxurious lobby with velvet furniture and soaring ceilings; rooftop pool and bar features unique views of Downtown; 24-hour fitness center to sweat off the effects of a night on Lower Broad. **Cons:** lobby is chopped up into multiple levels; area can feel a little deserted after dark; limited dining options. $ *Rooms from: $309 ⌆ 118 7th Ave. N, Downtown ☎ 615/392–1234 ⊕ www.hyatt.com/en-US/hotel/tennessee/holston-house-nashville/⇗ 191 rooms* ⦿ *No Meals.*

Noelle

$$ | HOTEL | Simple modern rooms with art deco touches can be found at Noelle. **Pros:** vinyl records and turntables available for guests to borrow during their stay; food and beverage credit offered at check-in; multiple drinking and dining options on premise. **Cons:** smaller rooms than at newer hotels; underground restaurant can feel a bit isolated; expensive valet parking is the only option for travelers with cars. $ *Rooms from: $399 ⌆ 200 4th Ave. N, Downtown ☎ 615/649–5000 ⊕ www.noelle-nashville.com ⇗ 224 rooms* ⦿ *No Meals.*

 # Nightlife

BARS

Heirloom Rooftop

BARS | Once a penthouse garden, this space has been converted into an open-air rooftop bar and lounge atop Holston House. Enjoy sweeping views of Downtown alongside craft cocktails and upscale bar bites. ⌆ *Holston House, 118 7th Ave. N, Downtown*

☎ 615/392–1234 ⊕ www.heir-
loomrooftopnashville.com.

CABARET AND
DANCE CLUBS

Skull's Rainbow Room

CABARET | A reimagined version
of a past Printers Alley staple,
Skull's Rainbow Room serves
classic entrées like steaks and
chops, ready to be washed
down with a boozy blend from
their classic cocktail list. Taking
center stage alongside food
and drink at this dimly lit yet
swanky lounge is the entertainment, alternating between live
jazz and live burlesque performances. ⊠ 222 Printers Alley,
Downtown ☎ 615/810–9631
⊕ www.skullsrainbowroom.
com.

Wildhorse Saloon

DANCE CLUB | Live music, barbecue, and dancing—lessons are
offered daily—are what makes the spacious Wildhorse Saloon so
popular. All ages (under 18 must be accompanied by an adult) are
welcome until midnight. The Wildhorse is undergoing renovations
to emerge as a newly rebranded club in partnership with country
music star Luke Combs, but they plan to keep the boots scootin'
and the beers flowing until the club emerges with a new name.
⊠ 120 2nd Ave. N, Downtown ☎ 615/902–8200 ⊕ wildhorsesa-
loon.com.

LIVE MUSIC

Bourbon Street Blues and Boogie Bar

LIVE MUSIC | A fixture in Printers Alley for more than a quarter
of a century, Bourbon Street Blues and Boogie Bar entertains
locals and tourists alike with a nightly lineup of R&B, blues, and
soul acts, some of which have been playing regular gigs on their
stage for years. A short menu of Cajun and creole snacks and
small plates nicely complements the raucous New Orleans–
inspired atmosphere and decor. ⊠ 220 Printers Alley, Downtown
☎ 615/242–5387 ⊕ www.bourbonstreetbluesandboogiebar.com.

Hard Rock Cafe

LIVE MUSIC | The Nashville branch of the Hard Rock Cafe is situated
where Broadway meets the Cumberland River. It's packed with

The Best
Rooftop Pools

Why walk around on a hot
sidewalk when you can
get away from it all at one
of Downtown's rooftop
pools? It seems like every
new property has included
these watery wonderlands
atop their buildings. Some
of our favorite spots can
be found at The Joseph,
JW Marriott Nashville,
Westin Nashville, Bobby
Hotel, Omni, and the Four
Seasons. Some rooftop
pools are even heated for
three-season use, so keep
that in mind for your next
visit.

rock memorabilia from around Nashville, like recording equipment used by Elvis Presley, and from around the world. If you want to party like a rock star, you can take over the mic at live band karaoke in the live music venue on the upper floor on Thursday nights. ⊠ *100 Broadway, Downtown* ☎ *615/742–9900* ⊕ *www.hardrockcafe.com/location/nashville.*

Layla's Honky Tonk

LIVE MUSIC | A stronghold in the row of classic honky-tonks on Broadway, Layla's offers an intimate dance floor and live music, often with a bluegrass twist. The best pairing to your beer can be found at the Chicago-style hot dog cart outside the front door. ⊠ *418 Broadway, Downtown* ☎ *615/726–2799* ⊕ *www.laylasnashville.com.*

Legends Corner

LIVE MUSIC | This no-frills, all-fun honky-tonk is a Broadway watering hole with plenty of live country music and room to dance. Don't miss the star-studded mural on the outside wall featuring Dolly Parton, Willie Nelson, Johnny Cash, Taylor Swift, and Merle Haggard, among others. ⊠ *428 Broadway, Downtown* ☎ *615/248–6334* ⊕ *www.legendscorner.com.*

Lonnie's Western Room

LIVE MUSIC | If you want to sing karaoke Downtown, this is the place to do it. No longer smoke-filled, it's still a carpeted time warp that will make you feel like you've gone back to the '70s. With an extensive catalog of songs to sing, Jell-O shots behind the bar, and an always unpredictable and wild crowd, you're guaranteed to make some kind of memories here. Whether or not you actually remember them is entirely up to you. ⊠ *308 Church St., Downtown* ☎ *615/613–7500* ⊕ *lonnieswesternroom.com.*

Ms. Kelli's Karaoke Bar

LIVE MUSIC | In some towns, singing at karaoke bars is a way to show off your lack of inhibition; in Nashville some performers sound like they're auditioning for a recording contract. Ms. Kelli's is a favorite among locals because even though the talent level is usually quite high, less experienced and confident singers are also warmly supported. ⊠ *207 Printers Alley, Downtown* ☎ *615/255–4423* ⊕ *www.facebook.com/MsKellisKaraoke.*

★ Robert's Western World

LIVE MUSIC | If you ask any native Nashvillian (even famous locals), they'll tell you that Robert's is the gold standard of honky-tonks in town, with live music and dancing nightly. The two-level bar has been a local staple for decades and features some of the absolute best live bands on Broadway from before lunchtime until after midnight. Peruse the boot collection on the infamous boot wall and enjoy a fried bologna sandwich. ✉ *416B Broadway, Downtown* ☎ *615/244–9552* ⊕ *robertswesternworld.com*.

The Stage on Broadway

LIVE MUSIC | The backdrop for many a movie and music video, The Stage is classic Lower Broadway in both looks and entertainment. With live music starting in the early afternoon and a convenient location across from Bridgestone Arena, it's a great stop before or after a game or concert. ✉ *412 Broadway, Downtown* ☎ *615/726–0504* ⊕ *www. thestageonbroadway.com*.

Tootsie's Orchid Lounge

LIVE MUSIC | Tootsie's gets its name from legendary former owner Hattie Louise "Tootsie" Bess and the bold color of the honky-tonk's walls and exterior, which also features one of the more famous Downtown murals of '80s country stars. A multilevel honky-tonk playground, you can see live music on all of its four floors, including the rooftop. Take note of the neon sign in the back alley for the famous Tootsie's Upstairs, a novelty relic of the '60s and '70s, when country legends would go sit in the private room and drink after shows at the Ryman. ✉ *422 Broadway, Downtown* ☎ *615/726–0463* ⊕ *www. tootsies.net*.

Snack Time: Fried Bologna

While Nashville is best known for hot chicken, another low-down local delicacy gets its share of attention: the fried bologna sandwich. Whether it's a thick-cut slab that is smoked over hickory before a pass across a hot griddle like at Martin's Bar-B-Que Joint, or thin slices piled high between two slices of white bread like they serve at Robert's Western World alongside a bag of chips, a Moon Pie (a popular dessert snack from nearby Chattanooga), and an ice-cold PBR beer for just $6 as part of Robert's Recession Special—a fried bologna sandwich will cure what ails you!

⭐ Performing Arts

CMA Fest

FESTIVALS | In the second week of June, CMA Fest hosts big-name country music stars at Nissan Stadium, Ascend Amphitheater, Riverfront Park, and Bridgestone Arena. Over the long weekend, Lower Broadway also hosts many free concerts. ✉ *Riverfront Park, Downtown* ☎ *615/244–2840* ⊕ *cmafest.com*.

Tennessee Performing Arts Center (*TPAC*)

CONCERTS | This multicultural center with elegant concert halls is the home of the Nashville Ballet, Nashville Opera, Nashville Repertory Theatre, and various touring performers, including the popular Broadway series in the center's large Andrew Jackson Hall. ✉ *505 Deaderick St., Downtown* ☎ *615/782–4000* ⊕ *www. tpac.org.*

 Shopping

Boot Country

SHOES | If it's time to replace or update your dancing boots, Boot Country offers a wide selection of cowboy boots, Western wear, and other wearable Nashville souvenirs. It is conveniently located for boot-scooters on Broadway and frequently offers promotions for discounts on new boots. ✉ *304 Broadway, Downtown* ☎ *615/259–1691* ⊕ *www.twofreeboots.com.*

Fifth + Broadway

SHOPPING CENTER | In addition to stand-alone restaurants and the Assembly Food Hall, Fifth + Broadway is also home to a host of retail opportunities. Those looking for boots can check out Ariat or Tecovas, while clothing shoppers can drop into outlets for Levi's, Nike, and Carhartt. Tech lovers can geek out at the large and airy Apple store on the corner of Fifth and Broadway. ✉ *5036 Broadway, Downtown* ☎ *615/416–6400* ⊕ *fifthandb.com.*

SoBro

While technically SoBro is short for "south of Broadway," for the purposes of defining the neighborhood, the southern side of the main drag running through Lower Broad is included in this designation. The neighborhood becomes less densely populated as it approaches its southern boundary at I–40, but commercial and residential expansion continues to push in that direction.

 Sights

Bridgestone Arena

SPORTS VENUE | Home to the Nashville Predators, the city's NHL team since 1998, visitors can catch a home game from October to April (tickets may be hard to get) and then hit the honky-tonks right outside the arena to celebrate the win. The arena also plays host to numerous concerts and other large-format events. The Nashville Visitor Center, also known as the Music City Shop at

Bridgestone, is located by the main entrance. If you make it inside, head to the elevator lobby outside of Section 109 on the building's main concourse to see the Brad Paisley–Rob Hendon mural. ⊠ *501 Broadway, SoBro* ☎ *615/770–2000* ⊕ *www.bridgestonearena.com.*

★ The Country Music Hall of Fame and Museum

PEDESTRIAN MALL | This tribute to country music's finest is a full city block long, filled with plaques and exhibits highlighting performers from the old-time favorites to the latest generation of stars, a two-story wall with gold and platinum country records, a theater, and Elvis Presley's solid-gold 1960 Cadillac limo. Tours of the Historic RCA Studio B recording studio are also run by the museum. Their extensive collection of memorabilia and rotating exhibits make this an essential stop for any music fan or history buff. ⊠ *222 Rep. John Lewis Way S, SoBro* ☎ *615/416–2001* ⊕ *www.countrymusichalloffame.org* ✆ *$27.95.*

The John Seigenthaler Pedestrian Bridge

BRIDGE | This 3,150-foot-long pedestrian-only truss bridge crosses the Cumberland River and connects Downtown to East Nashville. Its iconic look and location offer up one of the best views of the city and the perfect photo op. ⊠ *1st Ave. S and Cumberland River Greenway, SoBro.*

The Johnny Cash Museum

SPECIALTY MUSEUM | The legendary Man in Black has a dedicated space in Nashville. Performance costumes, handwritten lyrics, a wall of gold and platinum records—even a limestone wall from the home Cash shared with his beloved June—are among the items in this museum located between Broadway and the Country Music Hall of Fame and Museum. Interactive exhibits include presentations of Cash's music in formats ranging from 78rpm records to digital downloads. Clips of Cash's many appearances in films and on television are played in a small theater. ⊠ *119 3rd Ave. S, SoBro* ☎ *615/256–1777* ⊕ *www.johnnycashmuseum.com* ✆ *$25.95.*

Patsy Cline Museum

SPECIALTY MUSEUM | Honoring one of Nashville's most iconic former residents, the Patsy Cline Museum features artifacts like stage costumes, home furnishings, records, and more to honor the

The Country Music Hall of Fame and Museum has more than 500 musical instruments in its collection.

legacy of the late singer. The Johnny Cash Museum is the Patsy Cline Museum's downstairs neighbor, making this a convenient stop for country music fans (though they are separate museums charging separate admission). ✉ *119 3rd Ave. S, 2nd level, SoBro* ☎ *615/454–4722* ⊕ *www.patsymuseum.com* ✉ *$21.95.*

Walk of Fame Park

CITY PARK | **FAMILY** | This rare patch of green in Nashville's urban core features a walkway of stars commemorating many of the people who turned the city into Music City, USA. Visitors will find plaques with the names of iconic country stars like Johnny Cash, Reba McEntire, Loretta Lynn, Alan Jackson, and Dolly Parton alongside surprising names of stars with connections to Nashville from other genres such as Little Richard, Jimi Hendrix, Kid Rock, Steve Winwood, Peter Frampton, and the Fisk Jubilee Singers. It's "Music City," not just "Country Music City." ✉ *Nashville Music Garden, 121 4th Ave. S, SoBro* ⊕ *nashvilledowntown.com/go/ walk-of-fame-park* ✉ *Free.*

Restaurants

Bakersfield

$ | **MODERN MEXICAN** | One of the better options for a casual meal, Bakersfield specializes in Mexican street food that is authentic and quick. The bar also serves more than 100 types of tequila so you can get the full experience. **Known for:** extensive tequila selection; elevated Mexican street-food favorites; handmade tortillas.

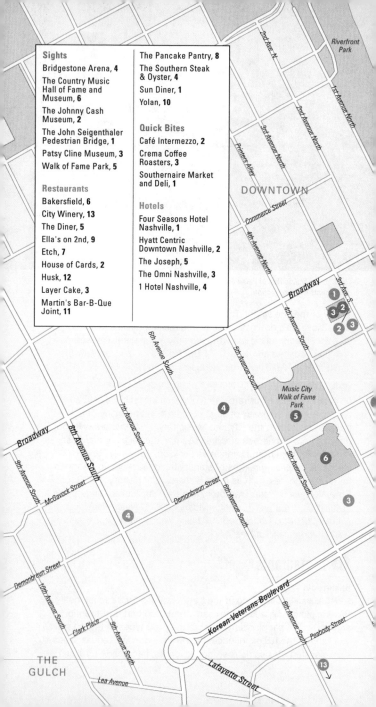

Sights

Bridgestone Arena, **4**

The Country Music Hall of Fame and Museum, **6**

The Johnny Cash Museum, **2**

The John Seigenthaler Pedestrian Bridge, **1**

Patsy Cline Museum, **3**

Walk of Fame Park, **5**

Restaurants

Bakersfield, **6**

City Winery, **13**

The Diner, **5**

Ella's on 2nd, **9**

Etch, **7**

House of Cards, **2**

Husk, **12**

Layer Cake, **3**

Martin's Bar-B-Que Joint, **11**

The Pancake Pantry, **8**

The Southern Steak & Oyster, **4**

Sun Diner, **1**

Yolan, **10**

Quick Bites

Café Intermezzo, **2**

Crema Coffee Roasters, **3**

Southernaire Market and Deli, **1**

Hotels

Four Seasons Hotel Nashville, **1**

Hyatt Centric Downtown Nashville, **2**

The Joseph, **5**

The Omni Nashville, **3**

1 Hotel Nashville, **4**

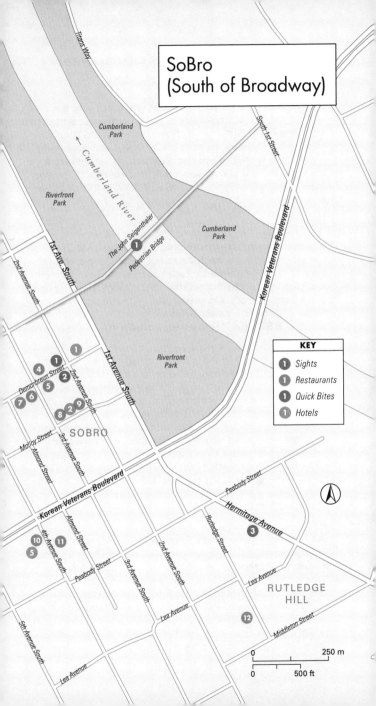

SoBro
(South of Broadway)

Titans Way

Cumberland Park

Cumberland River

Riverfront Park

The John Seigenthaler
Pedestrian Bridge **1**

South 1st Street

Korean Veterans Boulevard

Cumberland Park

1st Ave. South

2nd Avenue South

1st Avenue South

Riverfront Park

1

4 **1**

Demonbreun Street **2**

5 **2**

7 **6**

8 **2** **9**

2nd Avenue South

3rd Avenue South

Molloy Street

Almond Street

SOBRO

KEY

1 *Sights*

1 *Restaurants*

1 *Quick Bites*

1 *Hotels*

Korean Veterans Boulevard

Almond Street

Peabody Street

Hermitage Avenue

Rutledge Street

3

10 **11**

5

4th Avenue South

Peabody Street

3rd Avenue South

2nd Avenue South

Lea Avenue

Lea Avenue

**RUTLEDGE
HILL**

12

Middleton Street

5th Avenue South

Lea Avenue

0 ——— 250 m

0 ——— 500 ft

$ *Average main: $10* ✉ *201 3rd Ave. S, SoBro* ☎ *615/522–0970* ⊕ *www.bakersfieldtacos.com.*

City Winery

$$ | **AMERICAN** | As a restaurant, concert venue, and wine bar, the versatility of City Winery's offerings make it a standout in the city. The Barrel Room Restaurant and Wine Bar within City Winery serves hearty Southern-inspired fare for brunch and dinner with an extensive wine list. **Known for:** great place for dinner before the show; thoughtful wine selections; trendy brunch. $ *Average main: $19* ✉ *609 Lafayette St., SoBro* ☎ *615/324–1033* ⊕ *citywinery.com/nashville.*

The Diner

$$$ | **AMERICAN** | Despite its name, this eatery challenges diner conventions by occupying six stories of a Downtown building and serving upscale entrées like steaks, oysters, and sushi until the wee hours on weekends. Each luxe level features a different focus like fresh seafood or cocktails, and the rooftop view is one of the best in the city. **Known for:** oyster and sushi bars; first-floor coffee shop; rooftop views. $ *Average main: $25* ✉ *200 3rd Ave. S, SoBro* ☎ *615/782–7150* ⊕ *www.thediner.com.*

Ella's on 2nd

$$$ | **ITALIAN** | Tucked off the lobby of The Hyatt Centric, Ella's is open just about any time you're hungry (it's also where guests at the hotel get room service from). The California-inspired, Italian fare–focused menu has something for everyone: dinner highlights include crab risotto, braised short ribs, and pan-seared salmon piccata, while breakfast and lunch offer classics like lemon-ricotta pancakes and a grilled chicken Caprese sandwich. **Known for:** great cocktails; great starters like shrimp scampi al forno and whipped house-made ricotta; central location within walking distance of the sights of Broadway and the river. $ *Average main: $35* ✉ *The Hyatt Centric, 210 Molloy St., SoBro* ☎ *629/248–9515* ⊕ *www.ellason2nd.com.*

★ Etch

$$$$ | **ECLECTIC** | It's rare that a fine-dining restaurant is best known for an appetizer, but this is definitely the case for Etch's legendary roasted cauliflower dish, a work of art on a plate with browned florets atop a palette of three colorful and flavorful sauces. It's an ideal representation of the food at Etch, full of internationally-inspired flavors and artfully plated with precision. **Known for:** cultishly popular roasted cauliflower appetizer; deeply layered flavors courtesy of ingredients sourced from Latin America and North Africa; refined atmosphere without being too stuffy. $ *Average main: $39*

The Johnny Cash Museum is said to have the world's most extensive collection of Johnny Cash artifacts and memorabilia.

✉ *303 Demonbreun St., SoBro* ☎ *615/522–0685* ⊕ *etchrestaurant. com* 🕐 *Closed Sun. No lunch Sat.*

House of Cards

$$$$ | STEAK HOUSE | With a strict dress code and no-phone policy, House of Cards is a must-see for locals and tourists alike looking for an unusual night. The fine-dining meal price comes with a private magic show that rivals Hollywood's infamous Magic Castle. **Known for:** live magic show; speakeasy entrance; cigar menu. ⑤ *Average main: $55* ✉ *119 3rd Ave. S, lower level, SoBro* ☎ *615/730–8326* ⊕ *www.hocnashville.com* 🏛 *Jackets and button-up shirts are required for men, while women are encouraged to dress in formal or cocktail attire.*

★ Husk

$$$ | SOUTHERN | Southern charm abounds in both the decor and flavors at Husk, located in a converted historic home. With seasonal ingredients sourced from in and around Tennessee, the menu at this must-try restaurant staple (with other locations in Charleston and Savannah) is elevated and dynamic. **Known for:** attentive service; fresh local ingredients; small dynamic menu. ⑤ *Average main: $35* ✉ *37 Rutledge St., SoBro* ☎ *615/256–6565* ⊕ *husknashville.com.*

Layer Cake

$$$ | ECLECTIC | True to its name, Layer Cake offers a different drinking and dining experience on each of the restaurant's four levels. Intentionally designed to attract social media–savvy diners, there's something to enjoy (and photograph) in almost every corner of Layer Cake, from the subterranean Cherry Room and its VIP table service to the mix-and-mingle vibe of the street-level Wonder Room. **Known for:** ground zero for social media fans; DJ-fueled weekend dance party brunches; eclectic menu of international comfort food items. ⑤ *Average main: $25 ⊠ 127 3rd Ave. S, SoBro* ☎ *615/988–7698* ⊕ *www.layercakenashville.com.*

★ Martin's Bar-B-Que Joint

$$ | BARBECUE | Barbecue in the South is a very regional cuisine, with fans of each variation claiming their favorite to be the best. Martin's offers up authentic Tennessee Bar-B-Que with in-house prepared dry rubs and a massive whole-hog cinder-block pit that perfumes the air with the scent of hickory and pumps out delicious pork after a 24-hour slow cook. **Known for:** whole-hog barbecue; outdoor beer garden; rich Southern desserts. ⑤ *Average main: $15 ⊠ 410 4th Ave. S, SoBro* ☎ *615/288–0880* ⊕ *www. martinsbbqjoint.com/downtown.*

The Pancake Pantry

$$ | SOUTHERN | The original Hillsboro Village location opened in 1961, but this newer SoBro location brought the Pancake Pantry's signature scratch-made breakfasts—pancakes, omelets, and waffles—closer to the Downtown masses. Don't miss the irresistible homemade maple syrups; if you're not in the mood for breakfast, there are a range of sandwiches and salads, too. **Known for:** scratch-made pancakes; the line is worth the wait; late-night walk-up window Thursday to Saturday. ⑤ *Average main: $14 ⊠ 220 Molloy St., SoBro* ☎ *615/383–9026* ⊕ *thepancakepantry.com* ☽ *No dinner.*

The Southern Steak & Oyster

$$$$ | AMERICAN | An energetic addition to Nashville's dining scene, The Southern is an airy restaurant on the ground floor of The Pinnacle with a menu that features burgers and sweet potato fries, steak and oysters, salads, and a selection of creative cocktails. Its proximity to a number of major sights, including Bridgestone Arena, Lower Broadway, and the Country Music Hall of Fame and Museum means a steady stream of sports fans, locals, and visitors—and live music. **Known for:** seafood with a Southern twist; meat-centric entrées and creative cocktails; indulgent weekend brunch. ⑤ *Average main: $40 ⊠ 150 3rd Ave. S, Suite 110, SoBro* ☎ *615/724–1762* ⊕ *www.thesouthernnashville.com.*

Sun Diner

$ | DINER | A city that can party all night needs hangover recovery options, and that's where Sun Diner comes in, with Southern favorites and breakfast food options until late afternoon. Located steps away from the music of Broadway, the diner takes its name from legendary rockabilly and country record label Sun Records from Memphis. **Known for:** retro-themed decor; hearty Southern breakfast; convenient location. ⑤ *Average main: $12* ⊠ *107 3rd Ave. S, SoBro* ☎ *615/742–9099* ⊕ *thesundiner.com.*

Yolan

$$$$ | **ITALIAN** | Acclaimed chef Tony Mantuano has brought his talents from Chicago to Nashville with this elegant Italian restaurant that offers a changing tasting menu focused on different regional Italian cuisines. À la carte options inspired by dishes from across Italy are also available. The wine list features Italian bottles rarely seen at other local restaurants, and the pastry program is top-notch. **Known for:** inventive regional Italian cuisine; extensive wine list of rare Italian offerings; house-made pastas. ⑤ *Average main: $42* ⊠ *The Joseph, 403 4th Ave. S, SoBro* ☎ *615/231–0405* ⊕ *www.yolannashville.com* ◷ *No lunch.*

Coffee and Quick Bites

Café Intermezzo

$$ | **EUROPEAN** | Convenient to the Schermerhorn Symphony Center, Bridgestone Arena, and Ascend Amphitheater, Café Intermezzo is a favorite preshow destination for a quick bite before a concert. Serving all three meals of the day plus an extensive specialty coffee drink program, it's also a quiet spot to catch up with friends or meet for a business discussion. **Known for:** preshow destination; international breakfast menu; beautiful and delicious pastries. ⑤ *Average main: $15* ⊠ *205 Demonbreun St., SoBro* ☎ *615/840–7933* ⊕ *www.cafeintermezzo.com/location-nashville-tn.*

★ Crema Coffee Roasters

$ | **CAFÉ** | An early adopter of sustainable sourcing and zero-waste coffee bean roasting, Crema has introduced Nashville coffee lovers to new brews for years. Intentionally partnering with small farmers around the world, Crema advocates for living wages and also brews a fine cup of java to accompany a short list of breakfast dishes. **Known for:** sustainable sourcing and roasting practices; educational coffee-tasting classes; inventive specialty coffee drinks. ⑤ *Average main: $7* ⊠ *15 Hermitage Ave., SoBro* ☎ *615/255–8311* ⊕ *crema-coffee.com* ◷ *No dinner.*

Southernaire Market and Deli

$ | **SANDWICHES** | This cozy market combines the convenience of an urban bodega with the charm of a neighborhood market whose shelves are stocked with various sundries, food and drink items, and locally crafted souvenirs. But the real gem is that the butchers who cut the steak and chops for the attached Southern Steak & Oyster restaurant also prepare excellent deli sandwiches to carry out or eat at one of the few small tables in the shop. **Known for:** great spot for locally crafted souvenirs; excellent sandwiches; helpful selection of sundries for nearby hotel guests. ⑤ *Average main: $12* ⊠ *The Pinnacle at Symphony Place, 150 3rd Ave. S, SoBro* ☎ *615/490–8007* ⊕ *www.southernairemarket.com* ☾ *Closed weekends. No dinner.*

 ## Hotels

Four Seasons Hotel Nashville

$$$ | HOTEL | The Four Seasons signature style is on full display at this sleek glass tower overlooking Downtown and the Cumberland River, from luxurious linens and amenities in the spacious rooms to the infinity pool area that's like an urban oasis tucked away from the biggest crowds of Broadway. **Pros:** first-class amenities and services; easy access across the pedestrian bridge to Nissan Stadium on game days; concierge service offers advice and special opportunities at local sights. **Cons:** some amenities are shared with residents of the upper-floor condominiums; surrounding streets are often blocked for construction; lower-floor rooms can experience outdoor noise, especially those facing Broadway. ⑤ *Rooms from: $585* ⊠ *100 Demonbreun St., SoBro* ☎ *615/610–5001* ⊕ *www.fourseasons.com/nashville* ⌑ *235 rooms* ⑩ *No Meals.*

Hyatt Centric Downtown Nashville

$ | HOTEL | Just steps from the lights and sights of Lower Broadway, this boutique hotel offers guests a convenient escape filled with nods to the soul of Nashville. **Pros:** awesome rooftop pool; a branch of the Pancake Pantry is next door; Country Music Hall of Fame, Symphony Center, and Lower Broadway are easily walkable. **Cons:** noise from events at the nearby amphitheater may keep you up; valet parking is expensive; fantastic pool bar closes early during the week. ⑤ *Rooms from: $244* ⊠ *210 Molloy St., SoBro* ☎ *615/645–6037* ⊕ *www.hyatt.com/hyatt-centric/bnact-hyatt-centric-downtown-nashville* ⌑ *263 rooms* ⑩ *No Meals.*

The Joseph

$$ | HOTEL | This luxury hotel showcases art from the moment guests pull into the building's porte cochere and continues with impressive art installations throughout the building. **Pros:** gallery-worthy art pieces, many from the owner's private collection; premium spa offers a diverse menu of treatments; convenient access to Schermerhorn Symphony Center and

Ascend Amphitheater. **Cons:** small pool area can get crowded and necessitate staking out lounge chairs early in the day; on-site daytime food and beverage options are limited; few nearby options to purchase basic sundries. $ *Rooms from: $400* ⊠ *401 Korean Veterans Blvd., SoBro* ☎ *615/248–1990* ⊕ *www.thejosephnashville.com* ⊅ *297 rooms* ⦿ *No Meals.*

The Omni Nashville

$$ | HOTEL | Right next to the convention center, The Omni has stellar views, a luxe modern interior filled with wood and marble, a restaurant with a seriously good biscuit bar, and a coffee shop serving locally roasted Bongo Java coffee. **Pros:** ADA-accessible rooms available; the city's largest music venues and sports arenas are all within walking distance; excellent on-site dining and entertainment. **Cons:** free in-room Wi-Fi for Omni Select Guest members only; valet parking service is not free; in-room dining service can be slow. $ *Rooms from: $449* ⊠ *250 Rep. John Lewis Way S, SoBro* ☎ *615/782–5300* ⊕ *www.omnihotels.com/hotels/ nashville* ⊅ *800 rooms* ⦿ *No Meals.*

1 Hotel Nashville

$$ | HOTEL | This property's commitment to preserving the planet is evident from the time guests approach the entrance under a massive living plant wall to the moment they enter their room and discover details like chalkboards to reduce paper use, hangers made from 100% recycled paper, and water carafes repurposed from wine bottles. **Pros:** top-to-bottom commitment to sustainable practices; excellent proximity to events at Bridgestone Arena or the Ryman Auditorium; creative restaurant featuring regional dishes made using seasonal local ingredients. **Cons:** hallway noise can be heard in guest rooms; room service cuts off relatively early; little separation between bed and bath areas of guest rooms. $ *Rooms from: $449* ⊠ *710 Demonbreun St., SoBro* ☎ *615/510– 0400* ⊕ *www.1hotels.com/nashville* ⊅ *215 rooms* ⦿ *No Meals.*

Nightlife

BARS

Broadway Brewhouse

BARS | Less of a party scene and more of a place to sit and chat over a pint, Broadway Brewhouse's draft selection is rivaled by few places in town. The attached Mojo Grill serves a mash-up of Cajun and Tex-Mex food, plus some of the best chicken wings in town. ⊠ *317 Broadway, SoBro* ☎ *615/271–2838* ⊕ *www.broadwaybrewhousedowntown.com.*

★ Pinewood Social

GATHERING PLACE | Everything you need for a good time at work or play is at Pinewood Social, an all-day hangout featuring a coffee bar, craft cocktails, a bowling alley, bocce ball, and even two small outdoor dipping pools. This sceney spot is always bustling because the food is as good as the fun. ⊠ *33 Peabody St., SoBro* ☏ *615/751–8111* ⊕ *www.pinewoodsocial.com.*

6th & Peabody

BEER GARDENS | Home to sister companies Yee-Haw Beer and Ole Smoky Tennessee Moonshine, 6th & Peabody is your one-stop shop for beer and spirits tastings, live musical entertainment, outdoor yard games, and watching the big game. The front portion of the entertainment complex is dedicated to a tasting room and gift shop where guests can sample a flight of Ole Smoky's flavored 'shines. The building opens up into an indoor/outdoor space with massive television screens showing sports, a large stage where local acts perform throughout the week, and dining options from White Duck Taco Shop and Daddy's Dogs. They actually distill some of moonshine on-site, so smoking is definitely prohibited! ⊠ *423 6th Ave. S, SoBro* ☏ *615/647–8272* ⊕ *6thandpeabody.com.*

LIVE MUSIC

★ Acme Feed and Seed

LIVE MUSIC | This converted old feed store has a radio station, bar, and stage on the first floor, a sushi bar and cocktail emporium on the second, a private event space on the third, and a DJ hall and bar on the roof. The food menu includes eclectic street food in addition to the sushi, and the roster of music performers is more varied than most Downtown honky-tonks. ⊠ *101 Broadway, SoBro* ☏ *615/915–0888* ⊕ *www.acmefeedandseed.com.*

AJ's Good Time Bar

LIVE MUSIC | Country star Alan Jackson's Broadway honky-tonk occupies three levels, all dedicated to having a good time. Not every level is the same—while all feature beer and live music, check out the third floor for karaoke and the rooftop level for skyline views. ⊠ *421 Broadway, SoBro* ☏ *615/678–4808* ⊕ *www. ajsgoodtimebar.com.*

Ascend Amphitheater

LIVE MUSIC | This outdoor amphitheater is nestled into a hill between Broadway and the Cumberland River, making for great skyline views. Ascend Amphitheater regularly hosts popular musical artists and other touring acts, especially during the spring and summer months. ⊠ *310 1st Ave. S, SoBro* ☏ *615/258–5944* ⊕ *www.livenation.com/venue/KovZpZAEet7A/ ascend-amphitheater.*

City Winery

LIVE MUSIC | This versatility of City Winery's offerings makes it a standout in this music city showcasing everything from rock and soul to comedy. Most people eat in the main showroom before concerts, making it a full evening out. ⊠ *609 Lafayette St., SoBro* ☎ *615/324–1033* ⊕ *citywinery.com/nashville.*

Honky Tonk Central

LIVE MUSIC | Looming over the busiest corner of Lower Broad, the balconies of this three-story club teem with revelers enjoying great live music, food, and beverages. ⊠ *329 Broadway, SoBro* ☎ *615/742–9095* ⊕ *www.honkytonkcentral.com.*

The Listening Room Cafe

LIVE MUSIC | One of Nashville's greatest musical traditions is the "writer's round": a group of songwriters performing their compositions one after the other in a round, creating an intimate environment focused on the music. The Listening Room Cafe is one of the premiere places to experience a writer's round in Nashville, and its high-quality, straight-ahead Southern brunch, lunch, and dinner menus paired with its bar add a tasty twist to the music. ⊠ *618 4th Ave. S, SoBro* ☎ *615/259–3600* ⊕ *www.listeningroom-cafe.com/nashville.*

Nudie's Honky Tonk

LIVE MUSIC | Inspired by the glitz and glamour of rhinestone-loving Western clothier Nudie's Rodeo Tailors, Nudie's Honky Tonk is home to Nashville's longest bar. This multilevel space features a rooftop bar and is decorated with historic stage costumes designed by Nudie Cohn and worn by artists like Bob Dylan, Johnny Cash, Roy Rogers, and more. ⊠ *409 Broadway, SoBro* ☎ *615/942–6307* ⊕ *www.nudieshonkytonk.com.*

3rd & Lindsley

LIVE MUSIC | A local favorite, 3rd & Lindsley hosts musical acts from around town and around the world. This no-frills venue has ample room for dancing, and also has a full lunch and dinner menu in addition to a full bar. For some of the best bets for musical events in town, 3rd & Lindsley is a must. ⊠ *818 3rd Ave. S, SoBro* ☎ *615/259–9891* ⊕ *www.3rdandlindsley.com.*

 Performing Arts

Nashville Children's Theatre

THEATER | **FAMILY** | Performing classic shows for children since the 1930s, this theater company touts the title of the country's oldest continually running children's theater company. They also host drama workshops. ⊠ *25 Middleton St., SoBro* ☎ *615/254–9103 for* *main office, 615/252–4675 for box office ⊕ nashvillechildrensthea-tre.org 🎟 $22.50.*

Nashville Symphony

CONCERTS | Nashville's Symphony orchestra performs around 140 concerts a year, typically at the Schermerhorn Symphony Center, and often collaborates with visiting artists or other members of the Nashville arts community. ✉ *1 Symphony Pl., SoBro* ☎ *615/687–6500 for main office, 615/687–6400 for box office* ⊕ *www.nashvillesymphony.org.*

Schermerhorn Symphony Center

CONCERTS | The splendid home of the Nashville Symphony is a modern take on a great European concert hall. In addition to the symphony, the Schermerhorn hosts many other concerts and boasts an on-site café. ✉ *1 Symphony Pl., SoBro* ☎ *615/687–6500* ⊕ *www.nashvillesymphony.org.*

Shopping

The Goo Goo Chocolate Company

CHOCOLATE | The Goo Goo Cluster is a legendary Nashville candy confection so good that it deserves to have an entire store dedicated to it. A chocolate-covered cluster of nuts and nougat, every flavor of Goo Goo is available here along with the option to create your own customized Premium Goo Goo from a list of delicious ingredients. ✉ *116 3rd Ave. S, SoBro* ☎ *615/490–6685* ⊕ *googoo.com.*

Hatch Show Print

ART GALLERY | Hatch Show Print is home to the legendary let-terpress style that has single-handedly created the signature iconography of Nashville through its handmade show posters. Housed within the Country Music Hall of Fame and Museum, the print studio offers art for sale, as well as tours demonstrating their unique printing and design process. Hands-on experiences are also available at Saturday workshops. ✉ *224 Rep. John Lewis Way S, SoBro* ☎ *615/577–7710* ⊕ *www.hatchshowprint.com.*

THE GULCH

Updated by
Hilli Levin

⊙ Sights   🍴 Restaurants   🛏 Hotels   ⬤ Shopping   🍸 Nightlife

★★★☆☆   ★★★★★   ★★★★☆   ★★★★★   ★★★★★

NEIGHBORHOOD SNAPHOT

TOP EXPERIENCES

■ **Buzzy Upscale Eateries:** From local titans who have been serving up elevated Southern classics for more than a decade to exciting global cuisine from lauded transplants, this is the place to splash out on a decadent evening.

■ **Posh Hotels:** Experience some of Nashville's best accommodations with state-of-the-art amenities that are sure to make your trip relaxing and indulgent.

■ **Urban Southern Charm:** Although this district is characterized by extravagance, there are still cowboy boots, biscuits, locally made souvenirs, and genuine hospitality around every corner.

■ **Diverse Music Venues:** Find exciting local rock showcases, sultry jazz nights, open bluegrass jams, and more in the neighborhood's event spaces.

■ **Craft Cocktails with a View:** Several rooftop bars provide the perfect place to perch and enjoy views of the skyline while sipping specialty drinks crafted by some of the city's most seasoned bartenders.

PLANNING YOUR TIME

The Gulch is always bustling with residents, young professionals, and visitors, and there's rarely a slow hour to be found. Weekends are packed with foodies and urban explorers, so prepare to wait in lines for popular restaurants and attractions. Parking garages and paid lots are plentiful and most offer one free hour of parking each day, with daily rates running around $25. Metered spots max out at three hours during the day, with the option to extend starting after 6 pm. Most businesses close at midnight.

ART IN THE WILD

■ The city's most popular Insta-gram spot—the 20-foot-tall mural of two massive white wings by street artist Kelsey Montague—can be found at ✉ *302 11th Ave. S*; don't forget to use the #what-liftsyou hashtag. There's also a tiny set of wings for your pup's equally angelic photo op.

GETTING HERE

■ There's a WeGo bus route through The Gulch, but construction frequently closes or changes stops; taxis or rideshares are more reliable. Bike rentals are also available 24 hours a day at two different stations and can be checked out through the BCycle app or website. Electric scooter rental sta-tions are also easily found; use the cor-responding phone app to unlock one.

Nashville's Gulch neighborhood has one of the city's most interesting origin stories: Once a busy rail yard anchored by the commuter lines that ran through Union Station, the area fell out of favor after the rail services shut down in 1979. In the early 2000s, young investors and developers laid the foundation for this hip, walkable mixed-use neighborhood that has blossomed into one of Nashville's ritziest and most dynamic areas. Some might say the Nashville boom directly followed The Gulch's rise.

Now mainly a destination for foodies and savvy daring restaurateurs from across the country, The Gulch is characterized by its high-end condos, luxury hotels, plentiful boutiques, and diverse music venues where old and new Nashvilles rub elbows. From historic staples like bluegrass haven The Station Inn and the Union Station Nashville Yards hotel to the new rooftop oases serving up skyline views and inventive cocktails, it's clear this is a neighborhood where Southern tradition meets urban progress.

For our purposes, the borders of The Gulch are as follows: Church Street to the north, I–65 to the west, I–40 to the south, and Rosa L. Parks Boulevard (Route 41) and 8th Avenue South to the east.

Sights

★ Frist Art Museum
ART MUSEUM | FAMILY | Nashville has a unique and active arts community, and the city's main art museum reflects that. Instead of focusing on a beefy permanent collection like Atlanta's High Museum, The Frist, which opened in 2001, aims to expose the city's inhabitants and visitors to as many different and disparate artists, mediums, and movements as possible, with multiple rotating exhibitions from the masters of antiquity to modernists. Depending on when you're in town, you can catch anything from an extensive focus on a single artist to an exploration of

Impressionism. Visitors can dine in The Frist's alfresco café after perusing thought-provoking exhibitions in the 1930s art deco building that once served as a post office. The historic building is a work of art in and of itself, so build in some time to linger or drop by on a Saturday for an architecture tour. ⊠ *919 Broadway, The Gulch* ☎ *615/244–3340* ⊕ *fristartmuseum.org* ⊠ *$15* ⊗ *Closed Tues. and Wed.*

The Gulch's Must-See Murals 🎟

- *Candy Hearts* ⊠ *601 8th Ave. S*

- *Spread Love* ⊠ *1015 Nelson Merry St.*

- *WhatLiftsYou - Rainbow* ⊠ *1010 Martin Luther King Jr. Blvd.*

- *WhatLiftsYou - Wings* ⊠ *302 11th Ave. S*

Noble Park

CITY PARK | FAMILY | This recently constructed green space provides a welcome oasis in the middle of this high-rise district. A large shaded patio peppered with tables makes for an ideal spot to chow down on takeout from a nearby restaurant, and there are plenty of benches and even wooden loungers for soaking up some Southern sun. In the warmer months, the park hosts movie and music nights along with the occasional market. ⊠ *11th Ave. S, The Gulch* ⊕ *nashvilledowntown.com/go/noble-park* ⊠ *Free.*

Paddywax Candle Bar

OTHER ATTRACTION | Nashville's luxe Paddywax candles have become a national household staple with unique scent collections based on classic authors, national parks, and gourmand treats. Visitors to this brick-and-mortar outpost will not only be able to shop their established favorites, but they can also experience the fun of candle making with self-guided workshops or even grab an at-home kit for a DIY fix. ⊠ *408 11th Ave. S, The Gulch* ☎ *615/630–7130* ⊕ *thecandlebar.co* ⊠ *$45 for DIY custom candle pouring.*

★ Third Man Records

OTHER ATTRACTION | Serious Jack White fans won't want to miss his lauded label's Nashville outpost. Drop by to record your own two-minute song on a 1945 Voice-o-Graph machine, pop into the photo booth, dig through the stacks, or grab some exclusive merch. Check their social media and special events pages if you're looking to catch a live performance in the now-legendary Blue Room. Tours of the full operation are available on Fridays at 2 and 3 pm, but book online to snag a spot. ⊠ *623 7th Ave. S, The Gulch* ☎ *615/891–4393* ⊕ *thirdmanrecords.com* ⊠ *$20 for tours.*

The 1930s art deco building that houses the Frist Art Museum once served as a post office. Architecture tours are offered on Saturdays.

WhatLiftsYou Wings Mural

PUBLIC ART | **FAMILY** | For those who want the quintessential Gulch photo op, head to artist Kelsey Montague's Instagram-famous mural right off 11th Avenue South. The sprawling 20-foot white wings are filled with little design nods to the Music City like guitars, along with dreamy abstractions that add to the ethereal feeling. There's even a smaller set of wings that are perfect for kids or pets, so everyone can get their perfect shot. The line can get long, especially during the weekends, so this is a great way to kill some time while you're waiting for a restaurant table nearby. ⊠ *302 11th Ave. S, The Gulch.*

🍴 Restaurants

★ Adele's

$$$ | **SOUTHERN** | Fresh, open, airy, and never too buttoned-up, Adele's is a favorite for business lunches and date-night dinners alike. This high-end Southern eatery was an early part of the neighborhood's revitalization, and James Beard–winning chef Jonathan Waxman continues to dazzle with his accessible but polished cuisine. **Known for:** surprisingly addictive kale salad; Southern coconut cake; Sunday brunch buffet. $ *Average main: $25* ⊠ *1210 McGavock St., The Gulch* ☎ *615/988–9700* ⊕ *www.adelesnashville.com* ⊗ *No dinner Fri.–Sun.*

The Gulch

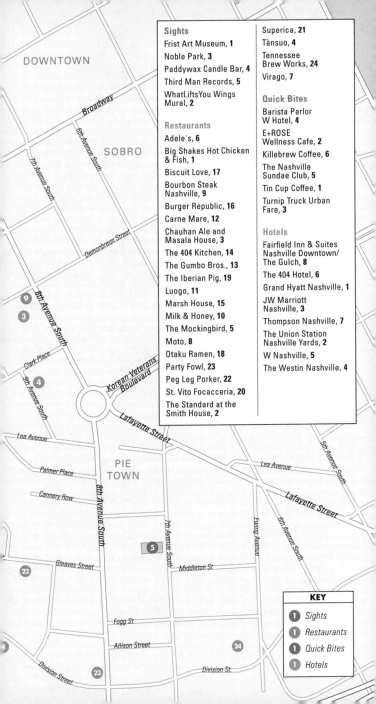

DOWNTOWN

Broadway

SOBRO

6th Avenue South

7th Avenue South

Demonbreun Street

8th Avenue South

Clark Place

9th Avenue South

Korean Veterans Boulevard

Lafayette Street

Lea Avenue

Palmer Place

PIE TOWN

Cannery Row

8th Avenue South

7th Avenue South

Gleaves Street

Middleton St

Ewing Avenue

Lea Avenue

Lafayette Street

5th Avenue South

6th Avenue South

Fogg St

Allison Street

Division Street

Division St.

Sights
Frist Art Museum, **1**
Noble Park, **3**
Paddywax Candle Bar, **4**
Third Man Records, **5**
WhatLiftsYou Wings Mural, **2**

Restaurants
Adele's, **6**
Big Shakes Hot Chicken & Fish, **1**
Biscuit Love, **17**
Bourbon Steak Nashville, **9**
Burger Republic, **16**
Carne Mare, **12**
Chauhan Ale and Masala House, **3**
The 404 Kitchen, **14**
The Gumbo Bros., **13**
The Iberian Pig, **19**
Luogo, **11**
Marsh House, **15**
Milk & Honey, **10**
The Mockingbird, **5**
Moto, **8**
Otaku Ramen, **18**
Party Fowl, **23**
Peg Leg Porker, **22**
St. Vito Focacceria, **20**
The Standard at the Smith House, **2**

Superica, **21**
Tànsuo, **4**
Tennessee Brew Works, **24**
Virago, **7**

Quick Bites
Barista Parlor W Hotel, **4**
E+ROSE Wellness Cafe, **2**
Killebrew Coffee, **6**
The Nashville Sundae Club, **5**
Tin Cup Coffee, **1**
Turnip Truck Urban Fare, **3**

Hotels
Fairfield Inn & Suites Nashville Downtown/ The Gulch, **8**
The 404 Hotel, **6**
Grand Hyatt Nashville, **1**
JW Marriott Nashville, **3**
Thompson Nashville, **7**
The Union Station Nashville Yards, **2**
W Nashville, **5**
The Westin Nashville, **4**

KEY
1 Sights
1 Restaurants
1 Quick Bites
1 Hotels

Big Shake's Hot Chicken & Fish

$ | **SOUTHERN** | Big Shake's juicy hot chicken really holds its own—especially when it comes to its Hot Mess sandwich loaded with coleslaw, pickles, and ghost pepper sauce—but it's also one of the rarer places in town where hot fish is also on the menu. Crispy, golden breaded catfish and whiting fillets also get the famous dry rub treatment here with four different spice levels; there's even a chicken and fish combo platter so diners can get the best of both worlds. **Known for:** hot catfish platter; Hot Mess chicken sandwich; loaded ghost fries. $ *Average main: $12* ✉ *421 11th Ave. N, The Gulch* ☎ *615/988–8044* ⊕ *www.bigshakeshotchicken.com.*

Biscuit Love

$$ | **SOUTHERN** | **FAMILY** | What started as a beloved Airstream food truck is now a brick-and-mortar staple in the neighborhood that's hailed for its daily scratch-made Southern-style biscuits. There are nine different biscuit entrees to choose from, made with a variety of meats, gravies, and toppings, but there are plenty of tempting "Without a Biscuit" options like the surprisingly tasty egg-topped Lindstrom made with shaved brussels sprouts, hazelnuts, and shredded Parmesan. **Known for:** biscuit donuts; long lines at peak hours; a chicken biscuit you'll never forget. $ *Average main: $13* ✉ *316 11th Ave. S, The Gulch* ☎ *615/490–9584* ⊕ *biscuitlove.com.*

Bourbon Steak Nashville

$$$$ | **STEAK HOUSE** | Celebrity chef Michael Mina's restaurant on the top floor of the JW Marriott features impressive offerings of both whiskey and beef along with unparalleled panoramic vistas of Downtown and beyond. In addition to wood-fired steaks, the restaurant's signature Maine lobster potpie is prepared table-side as dinner and a show. **Known for:** excellent whiskey selection; succulent Black Angus and Wagyu beef; table-side lobster potpie presentation. $ *Average main: $75* ✉ *JW Marriott, 201 8th Ave. S, 34th fl., Downtown* ☎ *629/208–8440* ⊕ *nashvillebourbonsteak.com* ☾ *No lunch.*

Burger Republic

$$ | **BURGER** | **FAMILY** | For those craving a burger that's a cut above the rest, Burger Republic offers up 12 different variations—like a fancier version of the In-N-Out classic or a Southern-inspired burger with a Jack Daniel's honey glaze—with a focus on locally sourced meats and ingredients. For the full artery-clogging experience, order a handmade shake spiked with your choice of booze. **Known for:** boozy milkshakes; Tennessee Burger featuring Jack Daniel's honey glaze; tater tot fondue. $ *Average main: $14* ✉ *420 11th Ave. S, The Gulch* ☎ *615/915–1943* ⊕ *burgerrepublic.com.*

Carne Mare

$$$$ | **STEAK HOUSE** | When done just right, a night at an American steak house can be an unforgettable dining experience, and Carne Mare's 30-day dry-aged shareable tomahawk and Wagyu cuts make for worthy splurges, while impressive seafood options like red snapper prepared table-side feel just as decadent. The passion of the hospitality and kitchen teams at the Nashville location is obvious in the loving attention given to each and every dish, cocktail, and dessert on the menu, and the classic and inviting interior delivers a dose of classic elegance with dark wood, leather, and low lighting. **Known for:** critically acclaimed steaks; top-notch service; 17-layer chocolate cake. ⑤ *Average main: $100 ⊠ 300 12th Ave. S, The Gulch* ☎ *615/379–9000* ⊕ *www.carnemarenashville. com* ☾ *No lunch.*

★ Chauhan Ale and Masala House

$$ | **INDIAN** | Chopped judge and beloved celebrity chef Maneet Chauhan made a splash when she announced that she would be opening her first restaurant not in New York or Chicago, but right here in Nashville. Her playful global Indian fusion is not to be missed, and although you'll find some of the best food in the city here by far, the ambience is never stuffy. **Known for:** happy hour weekdays 5–6:30; inventive cocktails and unconventional weekend brunch; tandoori chicken poutine and hot chicken pakoras. ⑤ *Average main: $19 ⊠ 123 12th Ave. N, The Gulch* ☎ *615/242– 8426* ⊕ *www.chauhannashville.com.*

The 404 Kitchen

$$$ | **AMERICAN** | Big on visual presentation and earning high marks in overall aesthetics, The 404 Kitchen is an excellent choice for anyone looking for a sumptuous evening. The menu is focused on elegant yet hearty Southern dishes like catfish and fried chicken, and everything is carefully laid out to ensure that every order lives up to the kitchen's high bar for quality. **Known for:** house-made burrata; decadent Southern brunch; more than 400 whiskies available. ⑤ *Average main: $27 ⊠ 507 12th Ave. S, The Gulch* ☎ *615/251–1404* ⊕ *www.the404nashville.com.*

The Gumbo Bros.

$$ | **CAJUN** | **FAMILY** | True Cajun favorites are notoriously hard to find outside of Louisiana, but two Louisiana State University alums have brought an authentic slice of New Orleans to The Gulch. Four different variations of gumbo are the main draw here, but alligator, catfish, and high-piled po'boys made with bread shipped in directly from the Big Easy all deserve nods as well. **Known for:** chicken and sausage gumbo; Louisiana fried alligator tail;

croissant beignets. $ *Average main: $17* ⊠ *505 12th Ave. S, The Gulch* ☎ *615/679–9063* ⊕ *www.thegumbobros.com.*

★ The Iberian Pig

$$ | TAPAS | For those who are looking for a great place to relax over shareable small plates and flowing glasses of Spanish wines, this venerable Atlanta-based chain delivers on relaxed European ambience. Explore the flavors of Spain with Ibérico ham tastings, tender grilled octopus, paella for two, or even an entire roasted pig for tables of six or more. **Known for:** Ibérico ham tastings; daily happy hour from 4 to 6; 25-plus tapas varieties. $ *Average main: $15* ⊠ *607 Overton St., The Gulch* ☎ *615/844–4242* ⊕ *www. iberianpig.com/nashville.*

Luogo

$$$ | ITALIAN | New York restaurateur Anthony Scotto has opened his latest Italian-American fine-dining destination right in the heart of The Gulch. Diners will be transported to the Amalfi Coast, with whitewashed interiors accented with bright blues and yellows, generous bowls of house-made pastas, and protein-focused entrées centered on classic Mediterranean flavors. **Known for:** pasta Bolognese; fritto misto; duck ragù. $ *Average main: $34* ⊠ *211 12th Ave. S, The Gulch* ☎ *615/988–8200* ⊕ *luogorestaurant. com* ☉ *Closed Mon. No lunch.*

Marsh House

$$$ | SEAFOOD | Southern seafood is no joke: where the Northeast focuses on lobster and clam, the South emphasizes fried Gulf oysters, shrimp, and gumbo. At Marsh House, they elevate these Southern staples to beautiful heights while also offering up a raw bar to behold and their signature seafood towers; now with daily brunch, you can choose a more low-key experience until 2 pm. **Known for:** seafood towers; oyster happy hour; raw bar. $ *Average main: $28* ⊠ *Thompson Nashville, 401 11th Ave. S, The Gulch* ☎ *615/262–6001* ⊕ *www.marshhouserestaurant.com.*

Milk & Honey

$$ | CAFÉ | FAMILY | What started as a tiny coffee-and-gelato shop in nearby Chattanooga, Tennessee, is now a full-service restaurant serving up one of The Gulch's most extensive brunch and lunch menus, with savory options like the shareable shakshuka (eggs poached in a tomato sauce) to comforting breakfast hash bowls. Once known mainly for its gelato, the bakery has also blossomed over recent years with crowd-pleasing homemade Pop-Tarts, brioche cinnamon rolls, and fluffy croissants that pair perfectly with any of their specialty coffee drinks. **Known for:** homemade gelato; shakshuka; buttermilk biscuits. $ *Average main: $15* ⊠ *214 11th Ave. S, The Gulch* ☎ *615/712–7466* ⊕ *milkandhoneynashville.com.*

The Mockingbird

$$$ | DINER | For a melting pot of global flavors, head to Food Network–featured chef Brian Riggenbach's playful modern diner. Start with the famous tatchos (nachos with tater tots) and then take a short trip around with world with Filipino *sisig* (a pork dish that's a bit sour), Korean-style bulgogi steak, and barbacoa (slow-roasted short ribs) smothered in adobo. **Known for:** The Mockingburger (double cheeseburger with charred onion and a secret sauce); peanut butter mousse pie; tatchos with lamb chili. $ *Average main: $25* ⊠ *121 12th Ave. N, The Gulch* ☏ *615/741–9900* ⊕ *www. mockingbirdnashville.com* ☉ *Closed Mon. and Tues.*

Moto

$$ | ITALIAN | The inside of this ritzy Italian restaurant can be a bit of a maze (it's so much bigger on the inside than expected from its small entrance on a side street), but thankfully it just means there's plenty of seating inside for hungry diners to dive into rich, decadent homemade pastas and gnocchi. **Known for:** black spaghetti made with squid ink; extensive wine list; whole branzino. $ *Average main: $20* ⊠ *1120 McGavock St., The Gulch* ☏ *615/736–5305* ☉ *www.mstreetnashville.com/moto.*

★ Otaku Ramen

$$ | RAMEN | Although ramen has always been hiding in Nashville's under-the-radar Japanese spots, Sarah Gavigan returned from 20 years in L.A. and made it her mission to get more Nashvillians interested in slurping it up. Start with either a salty clear *shio* broth or a richer shoyu, then choose one of three protein options plus additional toppings like burnt miso butter. **Known for:** tonkatsu ramen; hot chicken buns; cocktails with Japanese flair. $ *Average main: $15* ⊠ *1104 Division St., The Gulch* ☏ *615/942–8281* ⊕ *otakuramen.com.*

★ Party Fowl

$$ | SOUTHERN | Most Nashville hot chicken joints are smaller grab-and-go affairs, but this spacious sports bar provides table service and a full bar. Heat levels on these hot chicken dishes—you can find just about everything from a half bird to tacos to salads—range from mild to the scary spicy "Poultrygeist." All-day happy hour takes place on Tuesday and Sunday. **Known for:** pork fat–fried piggy chips; hot chicken tenders; brunch-for-two Bloody Mary. $ *Average main: $15* ⊠ *719 8th Ave. S, The Gulch* ☏ *615/624–8255* ⊕ *partyfowl.com.*

★ Peg Leg Porker

$ | BARBECUE | Owner and longtime pitmaster Carey Bringle says it all in his biography: "Smoke is in my veins." The line for the lunch rush is often out the door, but many agree that the dry ribs—hickory-smoked for more than 18 hours—are well worth the wait, as are Peg Leg's wings which are offered BBQ, dry, or hot. Standout sides include the smoked green beans and barbecue baked beans; as an appetizer, you can prime your palate with a platter of piled-high nachos. **Known for:** dry-rub ribs; pulled pork platter; fried pie. $ *Average main: $10* ⊠ *903 Gleaves St., The Gulch* ☎ *615/829–6023* ⊕ *peglegporker.com* ☾ *Closed Sun.*

★ St. Vito Focacceria

$$ | ITALIAN | What started as a beloved nomadic pop-up has now become Nashville's premiere destination for Sicilian cuisine, most notably Sicilian-style pizza—each pizza starts with a handmade focaccia base and is brought to life with toppings like fresh tomato, potato, and lemon or a four-cheese blend with pistachio. Shareable plates of veg rotate according to the season, and a choice selection of desserts and drinks make this a great choice for a chill and intimate evening. **Known for:** fresh-shaved Italian ice; rotating must-try specials; creamy potato. $ *Average main: $15* ⊠ *605 Mansion St., The Gulch* ☎ *615/880–6561* ⊕ *www.stvitonashville.com* ☾ *Closed Mon. and Tues.*

The Standard at the Smith House

$$$$ | AMERICAN | A beautiful and historic 24-room town house built in the 1840s is the setting for this unique restaurant, where dinner is served among fireplaces, oak floors, antiques, and paintings. Specialties include homemade crab bisque, grilled rack of lamb, and fried green tomatoes. **Known for:** antique decor; classic Southern side dishes; elevated steak-house fare. $ *Average main: $45* ⊠ *167 Rosa L. Parks Blvd., The Gulch* ☎ *615/254–1277* ⊕ *www. smithhousenashville.com* ☾ *Closed Sun. No lunch.*

Superica

$$ | MEXICAN | Atlanta-based chef Ford Fry has brought a location of his popular Tex-Mex chain to the Gulch, and the neighborhood is all the better for it. Customizable queso fundido makes for an ideal appetizer, and the tortillas are all made in the restaurant, taking their three different styles of tacos—street, *al carbon*, and traditional Tex-Mex—to new heights. **Known for:** queso fundido; puffy norteña-style tacos; skirt steak. $ *Average main: $20* ⊠ *605 Overton St., The Gulch* ☎ *615/709–3148* ⊕ *superica.com/nashville.*

Tànsuo

$$$ | CHINESE FUSION | Although the street view isn't much, jewel-toned hanging lanterns, cozy wraparound booths, and upbeat tunes await inside one of Nashville's top spots for Chinese fusion. The Chinese roasted duck is can't-miss, but order ahead or prepare to settle in and have a few cocktails while it's being prepped. **Known for:** dim sum and sake specials on Sundays; duck dishes;

General Tso brussels sprouts. $ *Average main: $35* ⊠ *121B 12th Ave. N, The Gulch* ☎ *615/782–6786* ⊕ *www.tansuonashville.com* ⊙ *Closed Mon. No lunch.*

★ Tennessee Brew Works

$ | **AMERICAN** | Enjoy some of the city's finest craft beers at this chilled-out multilevel taproom where the masterful brewing process—an in-house chemist is employed for ideal fermentation—is matched with a passion for locally sourced ingredients and history. The attention to detail also extends to their solid food menu with standout items such as their Five Beer Burger, hot chicken sandwich, beer bread grilled cheese, and more. **Known for:** Five Beer Burger; Saturday brewery tours; happy hour specials Monday through Friday. $ *Average main: $12* ⊠ *809 Ewing Ave., The Gulch* ☎ *615/436–0050* ⊕ *www.tnbrew.com.*

Virago

$$ | **SUSHI** | The best place to go for a lively night of cocktails and inventive sushi rolls, step inside Virago's new location with an updated sprawling modern interior and get ready for some of the freshest fish you can find in the entire landlocked state. Make a reservation if you're smart, and be sure to follow the business-casual dress code. **Known for:** half-price maki and 2-for-1 sake on Mondays; bao buns; wasabi martinis. $ *Average main: $20* ⊠ *1120 McGavock St., The Gulch* ☎ *615/254–1902* ⊕ *www. mstreetnashville.com/virago.*

☕ Coffee and Quick Bites

Barista Parlor W Hotel

$ | **CAFÉ** | Serious coffee connoisseurs shouldn't leave the city without a visit to one of Barista Parlor's outposts. The Gulch location is housed on the first level of the W, and everything inside—from the wood tables and platters to the art and barista aprons—are sourced from local makers and craftspeople, so you better believe they're serious about keeping it bespoke. **Known for:** bourbon vanilla latte; unique limited-run beans from around the world; homemade Pop-Tarts. $ *Average main: $7* ⊠ *300 12th Ave. S, The Gulch* ☎ *615/227–4782* ⊕ *baristaparlor.com.*

E+ROSE Wellness Cafe

$ | **VEGETARIAN** | **FAMILY** | Vegans, vegetarians, and anyone looking for a healthy pick-me-up can find light breakfast and lunch fare at this location of the popular local chain. Hearty salads with house-made dressings, bright fruit superfood bowls with crunchy cacao nibs, fresh-pressed juices, and inventive smoothies make it a treat to grab some nourishing food on the go. **Known for:** superfood smoothie bowls; rejuvenating green juices; extensive vegan options. $ *Average main: $12* ✉ *1201 Demonbreun St., Suite 110, The Gulch* ☎ *615/200–7684* ⊕ *eandrose.com*.

Killebrew Coffee

$ | **CAFÉ** | **FAMILY** | High-quality beans are the focal point of this airy and upscale coffee shop located on the ground floor of the Thompson Hotel. The friendly and professional staff serve up a rotating selection of specialty and seasonal lattes that keep things interesting along with sweet and savory breakfast bites. **Known for:** matcha latte; breakfast sandwich; Gulchie latte (vanilla and caramel). $ *Average main: $5* ✉ *Thompson Nashville, 401 11th Ave. S, The Gulch* ☎ *615/262–6001* ⊕ *www.killecoffee.com* ☾ *No dinner.*

The Nashville Sundae Club

$ | **ICE CREAM** | **FAMILY** | A little inner child indulgence is encouraged at this playful ice cream shop that also serves up cocktails, boozy milkshakes, scoops and cones, espresso drinks, and eight different varieties of hot chocolate. Sundaes with toppings like brownies, marshmallows, and cinnamon rolls are the focus, and there's also a banana split with all the fixings. **Known for:** quick breakfast bites; ice cream sandwiches; boozy milkshakes. $ *Average main: $5* ✉ *335 11th Ave. S, The Gulch* ☎ *615/252–5600* ⊕ *www.nash-villesundaeclub.com*.

Tin Cup Coffee

$ | **CAFÉ** | This quiet oasis on an otherwise bustling block beckons with a relaxing interior characterized by warm brick, weathered wood floors, and string lights. Pop in for solid brewed coffee and all the classic espresso drinks, plus quick and satisfying breakfast and lunch bites. **Known for:** quick service; biscuit sandwich; breakfast burrito. $ *Average main: $10* ✉ *1201 Demonbreun St., Suite 100, The Gulch* ☎ *615/964–7799* ⊕ *tincup.coffee* ☾ *Closed Sun. No dinner.*

Turnip Truck Urban Fare

$ | **AMERICAN** | **FAMILY** | Need quick access to a natural market in the middle of town? Head to Turnip Truck for Nashville's best local produce; hot bars filled with fresh and healthy options for breakfast, lunch, and dinner; locally made bath and beauty products; and plenty of tables inside and out for enjoying a quick and healthy meal or midday snack. **Known for:** all-day hot bar; locally made gift options; juice and smoothie bar. $ *Average main: $10* ✉ *321 12th Ave. S, The Gulch* ☎ *615/248–2000* ⊕ *www.theturniptruck.com*.

Hotels

Fairfield Inn & Suites Nashville Downtown/The Gulch
$ | **HOTEL** | This bright, clean, and reliable hotel is a favorite for business travelers and casual tourists alike. **Pros:** solid complimentary breakfast; rooftop bar with live music; good amenities for business travelers. **Cons:** rooms are comfy but lack design flair; few amenities available; daily parking fees can add up. $ *Rooms from: $260 ⊠ 901 Division St., The Gulch ☎ 615/690–1740 ⊕ www. marriott.com ⇱ 126 rooms ⧉ Free Breakfast.*

The 404 Hotel
$$ | **HOTEL** | Next door to The Station Inn sits this very private boutique hotel with just four loft-style king rooms, no lobby, keyless entry, and no common area. **Pros:** complimentary snacks and coffee; very spacious rooms; private and quiet. **Cons:** difficult to snag a booking; no on-site concierge; limited amenities. $ *Rooms from: $350 ⊠ 404 12th Ave. S, The Gulch ☎ 615/242–7404 ⊕ www.the404hotel.com ⇱ 4 rooms ⧉ No Meals.*

Grand Hyatt Nashville
$$ | **HOTEL** | Towering over the railroad line that bisects Downtown, this conveniently located hotel—easy walking access to both Downtown and Midtown without being in the middle of the Lower Broad craziness—embraces the historic nature of the city's past as a rail center with impressive symbolic artwork in the massive lobby. **Pros:** James Beard–winning chef's restaurant on-site; convenient access to all three interstates crossing in Downtown; short walk to Lower Broad without all the craziness associated with the main tourist district. **Cons:** lots of construction in the area can get noisy during the day; railroad tracks complicate walking access to The Gulch; feels a little isolated over the hill from the main strip of Broadway. $ *Rooms from: $323 ⊠ 1000 Broadway, The Gulch ☎ 615/622–1234 ⊕ www.hyatt.com ⇱ 591 rooms ⧉ No Meals.*

JW Marriott Nashville
$$$ | **HOTEL** | Nashville's tallest hotel casts a shadow over the Music City Center, making this contemporary luxury hotel a preferred home base for conventioneers. **Pros:** amazing skyline views from almost every guest room; celebrity-chef restaurant; a wide variety of room and suite types to choose from. **Cons:** no free Wi-Fi; pricey on-site dining options; no self-parking option and valet is very expensive. $ *Rooms from: $550 ⊠ 201 8th Ave. S, The Gulch ☎ 615/291–8600 ⊕ www.marriott.com ⇱ 533 rooms ⧉ No Meals.*

★ Thompson Nashville

$$$ | HOTEL | Award-winning for its architecture, this centrally located luxury boutique hotel is one of the best spots to stay in the city, as it affords guests the ability to explore, shop, and dine their way through the entire Gulch neighborhood on foot. **Pros:** central Gulch location; in-room stereo; great dining options. **Cons:** can be noisy; no pool; no in-room coffee/tea. $ Rooms from: $529 ⊠ 401 11th Ave. S, The Gulch ☎ 615/262–6000 ⊕ www.hyatt.com ⇋ 224 rooms ⦿ No Meals.

★ The Union Station Nashville Yards

$$ | HOTEL | With a 65-foot barrel-vaulted lobby ceiling, granite walls, huge stone fireplaces, stained-glass windows, crystal chandeliers, and even its own blend of Jack Daniel's whiskey, a stay at this renovated 1900 train station includes a unique peek into local history; the building was designated a National Historic Landmark in 1977. **Pros:** beautiful public spaces; unique setting, with notable architecture and history; rooms feel like city apartments rather than hotel rooms. **Cons:** elevators are small and dark (so hurrah for the wide open staircases); valet parking is expensive; hallways can be narrow and dim. $ Rooms from: $447 ⊠ 1001 Broadway, The Gulch ☎ 615/726–1001 ⊕ www.unionstationhotelnashville. com ⇋ 125 rooms ⦿ No Meals.

W Nashville

$$ | HOTEL | This luxury pick delivers with a convenient Gulch location, spacious rooms, sophisticated modern decor, and robust amenities. **Pros:** 24-hour room service; attentive and helpful staff; excellent dining options. **Cons:** pool can be booked by public and often gets crowded; not as walkable as other options; wait times for drinks and food can be long. $ Rooms from: $400 ⊠ 300 12th Ave. S, The Gulch ☎ 615/379–9000 ⊕ www.marriott.com ⇋ 406 rooms ⦿ No Meals.

The Westin Nashville

$$ | HOTEL | Across the street from the massive Music City Center convention facility, The Westin offers easy access to many desired destinations along with casual elegance and the chain's famously plush beds. **Pros:** extremely convenient location for conventioneers and tourists; attached Oak Steakhouse is a fine option for carnivores and seafood lovers; indoor and outdoor pool plus excellent spa and fitness facilities. **Cons:** lower floors have disappointing views unless they face Downtown; access to pool deck can be limited by private party bookings; valet parking is expensive and can be slow during peak traffic times. $ Rooms from: $329 ⊠ 807 Clark Pl., The Gulch ☎ 615/248–2800 ⊕ www.marriott.com ⇋ 456 rooms ⦿ No Meals.

Nightlife

BARS

Casa de Montecristo Cigar Lounge

BARS | This 6,000-foot cigar lounge and shop takes its selection seriously, with state-of-the-art humidors and an incredibly knowledgeable staff who are more than happy to walk visitors through the basics. Aficionados may even have luck tracking down elusive and exclusive cigars. The bar's focus is on pours of bourbon, whiskey, and craft beer, and there's live music every Thursday night. ✉ *600 9th Ave. S, Suite 130, The Gulch* 🕾 *615/800–3397* ⊕ *www.casademontecristo.com/nashville.*

The Pub

PUB | **FAMILY** | Walk into this wood-paneled wonderland and enjoy a little taste of London right in the heart of The Gulch. Anglophiles will be happy to find crispy fish-and-chips, a typical Sunday roast with all the fixings, and shepherd's pie, along with imported British ales that are rare to find on tap. Trivia nights happen every Monday, and it's a popular place for watching both local and overseas soccer games. ✉ *400 11th Ave. S, The Gulch* 🕾 *615/678–4840* ⊕ *experiencethepub.com/nashville.*

COCKTAIL LOUNGES

★ Gertie's Bar

COCKTAIL BARS | This inviting downstairs addition to The 404 Kitchen offers up 14 pages of hard-to-find whiskies from around the world on its menu, many of which are proudly displayed as part of the decor. You'll find some bottles here, all hand-selected by chef Matt Bolus, that you'd be hard-pressed to find in even the most exclusive whiskey bars in New York. Every dish from the restaurant upstairs is also available to order directly from the bar. ✉ *507 12th Ave. S, The Gulch* ✛ *Downstairs from The 404 Kitchen* 🕾 *615/251–1404* ⊕ *www.gertieswhiskeybar.com.*

★ L.A. Jackson

COCKTAIL BARS | At the top of the luxe Thompson Nashville is the city's premier rooftop bar, where the drinks are strong and the views are just as Instagrammable as the hip modern decor. Filled to the brim with friendly young professionals and travelers on the weekends, this is always a lively spot, especially when there's a local DJ spinning records. The Frozé is always a crowd-pleaser, and they offer a variety of small bites and cocktails along with brunch on the weekends. ✉ *Thompson Nashville, 401 11th Ave. S, The Gulch* 🕾 *615/262–6007* ⊕ *www.lajacksonbar.com.*

Pins Mechanical has duckpin bowling, bocce courts, pinball machines, ping-pong tables, and foosball tables.

LIVE MUSIC

The Blue Room

LIVE MUSIC | Jack White's Nashville bar and venue slings drinks from Thursday through Sunday, but there's almost always something happening during the week that's worth checking out. Independent film screenings that don't happen anywhere else in the city, touring bands from all over, funky little art markets, trivia, dance parties, and comedy nights are consistently found on the event calendar. ⊠ *623 7th Ave. S, The Gulch* ☎ *615/891–4393* ⊕ *theblueroombar.com* ☾ *Closed Sun.–Wed.*

Rudy's Jazz Room

LIVE MUSIC | Looking for an intimate listening room experience, but not a country music fan? Head to Rudy's for incredible local and traveling jazz musicians, Prohibition-style cocktails, a full dinner menu filled with New Orleans cuisine, and cozy mood lighting. Catch an all-ages jazz jam every Sunday night. ⊠ *809 Gleaves St., The Gulch* ☎ *615/988–2458* ⊕ *www.rudysjazzroom.com.*

Sambuca

LIVE MUSIC | This three-story eatery caters to those looking for a night of dinner, live music, and dancing. Bands start around 6:30 each night; if you're more of an early riser, you can opt for some tunes with your brunch instead. The style of music rotates, so be sure to check out the event calendar on their website. ⊠ *601 12th Ave. S, The Gulch* ☎ *615/248–2888* ⊕ *www.sambucanashville. com.*

★ The Station Inn

LIVE MUSIC | One of the last bastions of old Nashville that locals still frequent despite the influx of tourists, The Station Inn is without a doubt the best place to hear bluegrass, roots music, and Americana in the city. Inside the worn stone building you'll find cheap beer, folding tables, mismatched chairs, and a sea of red-and-white-checkered plastic tablecloths that prove this venue is charmingly frozen in time. ✉ *402 12th Ave. S, The Gulch* ☎ *615/255–3307* ⊕ *stationinn.com.*

TAPROOMS

Hops + Crafts

BREWPUBS | Curious about the Southeast's celebrated craft beer scene? Make a stop at this laid-back taproom to try one of their 36 rotating taps, order a bite from their small but solid food menu, and relax and refuel after a long day of walking and shopping. Hit up their nightly "Hoppy Hour" from 4–6 pm for different beer specials, and remember to check out the fridge for a six-pack to take home. ✉ *319 12th Ave. S, The Gulch* ☎ *615/678–8631* ⊕ *www.hopscrafts.com.*

THEMED ENTERTAINMENT

Pins Mechanical

THEMED ENTERTAINMENT | Let loose and have a night of play at this spacious and energetic duckpin bowling bar. With smaller lanes, pins and bowling balls, duckpin games offer a unique challenge, but there are also bocce courts, pinball machines, ping-pong tables, and foosball tables to float between for a full night of activities. Free video games and rounds of giant Jenga are a great way to pass the time while waiting for an open lane. Fruit-forward cocktails, punches, and boozy Slush Puppies are the main draw at the bar, and there's usually a food truck parked outside to provide a late-night bite. ✉ *1102 Grundy St., The Gulch* ☎ *615/610–7461* ⊕ *www.pinsbar.com/nashville.*

Shopping

CLOTHING AND ACCESSORIES

★ Blush Boutique

CLOTHING | A Nashville staple and frequently voted one of the best women's boutiques in town, Blush specializes in trendy colorful pieces that won't break the bank. Their focus is on "unique affordable fashion," and they definitely deliver on that promise. If you fall in love with their carefully curated selection during your trip, you can call to order your favorite pieces that pop up on their Instagram feed, even after you head back home. ✉ *606 12th Ave. S, The Gulch* ☎ *615/401–9599* ⊕ *blushboutiques.com.*

Lucchese Bootmaker

SHOES | Skip the two-for-one boot deals on Broadway in favor of the hand-stitched beauties at Lucchese. This luxury Texan brand is renowned for expert craftsmanship and attention to detail; if you're interested in raising some eyebrows, you can even find boots made of exotic materials like alligator, lizard, ostrich, and more. ⊠ *503 12th Ave. S, The Gulch* ☎ *615/242–1161* ⊕ *www. lucchese.com.*

Uncommon James

JEWELRY & WATCHES | Laguna Beach alum Kristin Cavallari relocated to Nashville in 2017 and opened her posh boutique soon after. You can snag a piece from her understated jewelry collection, in-house skin-care line, a branded tote or hat, or a few choice home goods characterized by clean lines and copper accents. Regardless of what you pick up, rest assured it will be chic and Instagram-ready. ⊠ *601 9th Ave. S, The Gulch* ☎ *615/712–7443* ⊕ *uncommonjames.com.*

MUSIC

Carter Vintage Guitars

MUSIC | Founded in 2012 by friendly and knowledgeable husband-and-wife duo Christine and Walter Carter, this gorgeous showroom is for serious musicians looking for a one-of-a-kind instrument. With price tags that also list the famous musicians who previously owned the piece, this is a shopping experience like no other. Take a vintage guitar, mandolin, or other fretted beauty into one of their private rooms and try it out for yourself. ⊠ *625 8th Ave. S, The Gulch* ☎ *615/915–1851* ⊕ *cartervintage.com.*

The Gibson Garage

MUSIC | Gibson's flagship experiential guitar shop combines the historic narrative of a museum with a hands-on music store. Staffed by some of the most knowledgeable gearheads that can be found, it's easy to take a Gibson for a test drive or track down a special accessory to get you the tone of your dreams. Branded apparel, gifts, and a book section ensure there's a little something for everyone. ⊠ *209 10th Ave. S, Suite 209, The Gulch* ☎ *615/933–6000* ⊕ *www.gibson.com/en-US/garage.*

GERMANTOWN AND MARATHON VILLAGE

Updated by
Brittney McKenna

⦿ Sights   🍴 Restaurants   🛏 Hotels   🛍 Shopping   🍸 Nightlife
★★★★☆   ★★★★★   ★☆☆☆☆   ★★★☆☆   ★★★☆☆

NEIGHBORHOOD SNAPSHOT

TOP EXPERIENCES

- **City House:** Enjoy Southern-inspired rustic Italian fare from James Beard–winning chef Tandy Wilson.

- **Tennessee State Museum:** Explore Tennessee's history through permanent and rotating exhibitions, with admission always free.

- **Oktoberfest:** Germantown plays host to Nashville's vibrant Oktoberfest celebration every fall, with dates varying.

- **Bearded Iris Brewing:** Enjoy some of Nashville's most celebrated brews, like the Homestyle IPA, in this large quirky space.

- **The Christie Cookie Company:** Take home a box of cookies as souvenirs or stop in for a snack—just don't miss out on these fresh-baked Nashville originals.

- **First Horizon Park:** Catch a Nashville Sounds baseball game while enjoying local concessions and on-site minigolf.

GETTING HERE

Germantown is easily accessible via bus. If it's a nice day, bike or walk from Downtown on the Music City Bikeway, which offers scenic views of the Cumberland River. Once in Germantown, points of interest are easily walkable.

BACK IN THE DAY

One of Germantown's largest structures is Werthan Lofts, a popular condo building that once housed a burlap bag mill, originally built in 1872. Trips through Germantown will yield similarly repurposed buildings, showing the area to be one of Nashville's best-preserved neighborhoods.

QUICK BITES

- **The Cupcake Collection.** Stop in for fresh-baked award-winning cupcakes in traditional and seasonal flavors. ✉ 1213 6th Ave. N ⊕ www.thecupcakecollection.com

- **Steadfast Coffee.** Reenergize with a refreshing coffee soda or a creative espresso concoction at this local coffee purveyor. ✉ 603 Taylor St. ⊕ steadfast.coffee

- **Red Bicycle Coffee.** Stop in for a quick but delicious lunch of savory crepes, tacos, and more at this friendly neighborhood eatery. ✉ 1200 5th Ave. N, Suite 104 ⊕ redbicyclecoffee.com

A historic neighborhood that has seen a boom in development and growth over the last decade, Germantown is a sight to behold with classic row houses, brick sidewalks, and a tree canopy that makes you forget you're a stone's throw from Downtown. It's also home to several of the city's best-loved and most acclaimed restaurants, as well as high-end shopping and destinations for sports fans and history buffs.

James Beard–winning chef Tandy Wilson's restaurant City House is a cornerstone of the neighborhood, beloved for its rustic Southern take on Italian food. A few blocks away, you'll find Philip Krajeck's Rolf & Daughters, another acclaimed Italian spot with cozy digs and a vibrant cocktail program. For more casual fare, grab a beer at Bearded Iris Brewing's flagship location, where you can find the celebrated brewery's fan favorites like the Homestyle IPA as well as rotating seasonal brews. Brewery hoppers can then head down to Preservation Co., an outpost of the popular Atlanta-based brand Monday Night Brewing, housed in a historic building and situated a stone's throw from another Atlanta transplant, the slick and vibey seafood house The Optimist.

Germantown is also dotted with coffee shops, making it the ideal destination for a leisurely but caffeinated afternoon. Local favorite Barista Parlor has a location just next door to City House, while newer local outfit Elegy Coffee has a convenient walkable spot serving up specialty espresso drinks and seasonal food offerings. Tempered Café and Chocolate offers a more refined café experience, serving homemade chocolates alongside meticulously chosen wines and artisanal cheeses. Book ahead at Tempered for a whiskey and chocolate pairing, a uniquely Nashville experience.

After fueling up on coffee and carbs, pop across Jefferson Street to find activities suited to any interest. The newly reopened Tennessee State Museum, housed in a stunning building with a grand marble atrium, is well worth a visit, housing local artifacts as well as rotating seasonal exhibitions. The Sounds minor-league baseball team plays at First Horizon Park, a newer stadium with fun family-friendly amenities like a Putt-Putt course and ping-pong tables, plus local fare served at concessions. Brooklyn Bowl Nashville plays host to local and national touring musicians, but plan ahead as events are ticketed. And just down the road is Top Golf, a great spot to kick back and work on your swing.

Must-See Murals

- *Harmony* ⊠ *1120 4th Ave. N*

- *Instagram Like* ⊠ *1230 4th Ave. N*

- *Kindness Is* ⊠ *1120 4th Ave. N*

Just over a mile from Germantown is Marathon Village. Housed in what remains of Marathon Motor Works (which produced automobiles in the early 20th century), Marathon Village features Corsair Distillery, Nelson's Green Brier Distillery, concert venue Marathon Music Works, an *American Pickers* store, and a number of shops and small businesses.

Sights

★ Corsair Distillery & Taproom

DISTILLERY | A highlight of Marathon Village is Corsair Distillery & Taproom, a microdistillery and brewpub offering eclectic locally-made spirits, beer, and pizza. Visitors can tour the facility, which is housed in a century-old automobile factory, and try full- and sample-size offerings of Corsair spirits in the distillery's taproom. Tours are offered every day but Tuesday and last about 30 minutes. ⊠ *1200 Clinton St., Suite 110, Marathon Village* ☎ *615/200–0320* ⊕ *www.corsairdistillery.com/marathon* 🍽 *$18 for tour with tasting; $10 for tour without tasting* ⊙ *Closed Tues.*

First Horizon Park

SPORTS VENUE | FAMILY | First Horizon Park is home to Nashville's triple-A baseball team, the Nashville Sounds. Game attendees will enjoy a variety of concessions, including craft cocktails and small bites at outfield bar The Band Box. And if you can't sit through an entire baseball game without getting fidgety, the park also has ping-pong tables and a minigolf course to keep you entertained. ⊠ *19 Junior Gilliam Way, Germantown* ☎ *615/690–4487* ⊕ *firsthorizonpark.com.*

Friday through Sunday guided tours and tastings (best to reserve online) can be booked for Nelson's Green Brier Distillery.

Fisk University

COLLEGE CAMPUS | Founded in 1866, Fisk is Nashville's oldest university. In 1930 it became the first historically black institution to gain accreditation by the Southern Association of Colleges and Schools (SACS), and the 40-acre campus is listed on the National Register of Historic Places as a historic district. Its students were instrumental in many of the sit-in demonstrations in Nashville. The Carl Van Vechten Art Gallery has an extensive art collection worth visiting, and the Jubilee Hall, the first permanent structure in the South built for the education of black students, is where you'll find a floor-to-ceiling portrait of the original Jubilee Singers, who started touring in 1871 to raise funds for the university; they performed for Queen Victoria. Tours are available. ✉ *1000 17th Ave. N, Germantown* ☎ *615/329–8500* ⊕ *www.fisk.edu.*

★ Fisk University Galleries

ART GALLERY | One of Nashville's best destinations for fine art is the campus of Fisk University, just north of Downtown. Visit the Carl Van Vechten Gallery to see works by Picasso, Cézanne, Renoir, and more. Elsewhere on campus, check out murals by Harlem Renaissance artist Aaron Douglas. For summer visitors, be mindful of limited hours. ✉ *1000 17th Ave. N, Germantown* ☎ *615/329–8720* ⊕ *www.fiskuniversitygalleries.org* ☾ *Closed Sun.*

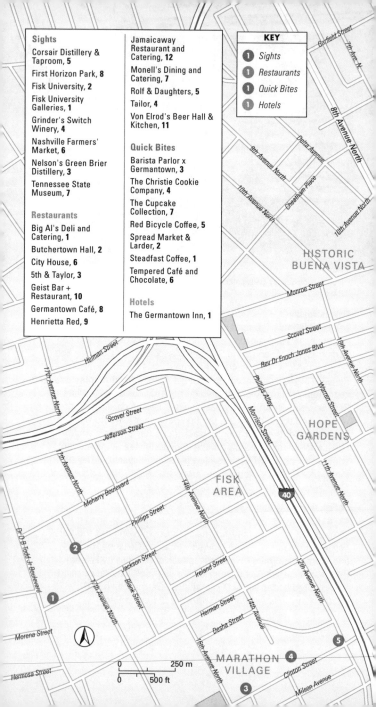

Sights

Corsair Distillery & Taproom, **5**

First Horizon Park, **8**

Fisk University, **2**

Fisk University Galleries, **1**

Grinder's Switch Winery, **4**

Nashville Farmers' Market, **6**

Nelson's Green Brier Distillery, **3**

Tennessee State Museum, **7**

Restaurants

Big Al's Deli and Catering, **1**

Butchertown Hall, **2**

City House, **6**

5th & Taylor, **3**

Geist Bar + Restaurant, **10**

Germantown Café, **8**

Henrietta Red, **9**

Jamaicaway Restaurant and Catering, **12**

Monell's Dining and Catering, **7**

Rolf & Daughters, **5**

Tailor, **4**

Von Elrod's Beer Hall & Kitchen, **11**

Quick Bites

Barista Parlor x Germantown, **3**

The Christie Cookie Company, **4**

The Cupcake Collection, **7**

Red Bicycle Coffee, **5**

Spread Market & Larder, **2**

Steadfast Coffee, **1**

Tempered Café and Chocolate, **6**

Hotels

The Germantown Inn, **1**

KEY

- **1** Sights
- **1** Restaurants
- **1** Quick Bites
- **1** Hotels

HISTORIC BUENA VISTA

HOPE GARDENS

FISK AREA

MARATHON VILLAGE

Garfield Street

7th Ave. N.

8th Avenue North

Delta Avenue

9th Avenue North

Cheatham Place

10th Avenue North

10th Avenue North

Monroe Street

Scovel Street

Rev Dr Enoch Jones Blvd.

10th Avenue North

Phillips Alley

Morrison Street

Warren Street

11th Avenue North

12th Avenue North

Hellman Street

17th Avenue North

Scovel Street

Jefferson Street

11th Avenue North

Meharry Boulevard

Phillips Street

14th Avenue North

Dr. D.B. Todd Jr Boulevard

17th Avenue North

Jackson Street

Blank Street

Ireland Street

Herman Street

14th Avenue

18th Avenue North

Desha Street

Clinton Street

Milson Avenue

Morena Street

Hermosa Street

I-40

0 250 m
0 500 ft

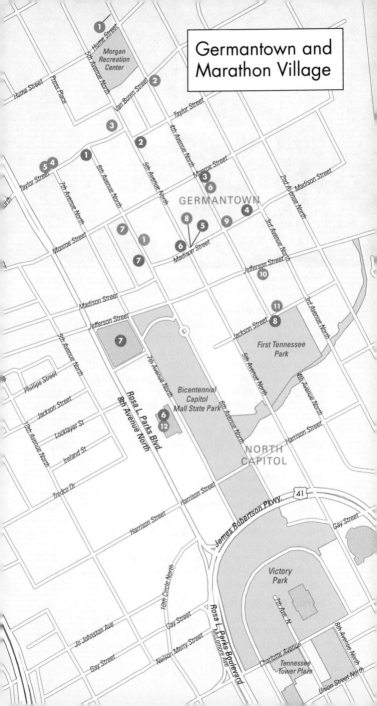

Permanent exhibits at the Tennessee State Museum range from First Peoples to the Civil War and Reconstruction and Tennesse Transforms.

Grinder's Switch Winery

WINERY | While there are a couple of distilleries on the Marathon Village property, the casual yet sophisticated setting of Grinder's Switch Winery ought to please the wine lover in your group. Expect everyday favorites like Cabernet Sauvignon, but their specialty is blends like their white table wine as well as fruited wines like Razzbury (raspberry) and Cou Rouge (strawberry). While you're there, pick up a curated local gift or craft in the winery's attached shop. If you're wondering where the wine is made, it comes from their vineyard in middle Tennessee. ⊠ *1310 Clinton St., Suite 125, Marathon Village* ☎ *615/679–0646* ⊕ *gswinery.com* 🖃 *$15 for tasting.*

★ Nashville Farmers' Market

MARKET | The Nashville Farmers' Market is the crown jewel of the Germantown area, bringing the community and surrounding neighborhood together with food, produce, and special events. Visit on a weekday to take advantage of the market's extensive restaurant offerings, which span myriad international cuisines. Come on the weekend for goods from local farmers and artisans. ⊠ *900 Rosa L. Parks Blvd., Germantown* ☎ *615/880–2001* ⊕ *www. nashvillefarmersmarket.org.*

Nelson's Green Brier Distillery

DISTILLERY | It wouldn't be a trip to Tennessee without some Tennessee whiskey, and Nelson's is home to Belle Meade Bourbon, a local favorite that has grown to national prominence. While on-site, you can tour the distillery, taste spirits, and shop the distillery's gift shop, which carries bottles, glassware, and other booze-centric gifts. Tours last about an hour and include four tastings; there's also an option for non-drinkers. ⊠ *1414 Clinton St., Germantown* ☎ *615/913–8800* ⊕ *greenbrierdistillery.com* ⊠ *$25 for tours.*

Tennessee State Museum

OTHER ATTRACTION | In 2018, the Tennessee State Museum relocated from Downtown to its own building in Germantown, right next to the popular Nashville Farmers' Market. Visitors to the museum will find thousands of artifacts and pieces of art in the museum's permanent collection, as well as periodic rotating exhibitions, all telling the story of Tennessee and its people. Admission to the museum is always free. ⊠ *Bill Haslam Center, 1000 Rosa L. Parks Blvd., Germantown* ☎ *615/741–2692* ⊕ *tnmuseum.org* ☉ *Closed Mon.*

 Restaurants

★ Big Al's Deli and Catering

$ | SOUTHERN | Tucked away in nearby Salemtown is Big Al's Deli, a neighborhood deli in every sense of the word. Owner Alfonso Hamilton serves home-cooked Southern food out of an otherwise nondescript converted house, making for a dining experience that feels like you're right at home. **Known for:** no-frills breakfast and lunch; friendly service; long waits but the food is worth it. ⑤ *Average main: $6* ⊠ *1828 4th Ave. N, Germantown* ☎ *615/594–5974* ⊕ *www.bigalsdeliandcatering.com* ☉ *Closed Sun.*

Butchertown Hall

$$ | BARBECUE | The name says it all: Butchertown Hall is the place to go for excellent elevated meat dishes, with a menu inspired by meat markets in Texas. Order smoked meats by the pound with sides like seasonal vegetables and shaved street corn, or opt for (slightly) lighter fare like oak-smoked brisket tacos and grilled lamb lollipops. **Known for:** elevated takes on traditional barbecue; tequila-heavy cocktail program; bright airy atmosphere. ⑤ *Average main: $22* ⊠ *1416 4th Ave. N, Germantown* ☎ *615/454–3634* ⊕ *www.butchertownhall.com* ☉ *No lunch Mon.–Thurs.*

★ City House

$$ | SOUTHERN | James Beard–winning chef Tandy Wilson has built a Nashville institution with City House, one of the first restaurants to take hold in Germantown. The menu changes seasonally but always features thoughtful salads, unusually delicious pizzas, and creative protein options, most of which lean heavily on pork. **Known for:** rustic Italian fare; pork- and meat-forward dishes; comfortable bright atmosphere. $ *Average main: $17* ✉ *1222 4th Ave. N, Germantown* ☎ *615/736–5838* ⊕ *cityhousenashville.com* ☾ *Closed Tues.*

5th & Taylor

$$$ | MODERN AMERICAN | Housed in a large artsy space, 5th & Taylor is a culinary playground for chef Daniel Lindley to push the boundaries of modern American cuisine. The menu often includes a number of Southern favorites, like tomato pie and beer-can chicken, all elevated by Lindley's finesse and knowledge of flavor. **Known for:** elevated dishes with Southern touches; large sophisticated dining space; extensive cocktail and beverage program. $ *Average main: $25* ✉ *1411 5th Ave. N, Germantown* ☎ *615/242–4747* ⊕ *5thandtaylor.com.*

Geist Bar + Restaurant

$$$$ | MODERN AMERICAN | Housed in a 100-plus-year-old blacksmith shop, Geist is as cozy and vibey inside as its food is delicious. A stone's throw from First Horizon Park, Geist offers a luxe alternative to the casual bar and ballpark fare nearby, instead serving creative takes on American dishes using regionally sourced ingredients. **Known for:** champagne garden; historic building; seasonal menu with local ingredients. $ *Average main: $40* ✉ *311 Jefferson St., Germantown* ☎ *615/920–5440* ⊕ *www.geistnashville.com.*

Germantown Café

$$ | SOUTHERN | One of the early restaurants to open in the now-bustling Germantown neighborhood was Germantown Café. Now a pillar of the neighborhood, this popular dining spot offers inventive takes on an eclectic Southern menu, serving up meals for lunch, dinner, and brunch (on the weekends). **Known for:** classic cocktails; elevated Southern fare; great happy hour. $ *Average main: $20* ✉ *1200 5th Ave. N, Germantown* ☎ *615/242–3226* ⊕ *germantowncafe.com.*

Henrietta Red

$$ | AMERICAN | Since opening in 2016, Henrietta Red has quickly become a Germantown staple, thanks to its creative menu and its hip airy digs. The project of chef Julia Sullivan and sommelier Allie Poindexter, the menu features vibrant seafood offerings (don't skip the raw bar!) alongside a carefully curated bar menu, as well as one of the area's best brunches. **Known for:** oysters; creative cocktails; inventive desserts. $ *Average main: $20* ✉ *1200 4th Ave. N, Germantown* ☎ *615/490–8042* ⊕ *www.henriettared.com* ☾ *Closed Mon.*

★ Jamaicaway Restaurant and Catering

$$ | JAMAICAN | FAMILY | A longtime favorite sit-down spot inside the Nashville Farmers' Market, Jamaicaway has a cozy setting, friendly owners, and scrumptious curried dishes. This dining experience makes you feel like you've stepped onto the island itself, where serenity and home-cooked food abound. **Known for:** famous curried dishes; vegetarian and vegan options (including curry tofu); friendly staff (family-owned and-operated). ⑤ *Average main: $13* ✉ *Nashville Farmers' Market, 900 Rosa L. Parks Blvd., Suite 120, Germantown* ☎ *615/255–5920* ⊕ *www.jamaicawayrestaurant.com* ⊘ *Closed Sat.*

Monell's Dining and Catering

$$ | SOUTHERN | Much of the dining in Germantown is high-end and experimental, making longtime local favorite Monell's Dining and Catering a welcome dose of Southern comfort food, all served family-style. Visit for breakfast, lunch, or dinner to fill up on Southern favorites like skillet-fried chicken, home-style meat loaf, and delicious biscuits. Just be sure to save room for dessert. **Known for:** skillet-fried chicken; home-cooked breakfast; family-style. ⑤ *Average main: $15* ✉ *1235 6th Ave. N, Germantown* ☎ *615/248–4747* ⊕ *monellstn.com/nashville.*

★ Rolf & Daughters

$$ | ECLECTIC | Chef Philip Krajeck has devised a simple innovative menu at Rolf & Daughters, a pillar of dining in both the Germantown neighborhood and greater Nashville. Menu staples include assorted seasonal, house-made pastas and creative takes on small plates and vegetable salads. **Known for:** innovative seasonal dishes; creative use of ingredients; cozy neighborhood atmosphere. ⑤ *Average main: $20* ✉ *700 Taylor St., Germantown* ☎ *615/866–9897* ⊕ *www.rolfanddaughters.com.*

Tailor

$$$$ | INDIAN | Diners at Tailor have the pleasure of enjoying one of the city's truly unique dining experiences. Chef Vivek Surti creates seasonally rotating menus inspired by his South Asian heritage that are served prix fixe over the course of a lively but leisurely two-and-a-half hours, with optional wine and beverage pairings for an additional cost. **Known for:** multicourse seasonal menu; inventive dishes; lively atmosphere. ⑤ *Average main: $125* ✉ *620 Taylor St., Germantown* ⊕ *www.tailornashville.com* ⊘ *Closed Mon.–Wed. No lunch.*

Von Elrod's Beer Hall & Kitchen

$$ | GERMAN | Von Elrod's Beer Hall & Kitchen was a welcome addition to the Germantown neighborhood when it opened in 2017. Housed in a large group-friendly space, the restaurant offers a casual alternative to the neighborhood's more-elevated offerings, serving house-made sausages and sides alongside a truly extensive beer menu. **Known for:** house-made sausage; extensive beer list; large outdoor space. $ *Average main: $14* ✉ *1004 4th Ave. N, Germantown* ☎ *615/866–1620* ⊕ *vonelrods.com.*

Coffee and Quick Bites

Barista Parlor x Germantown

$ | CAFÉ | The original East Nashville Barista Parlor was such a hit that the hip shop has since expanded to several locations around town, including this spot in Germantown. Conveniently located right next to popular dinner joint City House, baristas put an extraordinary amount of care into each cup of coffee brewed; you can taste that attention to detail each time you visit. **Known for:** ethically sourced ingredients; thoughtfully prepared coffee; hip trendy atmosphere. $ *Average main: $5* ✉ *1230 4th Ave. N, Germantown* ☎ *615/401–9144* ⊕ *baristaparlor.com.*

The Christie Cookie Company

$ | BAKERY | A trip to Nashville isn't complete without a stop at this Nashville-based bakery that makes gourmet cookies with real ingredients and recipes that have earned the brand national recognition. Their Germantown bakery now boasts a storefront where you can pick up a variety of cookies, milk, coffee, and Christie-branded goodies. **Known for:** fresh-baked cookies; gifts for sweets lovers; simple coffee drinks. $ *Average main: $5* ✉ *1205 3rd Ave. S, Germantown* ☎ *800/458–2447* ⊕ *www.christiecookies. com* ⊗ *Closed Sun.*

The Cupcake Collection

$ | BAKERY | This locally beloved cupcake shop serves a variety of tasty creative cupcakes at their storefront; preorders are also welcome. Classic flavors like red velvet and chocolate are always on hand, while seasonal cupcakes pop up throughout the year. **Known for:** homemade cupcakes in a variety of creative flavors; seasonal flavors; local gem. $ *Average main: $3* ✉ *1213 6th Ave. N, Germantown* ☎ *615/244–2900* ⊕ *www.thecupcakecollection. com* ⊗ *Closed Sat.*

Red Bicycle Coffee

$ | **CAFÉ** | There are a lot of coffee shops in Germantown, but only Red Bicycle has an extensive menu of sweet and savory crepes. This neighborhood café also serves a variety of sandwiches, tacos, pastries, and small snacks, all complemented by a menu of seasonally rotating coffee and espresso drinks and served by one of the friendliest staffs in town. **Known for:** sweet and savory crepes; assorted espresso beverages; creative tacos and sandwiches. ⑤ *Average main: $7* ⊠ *1200 5th Ave. N, Germantown* ☎ *615/516–1986* ⊕ *redbicyclecoffee.com.*

Spread Market & Larder

$ | **BAKERY** | If you're looking to pack a picnic lunch or grab a few things to eat on the go, stop by this neighborhood market for homemade bread and pastries, daily sandwiches, and other pantry items. There's a carefully curated wine, beer, and cider selection as well. **Known for:** curated international wine, beer, and cider offerings; cool neighborhood vibe; to-go food and snacks. ⑤ *Average main: $12* ⊠ *1330 5th Ave. N, Germantown* ⊕ *www.spreadthings.com* ۞ *Closed Mon. and Tues. No dinner.*

Steadfast Coffee

$ | **CAFÉ** | Germantown's Steadfast Coffee offers up the usual assortment of espresso drinks and café-style food options, but they also have some tasty menu items you'll be hard-pressed to find anywhere else. Their coffee soda, for example, is an unusual blend of espresso, soda water, and orange peel and has to be tried to be understood, while their "rested" coffee drinks bring out new flavors in old classics. **Known for:** creative espresso drinks; hip atmosphere; refreshing coffee soda. ⑤ *Average main: $5* ⊠ *603 Taylor St., Germantown* ☎ *615/891–7424* ⊕ *steadfast. coffee/pages/germantown.*

★ Tempered Café and Chocolate

$ | **CAFÉ** | Tempered Café is unlike any other café in Nashville, serving an extensive selection of handcrafted chocolates alongside a full menu of espresso drinks, breakfast and lunch plates—and yes, homemade hot chocolate and drinking chocolate. Tempered also has a full bar and offers chocolate and beverage pairings that are unlike anything you've ever tried before. **Known for:** creative handmade chocolates; rich drinkable chocolate; accompanying bistro and bar menu. ⑤ *Average main: $5* ⊠ *1201 5th Ave. N, Germantown* ☎ *615/454–5432* ⊕ *temperedfinechocolates.com* ۞ *Closed Mon.*

Hotels

The Germantown Inn

$$ | HOTEL | Situated in a gorgeous, recently renovated late-1800s brick home and carriage house, this inn is the epitome of cozy and upscale; the rooms pay tribute to influential American men and women (i.e., Thomas Jefferson and Rosa Parks). **Pros:** historic setting with modern touches; walking distance to great restaurants; free parking. **Cons:** lacks amenities of a conventional hotel like gym or pool; close quarters for some; historic charm isn't for everyone. ⓢ *Rooms from: $300* ✉ *1218 6th Ave. N, Germantown* ☎ *615/581–1218* ⊕ *germantowninn.com* ⇨ *10 rooms* ⦾ *Free Breakfast.*

Nightlife

BARS AND BREWERIES

Bearded Iris Brewing

BREWPUBS | Believe it or not, Germantown used to be one of Nashville's industrial hubs. You can see what remains of the neighborhood's old factories and warehouses on its eastern outskirts, where Bearded Iris Brewing lies. Housed in one of these old warehouses, Bearded Iris brews a variety of old-world-style beers that appeal to beer snobs and newbies alike and serves brews in a swanky-comfy setting that combines the best of old and new Germantown. ✉ *101 Van Buren St., Germantown* ☎ *615/928–7988* ⊕ *beardedirisbrewing.com/location/germantown.*

Frankie J's

BARS | Frankie J's is a laid-back queer oasis in the middle of busting Germantown, just steps away from beloved restaurants like 5th & Taylor and Butchertown Hall. Stop in for cocktails and casual fare before a Sounds game, or enjoy one of the bar's many weekly events like Trivia Time Tuesdays. Frankie J's is 21+, so don't bring the kids, but leashed dogs are welcome. ✉ *1314 6th Ave. N, Germantown* ☎ *615/930–3092* ⊕ *www.frankiejsnashville. com* ⊘ *Closed Mon.*

★ Green Hour

BARS | Located inside Tempered Café and Chocolate (and only open Thursday through Saturday), Green Hour is one of Germantown's best-kept secrets. It's the only bar in town that specializes in serving a wide variety of absinthe in traditional absinthe drips, making each drink ordered its own experiential treat. And if absinthe isn't your thing, the bar also serves a variety of classic cocktails and a small selection of beer. ⊠ *1201 5th Ave. N, Germantown* ☎ *615/454–5432* ⊕ *greenhournashville.com* ⊘ *Closed Sun.–Wed.*

Minerva Avenue

BARS | Drawing on the popularity of neighborhood pizza-and-beer joint Slim and Husky's, Minerva Avenue is the first true bar to open in the burgeoning Buchanan Arts District. The bar has an easygoing-meets-speakeasy vibe, with a phone out front to alert the host to grant you entrance to the cozy patio. Grab a fresh, locally sourced sandwich and wash it down with a boozy slushie or a signature cocktail. ⊠ *1002 Buchanan St., Germantown* ☎ *615/973–0962* ⊕ *www.minervaavenue.com.*

Neighbors Germantown

BARS | Neighbors has long been a popular bar in the west Nashville neighborhood of Sylvan Park, and in 2018 Germantown got its own outpost of the friendly watering hole. Located in close proximity to Germantown restaurants and to First Horizon Park, Neighbors is a great spot to pre-game before a Sounds game, toast to a good meal, or post up to watch the Nashville Predators. ⊠ *313 Jefferson St., Germantown* ☎ *615/873–1954* ⊕ *neighborsnashville.com.*

Preservation Co.

BREWPUBS | Atlanta-based Monday Night Brewing set up its first Nashville outpost in an old meatpacking plant in Germantown, an easy walk from local beer favorite Bearded Iris and from other Nashville-via-Atlanta transplant The Optimist. The space is large and lively and the brews are fresh and adventurous; Monday Night especially excels at making sour beers, so stop in for all your mouth-puckering needs. ⊠ *1308 Adams St., Germantown* ☎ *615/819–2622* ⊕ *mondaynightbrewing.com/location/preservation-co.*

COMEDY CLUBS

Third Coast Comedy Club

COMEDY CLUBS | If you're looking for laughs while you're in Music City, look no further than Third Coast Comedy Club. Nestled inside the Marathon Village complex, this local favorite plays host to sketch, improv, and stand-up shows most nights of the week. And if you're interested in brushing up on your own comedy chops, Third Coast also offers classes and workshops (check availability before visiting). ⊠ *1310 Clinton St., Suite 121, Marathon Village* ☎ *615/745–1009* ⊕ *www.thirdcoastcomedy.club.*

LIVE MUSIC

Brooklyn Bowl Nashville

LIVE MUSIC | Popular Brooklyn venue and activity space Brooklyn Bowl opened its Nashville outpost in 2021 and has since become a hot spot for local and national touring acts alike. Catch a concert while you throw strikes, or just take in your favorite artist within the venue itself while you sip on a spiked milkshake. Most events require tickets and/or reservations, so plan ahead. ⊠ *925 3rd Ave. N, Germantown* ☎ *615/953–5450* ⊕ *www.brooklynbowl.com/nashville.*

Marathon Music Works

LIVE MUSIC | This 14,000-square-foot open venue in the former automobile factory now known as the Marathon Village complex hosts mid-level artists in its standing-room-only, 1,500-person-capacity space. Plan ahead, as most events are ticketed. ⊠ *1402 Clinton Ave., Marathon Village* ☎ *615/891–1781* ⊕ *www.marathonmusicworks.com.*

 Performing Arts

Nashville Jazz Workshop

MUSIC | If jazz is your thing, be sure to check the calendar of the Nashville Jazz Workshop, which offers classes, performances, and various special events throughout the year. There are typically a couple of events taking place each day, with proceeds benefiting the nonprofit Workshop's mission of keeping jazz alive in Music City. ⊠ *1012 Buchanan St., Germantown* ☎ *615/242–5299* ⊕ *nashvillejazz.org.*

Shopping

ANTIQUES

Antique Archaeology

ANTIQUES & COLLECTIBLES | Fans of the History Channel's *American Pickers* series will want to check out Mike Wolfe's store in Marathon Village. All of the quirky items—signage, furniture and random finds—were personally selected or approved by Wolfe. The shop also carries show-branded merch, making for great souvenirs. ⊠ *1300 Clinton St., Suite 130, Marathon Village* ☎ *615/810–9906* ⊕ *www.antiquearchaeology.com.*

Bits & Pieces Antique Boutique

SECOND-HAND | From handcrafted jewelry and homemade soaps to vintage clothing and secondhand finds, you're certain to find something among the racks at this former warehouse turned antiques shop. It's the perfect spot for souvenirs and gifts or for a good old-fashioned treasure hunt. ⊠ *402 Madison St., Germantown* ☎ *615/499–4028* ⊕ *www.btsnpieces.com.*

FOOD

The Bang Candy Company

CANDY | If you have a sweet tooth, you can't skip a trip to the Bang Candy Company. Located in the Marathon Village complex, Bang specializes in handmade creatively flavored marshmallows, but it's far more than a one-trick pony. The shop also sells handmade syrups, chocolates, and other adventurous confections, as well as CBD Dream Drops, which blend tasty confections with relaxing CBD oil. ⊠ *1300 Clinton St., Suite 127, Marathon Village* ☎ *625/953–1065* ⊕ *www.bangcandycompany.com* ⊗ *Closed Mon.*

GIFTS AND SOUVENIRS

Abednego

SOUVENIRS | Whether you're buying for yourself or for a friend, Abednego is the perfect spot to buy a gift. The locally owned boutique carries a curated selection of women's clothing, accessories, and personal care supplies, as well as home decor, candles, and small trinkets. They have a cute selection of greeting cards, too, making it a one-stop gift shop. ⊠ *1212 4th Ave. N, Germantown* ☎ *615/712–6028* ⊕ *www.abednegoboutique.com* ⊗ *Closed Mon.*

Batch Nashville

SOUVENIRS | While visiting the Nashville Farmers' Market, be sure to stop at Batch Nashville, a highly curated shop featuring gifts, snacks, and treats from some of Nashville's (and the greater South's) best-loved creators. From artisanal chocolate bars to locally roasted coffee, the gifts at Batch are sure to please even your most finicky friends. ⊠ *Nashville Farmers' Market, 900 Rosa L. Parks Blvd., Germantown* ☎ *615/913–3912* ⊕ *batchusa.com.*

Jack Daniel's General Store

SOUVENIRS | If you can't make it down to Lynchburg to see the Jack Daniel's distillery in person, visit the famed whiskey maker's Nashville outpost for all your Jack Daniel's–branded gear needs. Located in Marathon Village, the sizable shop sells shirts, glassware, and accessories galore for you or the whiskey lover in your life. Note that the store does not sell alcohol. ⊠ *1310 Clinton St., Suite 101, Germantown* ☎ *629/702–2969.*

LEATHER GOODS
Nisolo

LEATHER GOODS | When Nisolo relocated from its Marathon Village location in 2015, it was one of the first businesses to open in what's now known as the Buchanan Arts District. Now, this stretch of historic Buchanan Street is bustling with galleries and restaurants, with Nisolo, a local pioneer of ethically made leather shoes and goods, as its retail anchor. Stop in for handcrafted leather chukkas, messenger bags, and much more. ✉ *1803 9th Ave. N, Germantown* ☎ *615/953–1087* ⊕ *nisolo.com.*

SYLVAN PARK AND THE NATIONS

Updated by
Rachel Heatherly

⦿ Sights	🍴 Restaurants	🛏 Hotels	🛍 Shopping	💬 Nightlife
★☆☆☆☆	★★★★☆	☆☆☆☆☆	★★☆☆☆	★★☆☆☆

NEIGHBORHOOD SNAPSHOT

TOP EXPERIENCES

■ **Mingle with Laid-back Locals:** There is no shortage of Southern hospitality to encounter on the streets, in shops, restaurants, or late-night dives of Sylvan Park and The Nations.

■ **Hunt for Treasures:** Browse through droves of vinyl records, movie posters, video games, and more at West Nashville's pop-culture memorabilia destination, The Great Escape, where you never know what you might find.

■ **Treats from a Time Machine:** Opened in 1951, Bobbie's Dairy Dip serves up nostalgia at its ice cream and burger stand.

■ **Art on the Outskirts:** Revel in bountiful creativity at OZ Arts.

■ **Kick Back at a Café:** Delicious caffeine kicks and fresh-baked goods in the roomy space of a transformed hosiery building makes Frothy Monkey a delight.

GETTING HERE

Located west of Downtown, Sylvan Park is situated south of 1–40 between the 440 and Briley Parkway junctions. The Nations is directly north of Sylvan Park over I–40, east of Briley Parkway. While parts of each neighborhood are walkable, a car is essential for traveling between most points of interest. The area's primary bus route runs along Charlotte Avenue in northern Sylvan Park.

ART IN THE WILD

■ Nashville is filled with murals, but none as large as the one on an abandoned silo in The Nations. The 15-story-high portrait of an elderly man is the work of Australian artist Guido van Helten, who chose his subject, Lee Estes, age 91, a longtime resident of the neighborhood, as a tribute to The Nations' past and changing future.

PLANNING YOUR TIME

■ While most businesses have adjacent parking lots, street parking is typically free and accessible on residential streets at all times, making it easy to stop by restaurants, stores, and more without the hassle or extra cost. If you're planning to dine on the weekends—starting from Thursday on—a reservation is your best bet.

Just a few miles from the bright lights of Broadway but far enough away to feel removed from the city, Sylvan Park and The Nations have become some of West Nashville's trendiest neighborhoods. Charm and convenience converge here, as do old and new with an influx of residential development, eateries, and local businesses along Charlotte and 51st avenues that complement the area's existing fixtures. Those seeking locally-owned businesses, roomy spaces, and a low-key atmosphere will find much to explore, from large catalogs of music memorabilia to vintage antiques and oddities.

Delicious dining options are never far away, and there are choices for every palate. Great barbecue and hot chicken can be found here, as well as multiethnic cuisine and cozy cafés. Sightseeing and attractions aren't the calling cards of Sylvan Park or The Nations, but the authentic experience of living like a local in Nashville is done best here at haunts, hidden gems, and watering holes where you can mingle with friendly faces.

Sylvan Park

One of Music City's most beloved residential neighborhoods, Sylvan Park is rich in charm and has remained relatively untouched despite the influx of residents and new construction seen in other parts of Nashville. Originally intended to be a satellite city adjacent to Nashville, the neighborhood bears its own identity with unique restaurants, shops, and varying architecture (Queen Anne to bungalows and cottages). Nashville Ballet and Nashville Opera also have main facilities in the community.

With multiple locations around the city, including the Nations, coffee lovers can get their caffeine fix and a good breakfast at Frothy Monkey.

The area is filled with intimate one-of-a-kind staples, many of which are located along the quiet Murphy Road. You'll also find outposts of eateries that Nashville is known for, but with shorter lines and wait times than their counterparts Downtown.

Sights

Richland Park

CITY PARK | FAMILY | The spacious greenery of Richland Park is situated opposite several of Charlotte Avenue's walkable independent shops and eateries. Covered picnic tables and a small playground share an easily accessible parking lot with a quaint public library branch and tennis courts. The Richland Park Farmer's Market operates every Saturday morning beside the playground. ✉ *4601 Charlotte Pike, Sylvan Park* ☎ *615/862–8400.*

 Restaurants

answer.

$$$ | ECLECTIC | This chef-driven restaurant, with its relaxed yet upscale feel and menu full of character, fits seamlessly into the Sylvan Park neighborhood that surrounds it. Their laid-back happy hour has familiar favorites with thoughtful touches, and their dinner entrées tout flavors that can satisfy even refined palates. **Known for:** enticing happy hour; seasonal menu; internationally inspired entrées. ⑤ *Average main: $25* ✉ *132 46th Ave. N, Sylvan*

Park ☎ 615/942–0866 ⊕ *www.answerrestaurant.com* ⊙ *Closed Sun. No lunch.*

Caffé Nonna
$$$ | **ITALIAN** | A long-standing staple of Sylvan Park, Caffé Nonna serves Italian dinner in an inviting and intimate café setting. Pasta is served with house-made sauces, the desserts are decadent, and the decent wine list rounds out the experience. **Known for:** classic dishes from scratch; Italian favorites; cozy seating area. ⑤ *Average main: $28* ⊠ *4427 Murphy Rd., Sylvan Park* ☎ 615/463–0133 ⊕ *www.caffenonna.com* ⊙ *Closed Sun. No lunch.*

★ Edley's Bar-B-Que
$$ | **SOUTHERN** | Edley's offers a taste of Southern cooking, and their sides are just as delicious as their melt-in-your-mouth meats. Make sure to try their brisket before it sells out for the day in either taco, sandwich, or platter form, and enjoy a craft beer or a signature spiked milkshake called a Bushwacker for refreshment. **Known for:** heaping barbecue platters; rich Southern sides; boozy Bushwackers. ⑤ *Average main: $15* ⊠ *4500 Murphy Rd., Sylvan Park* ☎ 615/942–7499 ⊕ *www.edleysbbq.com.*

Five Points Pizza West
$$ | **PIZZA** | **FAMILY** | Whopping pizza slices, determined by the day of the week, are cut from 20-inch pies and baked in retro gas-fired deck ovens at this laid-back neighborhood favorite. If you want a whole pie, those are available in 14- or 18-inch sizes with the same made-from-scratch dough and fresh pizza toppings as the slices, which all complement the extensive offering of craft beers. **Known for:** weekday lunch specials; New York–style thin crust; 16 rotating craft and local beer taps. ⑤ *Average main: $21* ⊠ *4100 Charlotte Ave., Sylvan Park* ☎ 615/891–1820 ⊕ *fivepointspizza. com/west-nashville.*

Hugh-Baby's
$ | **BURGER** | **FAMILY** | Made-to-order diner classics—some with a Southern twist—are served in a retro-style space at Hugh-Baby's. Burger patties ground fresh every day are joined by topping-laden hot dogs and barbecue sandwiches on the family-friendly menu. **Known for:** fresh hamburgers; children's play area; drive-through service. ⑤ *Average main: $6* ⊠ *4816 Charlotte Ave., Sylvan Park* ☎ 615/610–3340 ⊕ *www.hughbabys.com.*

McCabe Pub
$$ | **AMERICAN** | Burgers, beer, and pub food done right are the focus of this classic Sylvan Park establishment. Its brick interior feels vaguely European while the plant-filled outdoor patio looks out onto the neighborhood's main business intersection. **Known**

for: all-American entrées; neighborly staff; full bar featuring beer selection. ⑤ *Average main: $13* ⊠ *4410 Murphy Rd., Sylvan Park* ☎ *615/269–9406* ⊕ *www.mccabepub.com* ⊗ *Closed Sun.*

Pancho & Lefty's Cantina Sylvan Park

$$ | MEXICAN FUSION | Expect fresh ingredients and friendly neighborhood service at Pancho & Lefty's. There are plenty of savory tacos (don't miss the barbacoa or adobe chicken), fajitas, and quesadillas to choose from, which we suggest you complement with one or two of their signature margaritas or boozie slushies. **Known for:** award-winning inventive margaritas; slow-smoked meat selection; spacious covered patio. ⑤ *Average main: $17* ⊠ *4501 Murphy Rd., Sylvan Park* ☎ *615/647–8763* ⊕ *www.panchoandleftys.com/sylvan-park.*

Park Cafe

$$$ | AMERICAN | Park Cafe serves rich entrées, a selection of small plates, and a full wine program. In addition to their dinner service, they also feature an enticing happy hour with bar favorites like pizzas and fried pickles. **Known for:** quality meats; intimate dining room; Southern-inspired appetizers. ⑤ *Average main: $30* ⊠ *4403 Murphy Rd., Sylvan Park* ☎ *615/383–4409* ⊕ *www.parkcafenashville.com* ⊗ *Closed Sun.*

The Ridge

$$ | BARBECUE | Serving a wide variety of barbecue, burgers, Tex-Mex-inspired appetizers, and some of the best catfish in Nashville, this counter-serve spot is a great place to watch a game or celebrate happy hour. Located in a converted Sylvan Park house, the restaurant's excellent down-home cuisine is backed by its many cooking competition accolades that adorn the walls; don't miss a stop in The Attic Bar for a cocktail or two. **Known for:** barbecue platters; homey environment; family-owned hospitality. ⑤ *Average main: $15* ⊠ *333 54th Ave., Sylvan Park* ☎ *615/385–7800* ⊕ *theridgenashville.com.*

☕ Coffee and Quick Bites

★ Bobbie's Dairy Dip

$ | AMERICAN | FAMILY | This classic ice cream and burger stand feels like a blast from the past with retro decor, classic diner fare, ice cream, and milkshakes that can be enjoyed on their covered patio. The family-friendly staple embraces their throwback energy, even naming their delicious signature shake flavors after 1950s rockers. **Known for:** dipped soft-serve ice cream; creatively flavored milkshakes; hand-dipped corn dogs. ⑤ *Average main: $5* ⊠ *5301 Charlotte Ave., Sylvan Park* ☎ *615/864–5576.*

8th & Roast Charlotte Ave.

$ | **CAFÉ** | Look no further for a caffeine kick than 8th & Roast's ethically traded coffee with decadent flavor profiles. Small bites and syrups are made in-house, and natural light flows in through the shop's large windows. **Known for:** fresh coffee blends; roomy indoor seating; off-street free parking. $ *Average main: $5 ⊠ 4104 Charlotte Ave., Sylvan Park ☎ 615/988–4020 ⊕ www.8thandroast. com.*

Radish Kitchen

$$ | **AMERICAN** | Nutritious dishes brimming with fresh vibrant ingredients served in your choice of a grain bowl, wrap, or salad characterize the offerings at Radish Kitchen. Choose from hearty proteins like tamari-glazed salmon, crispy chicken, and falafel; colorful greens like chopped kale or a spring mix; grains (a mix of rice and quinoa); and toppings that range from almonds and goat cheese to lentils and mango at this convenient counter-service stop. **Known for:** easily-accessible dietary information; heaping healthy portions; speedy service. $ *Average main: $14 ⊠ 4101 Charlotte Ave., Sylvan Park ☎ 615/953–7058 ⊕ www.radishkitch-en.com.*

Star Bagel Cafe

$ | **CAFÉ** | This deli specializing in bagel sandwiches serves breakfast all day. In addition to bagels, the café offers granola, baked goods, coffee, and smoothies. **Known for:** flavored bagels; fresh smoothies; welcoming neighborhood atmosphere. $ *Average main: $6 ⊠ 4502 Murphy Rd., Sylvan Park ☎ 615/292–7993 ⊕ www.starbagel.com.*

Nightlife

Neighbors of Sylvan Park

BARS | An authentic neighborhood hangout as the name suggests, Neighbors is the spot in Sylvan Park to watch a game, hear some live music, and enjoy cheap beer on either their front patio or covered back deck. On the deck is where they smoke meats for sandwiches, quesadillas, loaded nachos, and more. ⊠ *4425 Murphy Rd., Sylvan Park ☎ 615/942–5052 ⊕ neighborsnashville. com/sylvan-park.*

 Performing Arts

Darkhorse Theater

THEATER | Darkhorse Theater is a meaningful addition to Nashville's independent alternative art scene. Housed in a former church, it's comprised of resident companies who share the performance

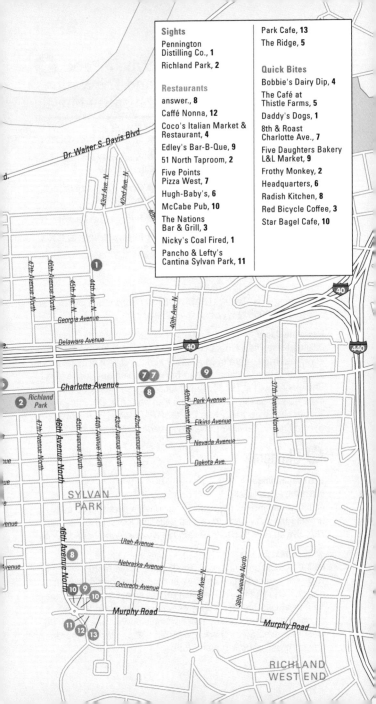

Dr. Walter S. Davis Blvd

Georgia Avenue

Delaware Avenue

Charlotte Avenue

Richland Park

Park Avenue

Elkins Avenue

Nevada Avenue

Dakota Ave.

SYLVAN PARK

Utah Avenue

Nebraska Avenue

Colorado Avenue

Murphy Road

Murphy Road

RICHLAND WEST END

space, with varied productions ranging from Shakespeare to the work of local playwrights and politically driven shows. ✉ *4610 Charlotte Ave., Sylvan Park* ☎ *615/297–7113* ⊕ *dark-horsetheater.weebly.com.*

Nashville Ballet

BALLET | Nashville Ballet is Tennessee's largest professional ballet company. Classes and community events are often hosted at the whopping 44,000-square-foot facility in Sylvan Park. Like their neighbors, the Nashville Opera, they also hold performances Downtown at the Tennessee Performing Arts Center (TPAC). ✉ *3630 Redmon St., Sylvan Park* ☎ *615/297–2966* ⊕ *www.nashvilleballet.com.*

Sylvan Park and The Nations Must-See Murals

- *Silo* ✉ 1407 51st Ave. N
- *Wish for Peace* ✉ 4816 Charlotte Ave.
- *Gender Equality* ✉ 5001 Charlotte Ave.
- *Honey* ✉ 343 53rd Ave. N
- *Import Flowers* ✉ 3636 Murphy Rd.

Nashville Opera

OPERA | Nashville's Opera company aims to celebrate a lesser-represented genre in Music City and to make it accessible and interesting to all audience members, including opera newbies. Shows are held at The Noah Liff Opera Center black-box theater each opera season. The company also performs Downtown at the Tennessee Performing Arts Center (TPAC). ✉ *3622 Redmon St., Sylvan Park* ☎ *615/832–5242* ⊕ *www.nashvilleopera.org.*

🛍 Shopping

Elle Gray Boutique

CLOTHING | This locally owned boutique sells chic on-trend women's apparel and accessories at reasonable prices. Stop by to browse the cozy shop for styled seasonal looks. ✉ *4429 Murphy Rd., Sylvan Park* ☎ *615/679–9854* ⊕ *www.ellegrayboutique.com.*

★ The Great Escape

MUSIC | A collector's heaven, The Great Escape features a wide-ranging collection of vinyl records, video games, comic books, CDs, and more. The vinyl record selection is one of the best in Music City, and their thrifty prices are often further discounted with frequent specials and sidewalk sales. ✉ *5400 Charlotte Ave., Sylvan Park* ☎ *615/385–2116* ⊕ *thegreatescapeonline.com* ⊙ *Closed Mon. and Tues.*

The Nations

West Nashville's last major urban enclave before the neighboring rolling hills, hiking trails, and green spaces, The Nations is approachable and neighborly with long-standing dive bars, varied dining options, locally-owned shops, a few breweries, and one of Nashville's foremost experimental contemporary-art venues.

You'll no doubt see joggers, cyclists, and families walking on the sidewalks of streets bearing state names, and new homes—known colloquially as "tall and skinnys" for their narrow appearance and quantity per plot of land—under construction. It's also an area under economic transition, which has caused tension among developers and longtime residents. Despite the changing landscape, down-to-earth local establishments remain strongholds and former industrial properties have been converted to multipurpose commercial spaces.

Sights

★ Pennington Distilling Co.

DISTILLERY | Tucked into a residential section of The Nations, Pennington Distilling Co. is known for its small-batch spirits—award-winning Tennessee whiskey, vodka, crafted cocktails, and boozy coffee—and the friendly experts who guide the distillery tours and tastings with care. Run by Nashville natives Jeff and Jenny Pennington, the distillery also offers immersive experiences like blend-your-own-bottle activities and craft cocktail classes. The hour-long tour does include a tasting, though tastings are offered separately. ⊠ *900 44th Ave. N, The Nations* ☎ *615/678–8986* ⊕ *penningtondistillingco.com* ⊠ *$10 for tours; $10 for tastings; $20 for tour and tasting* ☾ *Closed Sun. and Mon.*

Restaurants

Coco's Italian Market & Restaurant

$$ | ITALIAN | Dedicated to—and passionate about—all things Italian, Coco's is part grocery, part travel agency, and part Italian restaurant. Known for their grab-and-go pizzas, homemade meatballs, and baked ziti, all their house specialties remain proudly authentic to original family recipes, and you won't have to worry about breaking the bank. **Known for:** bocce courts; authentic Italian dishes and prepared meals; imported Italian wine list. ⑤ *Average main: $17* ⊠ *411 51st Ave. N, The Nations* ☎ *615/783–0114* ⊕ *cocositalianmarket.com.*

51 North Taproom

$$ | **AMERICAN** | This family-friendly spot delivers a comprehensive beer selection (30 rotating taps), traditional pub favorites like poutine fries and burgers, and elevated entrées like street-style tacos and lamb pops. A neighborhood gathering place, 51 North Taproom also offers a hearty weekend brunch and ample outdoor patio seating. **Known for:** local and regional craft beers on tap; patio dining; seitan (a plant-based meat substitute) options. ⑤ *Average main: $22* ⊠ *704 51st Ave. N, The Nations* ☎ *629/800–2454* ⊕ *www.51northtaproom.com.*

The Nations Bar & Grill

$$ | **AMERICAN** | Serving burgers nearly as big as their iconic neon sign, The Nations Bar & Grill keeps it real with substantial pub-style favorites that run the gamut from wings and Reubens to loaded tots and patty melts. Formerly an auto-repair shop, this no-nonsense neighborhood spot won't leave anyone hungry or thirsty; just leave room for the daily fried hand pies. **Known for:** large topping-heavy burgers; hearty chili; neighborhood pub atmosphere. ⑤ *Average main: $15* ⊠ *701 51st Ave. N, The Nations* ☎ *615/668–7582* ⊕ *www.nationsbarandgrill.com.*

Nicky's Coal Fired

$$ | **MODERN ITALIAN** | Quality ingredients and uncommon preparations come together at Nicky's Coal Fired for a unique pizza and Italian food experience. While coal-fired pizza is their specialty, Nicky's also offers house-made pasta and delectable Italian desserts. **Known for:** eclectic cocktail list; coal-fired pizza; Saturday and Sunday morning bagels. ⑤ *Average main: $24* ⊠ *5026 Centennial Blvd., The Nations* ☎ *615/678–4289* ⊕ *www.nickysnashville.com* ⊗ *No lunch.*

☕ Coffee and Quick Bites

The Café at Thistle Farms

$$ | **AMERICAN** | Created as a social enterprise, The Café employs female survivors of trafficking, prostitution, and addiction and partners with local food suppliers to create delicious locally sourced breakfast and lunch items like sandwiches, quiches, and baked goods. The Café also touts a full afternoon tea service, available by reservation. **Known for:** tea service; mission-driven purpose; fresh locally sourced breakfast and lunch entrées. ⑤ *Average main: $13* ⊠ *5122 Charlotte Pike, The Nations* ☎ *615/953–6440* ⊕ *www. thecafeatthistlefarms.org* ⊗ *Closed Sun.*

Daddy's Dogs

$ | HOT DOG | A hot dog stand housed in a converted gas station, Daddy's Dogs offers creative topping combos on a beef hot dog—the Georgia is topped with cream cheese, peaches, jalapeño, and a secret sauce, while the Carolina has coleslaw, bacon, secret sauce, and barbecue sauce. They also have a small selection of filling sides such as loaded tots, mac and cheese, and chili. **Known for:** creative topping combinations; juicy hot dogs; late-night service. *$ Average main: $11 ⊠ 5205 Centennial Blvd., The Nations* ☎ 615/802–8481 ⊕ www.daddysdogs.com.

Five Daughters Bakery L&L Market

$ | BAKERY | FAMILY | These heralded sweet treats are made from scratch daily, which will be of no surprise when you taste their savory signature croissant-donut hybrid, dubbed a Hundred Layer Donut. Five Daughters Bakery is as authentic as its name—owned and operated by a local family with five girls. **Known for:** layered pastries; gluten free and vegan options; buttercream-infused donuts. *$ Average main: $5 ⊠ 3820 Charlotte Ave., Suite 128, The Nations* ☎ 615/457–2961 ⊕ fivedaughtersbakery.com.

★ Frothy Monkey

$ | CAFÉ | Giant warehouse windows hearken back to The Nations' industrial roots and shed light on the stylish wood-laden interior of this coffee shop and all-day café. The variety of seating options makes Frothy Monkey a favorite for remote workers with laptops, and their health-focused menu features locally roasted coffee, fresh pastries, and farm-sourced ingredients for all meals. **Known for:** imaginative coffee beverages; elevated café food; cocktail offerings. *$ Average main: $10 ⊠ 1400 51st Ave. N, The Nations* ☎ 615/600–4756 ⊕ frothymonkey.com.

Headquarters

$ | CAFÉ | Blink and you could miss the narrow 9-foot-wide storefront of Headquarters, which serves locally roasted coffee, seasonal lattes, and locally sourced snacks. It's small in size but not personality; relax in the cozy interior or head outside to the inviting back patio and deck area. **Known for:** cozy surroundings; locally crafted flavored syrups; friendly baristas. *$ Average main: $5 ⊠ 4902 Charlotte Pike, The Nations* ☎ 615/386–6757 ⊕ www. hqsnashville.com.

Red Bicycle Coffee

$ | CAFÉ | More than just a coffee shop, Red Bicycle offers a wide selection of sweet and savory crepes, sandwiches, and tacos. A variety of seating options in the large space, including outdoor tables, make this a popular meeting place and workspace. **Known for:** all-day breakfast; creative crepe flavors; specialty lattes.

⑤ *Average main: $10* ✉ *712 51st Ave. N, The Nations* ☎ *615/457–1117* ⊕ *redbicyclenations.com.*

 Nightlife

Betty's Grill

BARS | This no-frills beer-only watering hole is the real deal: cheap beer and a straightforward food menu. Don't let appearances fool you, however: this is also one of the best places to see both touring and local live music acts up close. ✉ *407 49th Ave. N, The Nations* ☎ *615/297–7257.*

The Centennial

BARS | This classic dive is a stronghold in The Nations, providing all of the fixings necessary for fun: cheap beer, cornhole on the back patio, TVs, and friendly staff. But the real reason The Centennial has withstood the test of time is their simple yet surprisingly good food. ✉ *5115 Centennial Blvd., The Nations* ☎ *615/679–9746.*

Fat Bottom Brewing

BREWPUBS | Visiting the taproom at Fat Bottom Brewing turns enjoying the brewer's locally crafted beers into an experience. The large warehouse-like space features ample seating, multiple outdoor areas with yard games, and brewery tours Thursday through Saturday. ✉ *800 44th Ave. N, The Nations* ☎ *615/678–5715* ⊕ *www.fatbottombrewing.com.*

Southern Grist Brewing Company - The Nations Taproom

BREWPUBS | Local brewer Southern Grist serves pints and flights of their brews in their industrial-style taproom in The Nations. Their often fruity, sometimes sour, but always creative brews pair well with the in-house bites. ✉ *5012 Centennial Blvd., The Nations* ☎ *615/864–7133* ⊕ *www.southerngristbrewing.com.*

🎟 Performing Arts

OZ Arts

PERFORMANCE VENUES | Creativity is uninhibited at Nashville's foremost destination for contemporary performing and visual art experiences. The expansive venue was repurposed from a cigar storehouse into a cultural institution which hosts local and international artists. From dance and theater to live music and puppetry, nothing appears to be off-limits at OZ Arts. ✉ *6172 Cockrill Bend Circle, West Nashville* ☎ *615/350–7200* ⊕ *www.ozartsnashville.org* ☾ *Closed weekends.*

ABLE's flagship boutique in the Nations is known for its commitment to employing women in need, both locally and worldwide, to create their goods.

Shopping

★ ABLE

CLOTHING | Chic elevated basics are ABLE's hallmark, which they sell in their stylish flagship boutique. Popular around Nashville for their simple yet sophisticated leather bags, clothing, and jewelry, ABLE is also known for their commitment to employing women in need, both locally and worldwide, to create their goods. ⌧ *5022 Centennial Blvd., The Nations* ☎ *615/250–7216* ⊕ *www.ablecloth-ing.com.*

The Barefoot Cottage

SPECIALTY STORE | If it seems you've wandered onto the cover of a magazine, you've made it to The Barefoot Cottage. Elegantly staged home decor and furniture are on display alongside a selection of apparel and excellently curated gifts. ⌧ *3816 Charlotte Ave., The Nations* ☎ *615/707–9985* ⊕ *thebarefootcottage.com* ☻ *Closed Mon.*

Cool Stuff Weird Things

ANTIQUES & COLLECTIBLES | This flea market–style space selling salvaged items, vintage finds, and oddities lives up to its name. The friendly and unassuming environment is great for shoppers who live to dig for treasure. Take home one of their rustic, metal, lighted Nashville signs as a souvenir. ⌧ *4900 Charlotte Pike, The Nations* ☎ *615/460–1112* ⊕ *coolstuffweirdthings.com.*

Happily Grey

CLOTHING | Happily Grey is a boutique for those ahead of trends. Eclectic styles and designers make up the inventory of upscale women's and kids' fashion, accessories, and chic items for the home. ⊠ *3820 Charlotte Ave., Suite 147, The Nations* ⊕ *www. shophappilygrey.com* ⊗ *Closed Sun. and Mon.*

Judith Bright Jewelry L&L Market

JEWELRY & WATCHES | With custom-fit designs and in-store artisans, the Judith Bright Jewelry outpost in L&L Market is a standout for those looking for handmade timeless pieces. Opt for gemstones or birthstones in the locally-owned designer jewelry for a meaningful treasure. ⊠ *3820 Charlotte Ave., Suite 126, The Nations* ☎ *615/269–5600* ⊕ *judithbright.com* ⊗ *Closed Mon.*

MIDTOWN, WEST END, MUSIC ROW, AND EDGEHILL

Updated by
Rachel Heatherly

○ Sights   🍴 Restaurants   🛏 Hotels   ● Shopping   🍸 Nightlife

★★★☆☆   ★★★☆☆   ★★★☆☆   ★★★☆☆   ★★★☆☆

NEIGHBORHOOD SNAPSHOT

TOP EXPERIENCES

■ **Tour the "Home of 1,000 Hits":** Experience Historic RCA Studio B, where legendary acts like Elvis Presley recorded smash hits.

■ **Robust Dining:** Some of the most interesting dining options lie just beyond Downtown at neighborhood favorites.

■ **Visit the Parthenon:** The full-scale replica of the ancient Greek Parthenon in Centennial Park is a must-see.

■ **Unforgettable Nightlife:** Chic lounges, kitschy karaoke, and unpretentious bars can all be found here.

■ **Attend a Rock Show:** Located on the historic Rock Block, venues like Exit/In and The End, where many famous acts got their start, still operate.

■ **Elevated Boutique Stays:** Charm isn't lacking in the boutique hotels that make up the area's best accommodations.

GETTING HERE

Most of Downtown's main thorough-fares lead to Midtown, including Charlotte Avenue, Church Street/Elliston Place, and Broadway/West End.

PLANNING YOUR TIME

Midtown maintains a consistently busy level of traffic and people throughout the week and weekend. Plan to pay steep parking fees in Midtown, and reserva-tions are your best bet. West End, Music Row, and Edgehill offer free street parking on residential streets and unpaid parking lots for businesses. The area isn't particularly unsafe, but best to use the same safety precautions you would in any populous urban area.

ART IN THE WILD

■ Keep an eye out for public artwork throughout the city, including *Thread* and *Needle*, which appear on the Francis S. Guess Connector, a bridge located between Park Plaza and Charlotte Avenue. Formerly known as the 28th/31st Avenue Bridge, this connector was built to unite formerly segregated parts of the city (Midtown and the histori-cally Black North Nashville neighbor-hoods). The needle and thread are meant to symbolize that step toward unity.

VIEWFINDER

■ Even if you're not a Swiftie, take a walk in Centen-nial Park to find the bench officially dedicated to Taylor Swift by the city of Nashville in 2023. The park is men-tioned in her song "Invisible String." It's worth a photo—plaque and all.

Tucked between Downtown and the suburban enclaves of Green Hills and Belle Meade, Midtown and its adjacent neighborhoods are the perfect place for visitors to explore this rapidly growing city. The collection of sights, tastes, shops, and stays gives the area its draw, while its proximity to two premier universities—Vanderbilt and Belmont—gives it its youthful spirit. And the area is quickly accessible, with amenities like a direct bus route that travels in and out of Downtown and easy access to I–440, which circumnavigates the city.

Some of Music City's most interesting sights can be found in West End and Music Row. Consider visiting Centennial Park, which stands out among all premier green areas in Nashville for its scenic spaces and Parthenon, a full-scale replica of the Greek structure.

Traveling through Music Row, especially 16th and 17th Avenue South, can be an enthralling experience for music lovers, as recording studios, labels, entertainment management offices, and publishing houses line the streets. They are easy to spot by the numerous congratulatory yard signs decorating the lawns celebrating number 1 songs, albums, and accolades of their respective clients. But these neighborhoods aren't just a place where music is produced. This is also an area where music is performed. The Rock Block is located on Elliston Place in West End and features historic venues like Exit/In and The End, where famous acts like Jimmy Buffett, Red Hot Chili Peppers, Etta James, and more have taken the stage.

Visitors looking for unforgettable nightlife should explore the area's speakeasy-style cocktail lounges, which are acclaimed throughout the city. Beyond chic hangouts, there are laid-back neighborhood-style haunts and unique late-night offerings at Midtown's boutique hotels.

As the city expands, more luxury and boutique hotels have opened in Midtown and Music Row, offering stays for sophisticated business travelers, playful leisure trips, music lovers, and more. Each has its own personality and amenities like rooftop dining and bars.

Amid the ever-growing new additions to the area, there are mainstay shopping experiences that have been Nashville fixtures for some time. From discount designer shopping to a long-standing outfitter gear shop and a specialty running shoe store, the friendly service at each is as memorable as the products.

In short, Midtown, West End, Music Row, and Edgehill offer the best of both worlds: close proximity to the city's center with perks that make each neighborhood feel endearing and approachable.

Midtown

Just west of Downtown lies Midtown, a bustling urban area that continues to grow in conjunction with the city at large. Home to Nashville's prestigious Vanderbilt University—which was established by Cornelius Vanderbilt of the illustriously wealthy Vanderbilt family—there is an equal mixture of vibrant outposts and sophisticated offerings for visitors of all ages. Elevated and luxury hotel properties have infiltrated the area, bringing with them premium restaurants, rooftop bars, and intimate performance venues. Midtown's position in between Downtown and beloved neighborhoods like Music Row, West End, and Hillsboro Village makes it an excellent choice for visitors and locals alike.

Sights

Vanderbilt Arboretum

COLLEGE | FAMILY | More than 300 acres of Vanderbilt University's campus is a designated arboretum, with more than 6,000 trees, that can be explored using self-guided tours available via smartphone. Numerous trees have plaques that tell visitors the story of their ecological and historical significance, while others have QR codes that visitors can scan with their phones to learn more about a specific species. Visit the website for specific tour information and start locations. ⊠ *Vanderbilt University, 2301 Vanderbilt Pl., Midtown* ☎ *615/322–7311* ⊕ *www.vanderbilt.edu/trees.*

A large portion of Vanderbilt University's campus is a designated arboretum that can be explored using self-guided tours available via smartphone.

🍴 Restaurants

The Chef & I

$$$$ | **AMERICAN** | If you're looking for a dinner menu that won't necessarily break the bank, check out this stripped-down, rock-and-roll-inspired intimate restaurant, which is centered around hearty well-seasoned proteins paired with the freshest possible local produce. This is upscale American that delivers. **Known for:** flexibility with dietary restrictions; generous portions; continually evolving menus. ⑤ *Average main: $45* ✉ *1922 Adelicia St., The Gulch* ☎ *615/730–8496* ⊕ *www.thechefandinashville.com* ⊘ *No lunch.*

Henley

$$$ | **BRASSERIE** | Located off the lobby of the Kimpton Aertson Hotel, this stylish restaurant and bar serves up New American cuisine like country-fried oysters, pea tortellini, and smoked chicken in a Gatsby-inspired interior (see the pair of emotive eyes artistically fashioned above the full bar). Cocktails here are worth the price, especially during weekday happy hours, and live music often accompanies. **Known for:** personable bartenders; refreshing cocktails; breakfast seven days a week. ⑤ *Average main: $29* ✉ *Kimpton Aertson Hotel, 2023 Broadway, Midtown* ☎ *615/340–6378* ⊕ *henleynashville.com* ⊘ *No lunch weekdays.*

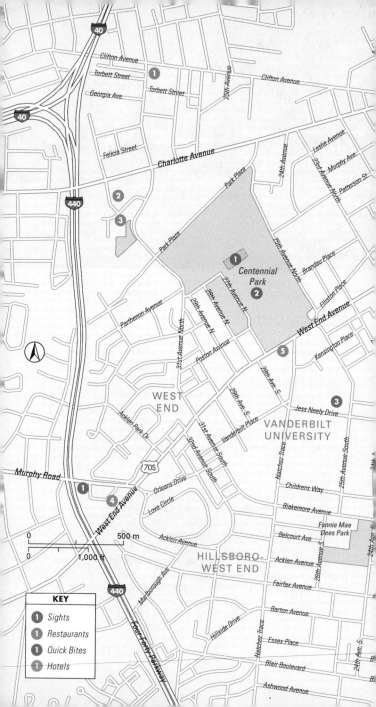

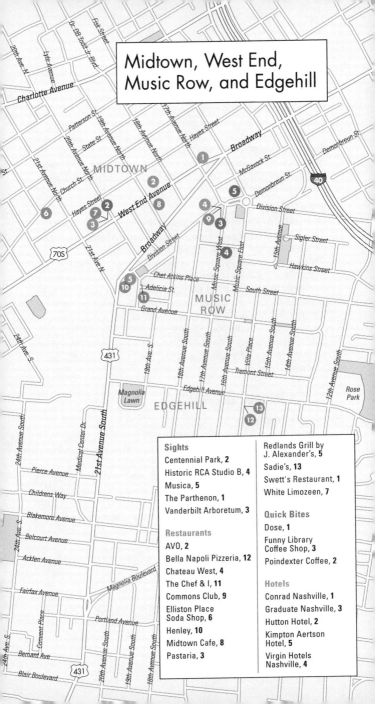

Midtown, West End, Music Row, and Edgehill

Sights
Centennial Park, **2**
Historic RCA Studio B, **4**
Musica, **5**
The Parthenon, **1**
Vanderbilt Arboretum, **3**

Restaurants
AVO, **2**
Bella Napoli Pizzeria, **12**
Chateau West, **4**
The Chef & I, **11**
Commons Club, **9**
Elliston Place
Soda Shop, **6**
Henley, **10**
Midtown Cafe, **8**
Pastaria, **3**
Redlands Grill by
J. Alexander's, **5**
Sadie's, **13**
Swett's Restaurant, **1**
White Limozeen, **7**

Quick Bites
Dose, **1**
Funny Library
Coffee Shop, **3**
Poindexter Coffee, **2**

Hotels
Conrad Nashville, **1**
Graduate Nashville, **3**
Hutton Hotel, **2**
Kimpton Aertson
Hotel, **5**
Virgin Hotels
Nashville, **4**

Midtown Cafe

$$$ | AMERICAN | If you love a decadent late breakfast or a sumptuous meal before heading out for a night on the town, then Midtown Cafe is the perfect place to stop for everything from soups to desserts. The café also offers diners a shuttle service to some of Nashville's premier performing arts venues, including the Schermerhorn Symphony Center, TPAC, and Ryman Auditorium. **Known for:** late breakfast and brunch options; Southern hospitality; complimentary valet parking for lunch and dinner. $ *Average main: $34* ⊠ *102 19th Ave. S, Midtown* ☎ *615/320–7176* ⊕ *www.midtowncafe.com* ☻ *No dinner Sun.*

White Limozeen

$$$ | SEAFOOD | This rooftop restaurant and bar is known for its picture-perfect all-pink ambience, including a giant sculpture of Dolly Parton's face. The menu features spunky cocktails like the Grey Goose and Campari Anti Hero or the smoky mezcal Fixin to Leave, shareable bites like a grazing board or classic crudité, and mains like caviar (even if it's not a special occasion), marinated mussels, and smoked chicken. **Known for:** indoor-outdoor seating; patio is available for walk-ins only; scenic view of the city. $ *Average main: $25* ⊠ *101 20th Ave. N, Midtown* ☎ *615/551–2700* ⊕ *graduatehotels.com/nashville/restaurant/white-limozeen* ☞ *Reservations are required for table dining and pool access. Restaurant is 21+ after 7 pm.*

Coffee and Quick Bites

Poindexter Coffee

$ | CAFÉ | Situated in the bright lobby of Graduate Nashville, this is a great sport for anyone (guest or not) to order classic caffeinated drinks, pastries, and savory sandwiches. Plan to stay a bit, as the mix-matched couches and accent chairs are the perfect place to enjoy your treats. **Known for:** Instagram-worthy decor; coffee cocktails; Southern breakfast options. $ *Average main: $8* ⊠ *101 20th Ave. N, Midtown* ⊕ *graduatehotels.com/nashville/restaurant/poindexter*.

Hotels

Conrad Nashville

$$$ | HOTEL | Midtown's only luxury hotel, the Conrad sits in the heart of the neighborhood, with expansive views of Downtown, sophisticated design, and attentive service. **Pros:** sophisticated on-site dining and two bars; state-of-the-art wellness options;

White Limozeen, located on the roof of the Graduate Hotel, is a must-visit for creative cocktails, shareable bites, and whimsical decor.

spacious suites. **Cons:** requires transportation to Downtown; lacks overt Music City atmosphere; pricier than other neighborhood hotels. Ⓢ *Rooms from: $599* ✉ *1620 West End Ave., Midtown* ☎ *615/327–8000* ⊕ *www.hilton.com/en/hotels/bnaleci-con-rad-nashville* ⤳ *234 rooms* ⦿❘ *No Meals.*

Graduate Nashville

$$$ | HOTEL | A bright and whimsical world awaits you inside this Midtown hotel—have your camera ready because you're going to want to take a picture everywhere you look. **Pros:** guests receive a coffee coin that can be used at Poindexter, the hotel's on-site coffee shop; approachable design and amenities; family suites available. **Cons:** no room service; small pool with limited hours; not suited for those seeking a low-key atmosphere. Ⓢ *Rooms from: $550* ✉ *101 20th Ave. N, Midtown* ☎ *615/551–2700* ⊕ *graduateho-tels.com/nashville* ⤳ *205 rooms* ⦿❘ *No Meals.*

Hutton Hotel

$ | HOTEL | As one of the neighborhood's first boutique hotels, the Hutton is a reflection of its proximity to Music Row, with nods to music just about everywhere. **Pros:** on-site entertainment; Peloton-equipped gym; great location. **Cons:** no pool; older than other boutique hotels in the neighborhood; rooms are on the small side. Ⓢ *Rooms from: $179* ✉ *1808 West End Ave., Midtown* ☎ *615/340–9333* ⊕ *www.huttonhotel.com* ⤳ *250 rooms* ⦿❘ *No Meals.*

Kimpton Aertson Hotel

$$ | HOTEL | FAMILY | Nestled between Vanderbilt University's campus and Downtown, this LEED-certified hotel—named in honor of an ancestor of the Vanderbilts—is decked out in artwork like prints by Hatch Show Print, Music City's legendary print shop, and all rooms feature views of the greenery and bustle of Midtown. **Pros:** on-site spa; next-door nightlife and restaurants; large pool deck with views of Midtown. **Cons:** slow valet parking; relatively small hotel; pricey nonattached parking garage. ⑤ *Rooms from: $349* ✉ *2021 Broadway, Midtown* ☎ *615/340–6376* ⊕ *www.aertsonhotel.com* ⇌ *180 rooms* ⭐ *No Meals.*

Must-See Murals

■ *Hold Fast* ✉ *128 31st Ave. N*

■ *It's a Southern Thing* ✉ *2555 West End Ave.*

■ *Heiroglitches* ✉ *2813 West End Ave.*

Nightlife

BARS

Cross-Eyed Critters Watering Hole

BARS | Let loose and sing a tune at Cross-Eyed Critters Watering Hole, located inside the Graduate. Styled like a Western saloon, this karaoke bar is campy and fun. A band of animatronic farm animals—the namesake critters—back those who take the stage. ✉ *Graduate Nashville, 101 20th Ave. N, Midtown* ☎ *615/551–2700* ⊕ *graduatehotels.com/nashville/restaurant/cross-eyed-critters-watering-hole* ☾ *Closed Sun.–Wed.* ☞ *21+ only.*

★ The Patterson House

COCKTAIL BARS | One of Nashville's long-standing speakeasy-style bars offers a Prohibition-era feel, which makes it one of the city's most popular nightspots. The amazing drinks, crafted by knowledgeable mixologists, enhance its popularity. ✉ *1711 Division St., Midtown* ⊕ *thepattersonnashville.com.*

LIVE MUSIC

Analog

MUSIC | This intimate performance venue—look for the retro marquee outside the Hutton Hotel—hosts multi-genre entertainment throughout the week. Mood lighting, crushed velvet curtains, and comfortable seating options add to the chill vibe. ✉ *Hutton Hotel, 1808 West End Ave., 2nd fl., Midtown* ☎ *615/340–9333* ⊕ *www.analognashville.com.*

West End

West End connects Midtown to West Nashville neighborhoods like Sylvan Park and Belle Meade. This understated area offers iconic performance venues, niche shopping experiences, and Centennial Park, a premier urban green space that features one of Nashville's most recognizable sights, the Parthenon. Adjacent to the park, Centennial Sportsplex (⊕ *www.nashville.gov/departments/parks/centennial-sportsplex*) hosts practice sessions (free to the public) for the Nashville Predators; check the website for the schedule.

Noteworthy Elliston Place is part of West End. It's home to some of Nashville's beloved historic landmarks, like rock venue Exit/In and the long-standing Elliston Place Soda Shop.

Sights

Centennial Park
CITY PARK | FAMILY | Home to the Parthenon, this 132-acre park has a 1-mile walking trail, Lake Watauga, the Centennial Art Center, Musicians Corner, sunken gardens, and a bandshell. It's home to the bench that was famously dedicated to Taylor Swift by the city of Nashville in 2023 to honor the park's mention in Swift's song "Invisible String." It's also a great place to explore an outdoor festival or hear live music. ⊠ *2500 West End Ave., West End* ☎ *615/862–8400* ⊕ *www.nashville.gov/departments/parks/parks/centennial-park.*

The Parthenon
NOTABLE BUILDING | FAMILY | An exact copy of the Athenian original, Nashville's Parthenon was constructed for Tennessee's 1897 Centennial Exposition. Across the street from Vanderbilt University's campus in **Centennial Park**, it's a magnificent sight, perched on a gentle green slope beside a duck pond. Inside are the 63-piece Cowan Collection of American Art, temporary exhibits, and the 42-foot *Athena Parthenos,* the tallest indoor sculpture in the Western world. ⊠ *2500 West End Ave., West End* ☎ *615/862–8431* ⊕ *www.nashville.gov/departments/parks/parthenon* ⊠ *$10.*

 Restaurants

AVO
$$ | VEGETARIAN | A plant-based restaurant, AVO is located in the mindful-lifestyle district called ONEC1TY. As such, it offers

decadent vegan options, a weekday happy hour, and thoughtful waitstaff trained to offer helpful information for those with specific nutritional needs. **Known for:** seasonal produce; happy hour featuring vegan cocktails; knowledgeable waitstaff. $ *Average main: $16* ⊠ *4 City Blvd., Suite 104, West End* ☎ *615/329–2377* ⊕ *www.eatavo.com* ⊗ *Closed Mon.*

Chateau West

$$$ | **FRENCH FUSION** | A Southern answer to French cuisine, Chateau West serves French-inspired lunch, dinner, and Sunday brunch. Their upscale yet relaxed setting matches the quality and accessibility of their entrées. **Known for:** French cuisine; Sunday brunch; chateau-like setting. $ *Average main: $30* ⊠ *3408 West End Ave., West End* ☎ *615/432–2622* ⊕ *www.chateauwestrestaurant.com.*

★ Elliston Place Soda Shop

$ | **AMERICAN** | **FAMILY** | Open since 1939, Elliston Place has retained much of its mid-century decor, including vintage jukeboxes at the tables (though the boxes themselves no longer play) and a lovely soda counter, complete with a fountain. Come for great burgers, frothy ice-cream sodas, and delicious chocolate shakes—or breakfast. **Known for:** flaky buttermilk biscuits; Southern meat and three option; delectable banana splits. $ *Average main: $12* ⊠ *2105 Elliston Pl., West End* ☎ *615/219–2704* ⊕ *www.ellistonplacesodashop.com* ⊗ *Closed Sun. No dinner.*

Pastaria

$$$ | **ITALIAN** | **FAMILY** | This spacious Italian restaurant located in the ONEC1TY community is known for its pastas and wood-fired pizzas. There are plenty of dish variations with veggies and savory meats, and the kids' menu has classic dishes and a gelato scoop that will pass the taste test for even the pickiest young eaters. **Known for:** gluten-free pasta options; laid-back atmosphere; free parking in garage. $ *Average main: $26* ⊠ *8 City Blvd., West End* ☎ *615/915–1866* ⊕ *eatpastaria.com/nashville* ⊗ *No lunch weekends.*

Redlands Grill by J. Alexander's

$$$ | **AMERICAN** | Part of a restaurant group, this spot has a decidedly upscale feel, with dark wood paneling, low lighting, and a great wine list. The menu includes wood-fired pork chops, rotisserie chicken, hearty salads, and fresh seafood. **Known for:** superb cocktails; perfectly cooked steaks; friendly and knowledgeable staff. $ *Average main: $27* ⊠ *2609 West End Ave., West End* ☎ *615/340–9901* ⊕ *jalexanders.com/tennessee/nashville/2609-west-end-ave.*

★ Swett's Restaurant

$ | SOUTHERN | FAMILY | Nashville is known for its meat-and-three-style restaurants, and Swett's is one of its most famous; past patrons run the gamut from presidents to pop stars and everyone in between. If you're looking for Southern staples like collard greens, baked mac and cheese, and entrées that range from fried catfish to barbecued ribs, this family-owned restaurant is the place to be. **Known for:** cafeteria-style dining; down-home Southern cooking; popular pies and cobblers. ⑤ *Average main: $12* ⊠ *2725 Clifton Ave., Nashville* ☎ *615/329–4418* ⊕ *swettsrestaurant.com.*

Coffee and Quick Bites

Dose

$ | AMERICAN | Located on the border of West End and Sylvan Park, Dose is one of the neighborhood's better-kept secrets, allowing it to be quieter and less crowded than larger chains closer to Down-town or Vanderbilt University. This is a good thing, because their daily fresh-baked goods, specially blended coffees, and delicious breakfast and lunch options are ones you're going to want to keep all to yourself. **Known for:** great sandwiches; fresh-baked goods; low-key (but friendly) atmosphere. ⑤ *Average main: $8* ⊠ *3431 Murphy Rd., West End* ☎ *615/457–1300* ⊕ *dosenashville.com/west-end* ☉ *No dinner.*

Nightlife

Elliston Place is home to the area historically known as the Rock Block for its live music venues like The End and Exit/In.

BARS

The Corner Bar

BARS | Like many of its neighbors on the Rock Block, The Corner Bar is heavy on local flavor and flair; its unpretentious clientele, great beer selection, and karaoke make it a favorite among nearby residents. It's open into the wee hours of the morning; stop by for a late-night bite or drink. ⊠ *2200 Elliston Pl., West End* ☎ *615/320–4979.*

SandBar Nashville

BARS | Locally owned and operated, SandBar Nashville has a coastal vibe in the middle of the city. It's best to visit on sunny days when you can sip on something refreshing—like their boozy juice pouches—and watch a sand volleyball game from the patio. ⊠ *3 City Ave., Suite 500, West End* ⊕ *www.sandbarnashville.com.*

LIVE MUSIC

The End

LIVE MUSIC | This grungy rock-and-roll dive bar is known for break-out performances by a host of famous bands like The Flaming Lips, The White Stripes, and R.E.M. Located on Elliston Place, in the strip historically known as the Rock Block, this is a small venue with a big reputation. Check out their website for upcoming events. ✉ *2219 Elliston Pl., West End* ☎ *615/321–4457* ⊕ *endnashville.com.*

Exit/In

LIVE MUSIC | Showcasing cutting-edge blues, rock, heavy metal, and hip-hop bands from the United States and beyond, the Exit/In is the place to be if you want to hear an array of genres in an unpretentious atmosphere. ✉ *2208 Elliston Pl., West End* ⊕ *exitin.com.*

Shopping

Cumberland Transit

SPORTING GOODS | As Nashville's oldest outdoor outfitter and bike shop, Cumberland Transit has everything you need for an adventure. The store specializes in gear for camping, biking, and climbing, as well as a selection of men's and women's clothing by popular brands like Teva, Patagonia, HOKA ONE ONE, and more. ✉ *2807 West End Ave., West End* ☎ *615/321–4069* ⊕ *cumberlandtransit.com* ⊘ *Closed Sun.*

Dead Ahead Tattoo Co.

SPECIALTY STORE | Looking for a longer-lasting souvenir than T-shirts and baseball caps? Then visit one of the artists at Dead Ahead Tattoo Co., one of the pioneer studios in Nashville's budding tattoo tourism industry. Clients have traveled from as far as Canada for new ink. ✉ *2916 West End Ave., West End* ☎ *615/490–3857* ⊕ *deadaheadtattoo.com.*

The French Shoppe

CLOTHING | Located in Park Place, this boutique is known for sophisticated women's clothing. In need of evening wear at the last minute? The French Shoppe also has stunning ballroom gowns in stock. ✉ *2817 West End Ave., Suite 120, West End* ☎ *615/327–8712* ⊕ *www.frenchshoppe.com* ⊘ *Closed Sun.*

★ Team Nashville

SPECIALTY STORE | A haven for runners, walkers, and swimmers, Team Nashville is stocked to the brim with shoes and other performance gear. This neighborhood store has been operating for more than 40 years and is known for its exceptionally friendly staff who are committed to helping customers find the best fit. ⊠ *3205 West End Ave., West End* ☎ *615/383–0098* ⊕ *www.teamnashvillesports.com* ☉ *Closed Sun.*

★ United Apparel Liquidators West End

CLOTHING | This West End shop is the best spot in Music City for heavily discounted designer clothing—up to 70–90% off retail. While the prices are akin to consignment deals, these assorted fashion pieces arrive at the store directly from the respective designer or retailer. ⊠ *2918 West End Ave., West End* ☎ *615/340–9999* ⊕ *store.shopual.com.*

Music Row and Edgehill

Music Row is one of Nashville's most famous historical districts; it is a series of streets just southwest of Downtown that serves as home to many of the recording studios, record labels, and publishing houses that have played a vital role in establishing the genre of country music. Unsurprisingly, this area neighbors Belmont University, an acclaimed school for music performance and business. Edgehill is a primarily residential district that seamlessly connects with Music Row. Its quieter atmosphere is great for those looking for a low-key experience that locals love.

Sights

★ Historic RCA Studio B

HISTORIC SIGHT | Music lovers will revel in the behind-the-scenes peek into Music Row's storied past at Historic RCA Studio B. Known as Nashville's "Home of 1,000 Hits," visitors are permitted into the studio space where hits like Dolly Parton's "I Will Always Love You," Roy Orbison's "Only the Lonely," and many more were recorded; guides provide history, commentary, and priceless stories about the likes of Elvis Presley, who recorded more than 240 songs at the studio. Tours depart daily from the Country Music Hall of Fame and Museum and are only available as an add-on to museum admission. ⊠ *1611 Roy Acuff Pl., Edgehill* ☎ *615/416–2001* ⊕ *countrymusichalloffame.org/experiences/studio-b* ⊠ *$49.95; $71.95 with Country Music Hall of Fame and Museum entrance, Hatch Show Print Tour, and Historic RCA Studio B Tour.*

Musica

PUBLIC ART | Sitting squarely in the Music Row roundabout (also known as Buddy Killen Circle), *Musica* was originally a point of controversy but now represents the artistic and cultural diversity of this thriving city. *Musica* is a bronze statue depicting nine dancing nude figures—including African American, Asian American, Native, and Latinx men and women—enthralled by music. At its pinnacle stands a woman holding a tambourine. The 14- and 15-foot-tall figures stand on limestone boulders, which are native to the area. ⊠ *Buddy Killen Circle, 1600 Division St., Music Row* ⟐ *At the convergence of 16th and 17th Aves. S and Division St.*

🍴 Restaurants

Bella Napoli Pizzeria

$$ | ITALIAN | Bella Napoli's brick-oven-baked pizzas and decadent pasta dishes will send you searching for this quaint eatery tucked in an alleyway on the back end of Edgehill Village. On warm nights, you can kick back on the romantically lit patio and enjoy good food, your favorite bottle of wine, and occasional live music. **Known for:** authentic Italian pizza; friendly service; beautiful patio seating. ⑤ *Average main: $18* ⊠ *1200 Villa Pl., Suite 206, Edgehill* ☎ *615/944–2819* ⊕ *bellanapolipizzeria.com* ⊗ *Closed Mon. and Tues.*

Commons Club

$$$ | AMERICAN | Located on the lobby level of Virgin Hotels Nashville, the cuisine at Commons Club ranges from Southern staples like the Nashville meat and three to seafood dishes and oven-fired flatbreads. Entering through the front doors, you'll walk past an eclectic inviting lounge area with plenty to look at, but continue on to the dining room for intimate seating, a pool table, a full bar, and frequent programming including songwriter showcases. **Known for:** live music programming; lively atmosphere; elevated bar bites. ⑤ *Average main: $26* ⊠ *1 Music Sq. W, Music Row* ☎ *615/808–8888* ⊕ *virginhotels.com/nashville/eat-drink/commons-club.*

Sadie's

$$ | MEDITERRANEAN | Serving up classic Mediterranean fare with an American twist, this light and airy space is a go-to lunch spot in the Edgehill neighborhood; a few dishes are guaranteed to have you in and out in 30 minutes. Menu items range from whipped feta with honeycomb or grilled romaine salad to traditional falafel or kebabs grilled over an open flame. **Known for:** express lunch options; stylish restaurant interior; charming patio seating. ⑤ *Average main: $18* ⊠ *1200 Villa Pl., Edgehill* ☎ *615/988–1200* ⊕ *www. sadiesnashville.com.*

Coffee and Quick Bites

Funny Library Coffee Shop

$ | **CAFÉ** | Located on the lobby level of the Virgin Hotels Nashville, the only thing funny about this coffee shop is its eccentric decor. Serving La Colombe coffee, baked goods, and breakfast bites, this is a great space to stretch out and work, relax, meet a friend, or plan the day's events. **Known for:** spacious lounge seating; reasonably priced coffee drinks; alcoholic beverages on the menu. $ *Average main: $8 ⊠ 1 Music Sq. W, Music Row ☎ 615/667–8000 ⊕ virginhotels.com/nashville/eat-drink/funny-library.*

🛏 Hotels

Virgin Hotels Nashville

$$$ | **HOTEL** | The stylish spirit of the Virgin brand delivers at this Music Row property, where there's plenty of guest programming, a speakeasy, a coffee shop, rooftop The Pool Club, and the lobby-level Commons Club restaurant. **Pros:** songwriter showcases in lobby; The Pool Club rooftop bar; walkable nightlife and dining options. **Cons:** small pool; limited parking; pricey overnight parking fees. $ *Rooms from: $450 ⊠ 1 Music Sq. W, Nashville ☎ 615/667–8000 ⊕ virginhotels.com/nashville ⇥ 262 rooms ⦾ No Meals.*

🍸 Nightlife

BARS
★ Old Glory

COCKTAIL BARS | Housed in an old steam-cleaning facility with most of the building's original 1920s fixtures—all except the sign—drinks and company take center stage at Old Glory. There isn't an expansive food menu, but there are craft drinks that highlight fresh and seasonally available ingredients. You'll find this spot by looking for the large golden triangle accenting the entrance door. ⊠ *1200 Villa Pl., Suite 103, Edgehill ⊕ oldglorynashville.com ☞ Reservations available for parties of 10 or more.*

LIVE MUSIC
The Electric Jane

LIVE MUSIC | The Electric Jane is a modern and swanky take on a supper club, offering up a mystical dinner and a show. Come on Saturday, when you can experience a themed drag brunch. ⊠ *1301 Division St., Music Row ☎ 615/964–7175 ⊕ theelectric-jane.com.*

Shopping

Billy Reid

CLOTHING | "Lived-in luxury" clothing brand Billy Reid is based in Florence, Alabama, but luckily for Tennesseans the store has an outpost in Nashville, too. Visit the Edgehill Village store for stylish comfortable pieces that will seamlessly integrate into any wardrobe. ⊠ *1200 Villa Pl., Suite 403, Edgehill* ☎ *615/292–2111* ⊕ *www. billyreid.com.*

Haven

CLOTHING | A thoughtfully curated women's clothing boutique in a chic urban setting, Haven offers trend-forward bohemian pieces that stand out in any crowd or closet. ⊠ *1200 Villa Pl., Suite 300, Edgehill* ☎ *615/812–1433* ⊕ *www.instagram.com/havenstyle* ☾ *Closed Sun.*

HILLSBORO VILLAGE AND BELMONT

Updated by
Brittney McKenna

⦿ Sights   🍴 Restaurants   🛏 Hotels   ⦿ Shopping   🍸 Nightlife

★★☆☆☆   ★★★★☆   ★★☆☆☆   ★★★★☆   ★★★★☆

NEIGHBORHOOD SNAPSHOT

TOP EXPERIENCES

■ **The Belcourt Theatre:** Catch the latest indie film or a cult classic at this beloved independent movie theater.

■ **The Villager Tavern:** Rub shoulders with locals at this long-running dive, known for its darts and jukebox.

■ **Fido:** Grab a great espresso drink or a full meal at this Bongo Java–affiliated eatery.

■ **Fannie Mae Dees Park:** Take the kids to play on the iconic mosaic dragon, or snap a grid-worthy photo for yourself.

■ **AB Hillsboro Village:** Catch a show from a local musician at this new neighborhood venue.

GETTING HERE

Hillsboro Village is close to Downtown and accessible via bus. It's also an easy neighborhood to bike to and boasts a nearby BCycle station if you need to rent some wheels. Once you've arrived in or near Hillsboro Village, the area's businesses and attractions are all within easy and safe walking or biking distance.

PLANNING YOUR TIME

There is plenty of parking in Hillsboro Village, both in paid lots and—if you're lucky—on the street. Most bars and restaurants in the area cater to nearby college students and stay open late, but specialty shops and attractions like The Belmont Mansion operate on limited hours. If you plan to check out The Belcourt Theatre, visit the schedule on their website first; popular showings will sell out in advance.

VIEWFINDER

■ One of Nashville's oldest murals is across the street from The Belcourt Theatre entrance. It depicts a large dragon beneath the words "Hillsboro Village" in homage to neighboring Fannie Mae Dees Park, known colloquially as "Dragon Park" for its large climbable dragon statue. Both landmarks make for great photo ops.

WORTH A TRIP

■ Vanderbilt and Belmont, each a short walk from Hillsboro Village, boast visit-worthy campuses. Vanderbilt's campus is an actual arboretum that makes for especially lovely walks in the fall. Belmont offers tours of its historic Belmont Mansion' it's also home to the Gallery of Iconic Guitars, featuring an extensive collection of rare and unusual guitars.

Hillsboro Village is one of Nashville's quaintest neighborhoods, playing host to some of the city's more exciting new fast-casual dining options and serving as stomping grounds for both Belmont University and Vanderbilt University students. Being so close to Belmont, the vibrant stretch of shops and restaurants on Belmont Boulevard—directly adjacent to the university—is almost an extension of Hillsboro Village, as walking between the two destinations is not only possible but quite pleasant on nice days.

Hillsboro Village is home to a number of vintage Nashville main-stays, like Pancake Pantry—a must-visit for breakfast lovers—and the historic Belcourt Theatre, which anchors the neighborhood in the city's history. New eateries like the brick-and-mortar Grilled Cheeserie (an offshoot of the popular food truck) and Austin transplant Hopdoddy Burger Bar bring new flavor to the area, while newer shops like Wilder and Hester & Cook offer plenty of reasons for a leisurely stroll, with coffee from Fido and shopping bags in hand.

Over on Belmont Boulevard, diners can enjoy a new location of Athens Family Restaurant, as well as an updated take on longtime boulevard favorite International Market, now run by original owner Patti Myint's son Arnold Myint, a celebrated restaurateur and drag performer. Check out the Gallery of Iconic Guitars, aka the GIG, while you're in the area to see beautiful instruments with storied histories. The Belmont Mansion will appeal to history buffs and aesthetic fiends alike, as the Civil War–era mansion plays host to a number of informative tours; the home itself, extravagant and luxuriously decorated, looks like something out of *Gone with the Wind*.

One could easily spend an entire day in the neighborhood: breakfast at Pancake Pantry, a couple hours browsing shops like United Apparel Liquidators (UAL for short) and Wilder, lunch at Proper Bagel near Belmont, an afternoon matinee at the Belcourt,

Fannie Mae Dees Park, also known as Dragon Park, is home to a large colorful dragon sculpture. It's a great spot for photo ops.

a quick walk back to dinner at International Market, and a nightcap and darts at longtime local dive The Villager Tavern. With a couple of new hotels in the area, like the conveniently located Moxy Nashville Vanderbilt at Hillsboro Village, you can stay where you play, too.

Bordering the southern section of Hillsboro, Green Hills is an affluent neighborhood known for high-end shopping; the Bluebird Cafe, one of the city's most famous live music venues; and Parnassus Books owned by best-selling author Ann Patchett.

Sights

Belmont Mansion

HISTORIC HOME | This 1850s Italian-style villa was the home of Adelicia Acklen, a wealthy plantation owner who married "once for money, once for love, and once for the hell of it." On Belmont University's campus, it's rich with historical and architectural details, with guided tours suited to varying interests. The property now also features Freedom Plaza, a monument built in 2021 honoring the many enslaved people who lived and worked on the property. The last tour of the day starts at 3:30. ⊠ *1900 Belmont Blvd., Hillsboro Village* ☎ *615/460–5459* ⊕ *www.belmontmansion. com* ☒ *$15.*

Fannie Mae Dees Park

CITY PARK | FAMILY | While Hillsboro Village itself offers plenty of charming outdoor walking space, the nearby Fannie Mae Dees

Park is the perfect place to stop for a picnic with your Fido goodies. Take the little ones to play on the playground, and check out the large dragon statue. Kids can play on it, but, with its bright colors and funky design, it's just as fun for adults who love a good photo op. ✉ *2400 Blakemore Ave., Hillsboro Village* ☎ *615/862–8400* ⊕ *www.nash-ville.gov/departments/parks/permits-rentals-and-reservations/picnic-shelters/fannie-mae-dees.*

Must-See Murals

- *Hillsboro Village Dragon* ✉ 2102 Belcourt Ave.

- *Hillsboro Village* ✉ 2013 Capers Ave.

Gallery of Iconic Guitars

SPECIALTY MUSEUM | Guitars are a dime a dozen in Nashville, but the axes on display at the Gallery of Iconic Guitars on Belmont University's campus are truly one-of-a-kind. From vintage instruments to guitars owned by legendary musicians, the guitars in Belmont's collection live up to their "iconic" name. The gallery sits within the heart of Belmont University, internationally renowned for its various music programs. Check the GIG's website before visiting, as University closures or holidays may affect hours. ✉ *1907 Belmont Blvd., Hillsboro Village* ☎ *615/460–6984* ⊕ *www.thegigatbelmont.com* 🎫 *$5.*

🍴 Restaurants

Athens Family Restaurant

$ | GREEK FUSION | Once featured on the Food Network, the Athens Family Restaurant is a diner that has all the appearances of a classic greasy spoon but instead serves delicious Greek food for all three meals. Enjoy gyro, pitas, and Greek sides, as well as American diner favorites like burgers and breakfast sandwiches. **Known for:** Greek cuisine; filling breakfasts; family-friendly diner environment. 💲 *Average main: $10* ✉ *2017 Belmont Blvd., Hillsboro Village* ☎ *615/383–2848* ⊕ *www.athensfamilyrestaurant.com.*

Biscuit Love

$ | AMERICAN | Biscuit Love opened its first outpost in The Gulch, and the hip new breakfast spot was so popular that lines poured out the door each morning. Now the beloved eatery is open in Hillsboro Village, serving up homemade biscuits and breakfast plates until 3 pm each day. **Known for:** sweet and savory biscuits; extensive breakfast menu; biscuit donuts ("bonuts"). 💲 *Average*

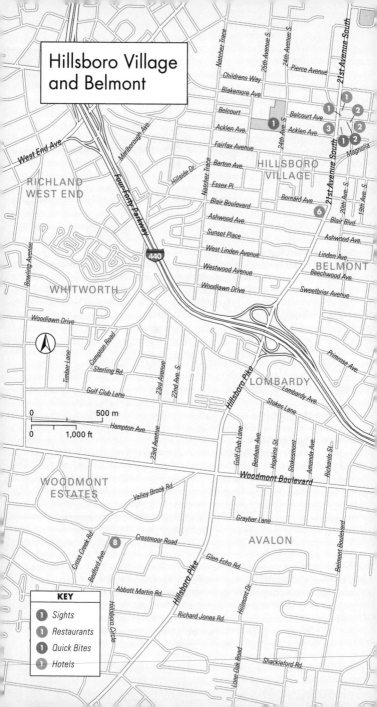

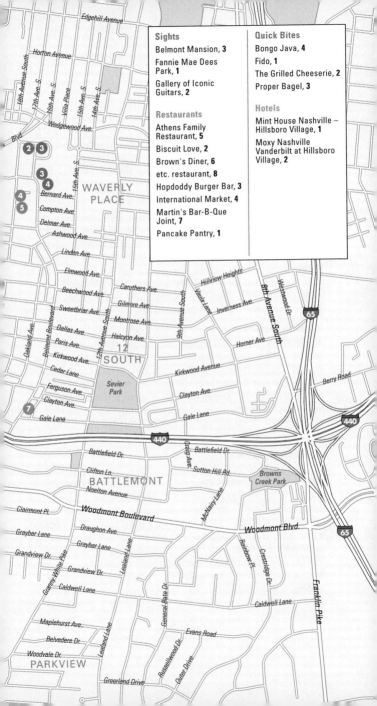

Sights

Belmont Mansion, **3**

Fannie Mae Dees Park, **1**

Gallery of Iconic Guitars, **2**

Restaurants

Athens Family Restaurant, **5**

Biscuit Love, **2**

Brown's Diner, **6**

etc. restaurant, **8**

Hopdoddy Burger Bar, **3**

International Market, **4**

Martin's Bar-B-Que Joint, **7**

Pancake Pantry, **1**

Quick Bites

Bongo Java, **4**

Fido, **1**

The Grilled Cheeserie, **2**

Proper Bagel, **3**

Hotels

Mint House Nashville – Hillsboro Village, **1**

Moxy Nashville Vanderbilt at Hillsboro Village, **2**

main: $10 ✉ *2001 Belcourt Ave., Hillsboro Village* ☎ *615/610–3336*
⊕ *www.biscuitlove.com* ☉ *No dinner.*

★ Brown's Diner

$ | **AMERICAN** | One of Nashville's oldest restaurants still in oper-
ation, the famed Brown's Diner first opened its doors in 1927.
This spot, housed in a large trailer, is popular with celebrities
and regular ol' locals, and the burger is one of the best in town.
Known for: classic no-frills burgers; friendly service; historic restaurant. $ *Average main: $7* ✉ *2102 Blair Blvd., Hillsboro Village*
☎ *615/269–5509* ⊕ *thebrownsdiner.com.*

etc. Restaurant

$$$ | **AMERICAN** | Tucked away behind the Mall at Green Hills, this
restaurant is the kind of place an out-of-towner could easily miss.
The menu, though, makes getting out the GPS worth it, as new
American favorites are reimagined using international ingredients.
Known for: extensive dessert menu; generous happy hour; hard to
find, but worth looking for. $ *Average main: $30* ✉ *3790 Bedford
Ave., Green Hills* ⊕ *About 8 minutes southwest of Hillsboro
Village* ☎ *615/988–0332* ⊕ *etc.restaurant.*

Hopdoddy Burger Bar

$ | **AMERICAN** | Hopdoddy Burger Bar has been popular in Texas
for some time now, but the new Hillsboro Village location marks
its first outpost in Nashville. The restaurant serves up a variety
of freshly made burgers, as well as thick creamy milkshakes and
perfectly crisp fries. **Known for:** craft burgers and local beer; free
samples of beer, fries, and shakes while you wait; house-made
margaritas. $ *Average main: $7* ✉ *1805 21st Ave. S, Hillsboro
Village* ☎ *615/823–2337* ⊕ *www.hopdoddy.com.*

International Market

$$ | **THAI** | Patti Myint's original incarnation of International Market
fed thousands of diners during its initial run from 1975 to 2019,
serving fresh Thai food and Asian-inspired dishes in a friendly grocery setting. Myint's son, the restauranteur and acclaimed drag
queen Arnold Myint, kept his late mother's legacy alive by opening
a new International Market across the street from its old location,
retaining many of the elder Myint's original recipes, like Patti's
Pad Thai, while adding some of his own, including creative takes
on curry and stir-fries. **Known for:** authentic Thai dishes; casual
setting; crispy fried chicken. $ *Average main: $15* ✉ *2013 Belmont
Blvd., Hillsboro Village* ☎ *615/297–4453* ⊕ *www.im2nashville.com*
☉ *Closed Sun.–Tues.*

The collection at the Gallery of Iconic Guitars, located at Belmont University, ranges from vintage instruments to guitars owned by legendary musicians.

★ Martin's Bar-B-Que Joint

$ | **BARBECUE** | Martin's proudly proclaims that they don't own a microwave or freezer and that they are committed to the western Tennessee style of whole-hog barbecue, smoking their hogs for a full day and serving them until they run out—period. This is the type of place where you may find yourself stupefied by just how much you've managed to eat. **Known for:** large portions; delicious beef brisket; veggie sides. $ *Average main: $11* ✉ *3108 Belmont Blvd., Belmont* ☎ *615/200–1181* ⊕ *www.martinsbbqjoint.com.*

Pancake Pantry

$ | **AMERICAN** | **FAMILY** | Breakfast is the specialty at this Nashville institution with 20 kinds of pancakes (sweet and savory) and homemade syrups. A favorite with locals, students, and celebrities, there are good soups and sandwiches for lunch—or you can stick with the pancakes, which are served till closing in late afternoon. **Known for:** 20 kinds of pancakes; sweet and savory homemade syrups; long wait times. $ *Average main: $12* ✉ *1796 21st Ave. S, Hillsboro Village* ☎ *615/383–9333* ⊕ *thepancakepantry.com* ☽ *No dinner.*

☕ Coffee and Quick Bites

Bongo Java

$ | **AMERICAN** | The Belmont Boulevard location of Bongo Java is a popular hangout for Belmont students. Accordingly, its food menu is more college-centric (think breakfast sandwiches) than Fido's, though in recent years the local coffee favorite has expanded its menu (and remodeled its building) to suit the needs of the rapidly growing neighborhood. **Known for:** ethically sourced coffee; inventive espresso drinks; all-day breakfast. $ *Average main: $5* ✉ *2007 Belmont Blvd., Hillsboro Village* ☎ *615/385–5282* ⊕ *www. bongojava.com/pages/bongo-java.*

★ Fido

$ | **AMERICAN** | Local favorite Fido is part of the Bongo Java family and has one of the coffee shop group's more extensive food menus. In addition to Fido's own take on the creatively made, ethically sourced espresso drinks found at other Bongo locations, the restaurant serves locally sourced breakfast, lunch, and dinner; try the burger. **Known for:** fresh local food; creative espresso drinks; funky environment. $ *Average main: $10* ✉ *1812 21st Ave. S, Hillsboro Village* ☎ *615/777–3436* ⊕ *www.bongojava.com/pages/fido.*

The Grilled Cheeserie

$ | **AMERICAN** | Long before The Grilled Cheeserie opened a brick-and-mortar shop, it was one of Nashville's most beloved food trucks, slinging grilled cheese and tater tots to long lines of eaters who often tracked the truck down. Now, though, it's easier to indulge in some melty goodness at the restaurant's first permanent location. **Known for:** inventive twists on grilled cheese; seasoned tater tots; homemade soup. $ *Average main: $8* ✉ *2003 Belcourt Ave., Hillsboro Village* ☎ *615/203–0351* ⊕ *grilled-cheeserie.com.*

Proper Bagel

$ | **AMERICAN** | Some say you can't get a proper bagel outside New York City, but Belmont Boulevard's Proper Bagel makes a good argument otherwise. Each day, the small eatery prepares a variety of freshly made bagels alongside numerous flavored cream cheese options. **Known for:** house-made bagels and cream cheese; variety of salads and sides; minimalist modern atmosphere. $ *Average main: $12* ✉ *2011 Belmont Blvd., Hillsboro Village* ☎ *615/928–7276* ⊕ *properbagel.com.*

Hotels

Mint House Nashville – Hillsboro Village

$$ | **APARTMENT** | Mint House's Hillsboro Village location offers spacious studio and one-bedroom rentals with far more amenities than offered by most hotels, including in-room kitchens, laundry, and seating areas. **Pros:** walkable neighborhood; in-room kitchens; spacious suites. **Cons:** can get expensive during peak seasons; neighborhood noise; not for fans of traditional hotels. $ *Rooms*

from: $300 ⊠ 1700 21st Ave. S, Hillsboro Village ☎ 855/972–9090 ⊕ minthouse.com/nashville/hillsboro-village ⥏ 17 units ⵙ No Meals.

Moxy Nashville Vanderbilt at Hillsboro Village

$ | HOTEL | Walk out the front door of the Moxy Nashville and find yourself in the middle of bustling Hillsboro Village, steps away from local attractions like The Belcourt Theatre, Pancake Pantry, and more. **Pros:** good for business travelers; walkable to local businesses; on-site food and beverage. **Cons:** limited in-room amenities; loud nearby foot traffic; no in-room closets. ⑤ Rooms from: $270 ⊠ 1911 Belcourt Ave., Hillsboro Village ☎ 615/385–1911 ⊕ www.marriott.com/en-us/hotels/bnaov-moxy-nashville-vander-bilt-area/overview ⥏ 130 rooms ⵙ No Meals.

Nightlife

BARS

Double Dogs

BREWPUBS | If you're looking to watch the big game in Hillsboro Village, look no further than Double Dogs. This brewpub has TV screens on TV screens, so they're sure to be broadcasting whichever sporting event you're after, which you can enjoy with a long list of craft beers. It's also a full restaurant, making it a nice spot for a casual meal. ⊠ 1807 21st Ave. S, Hillsboro Village ☎ 615/292–8110 ⊕ doubledogs.biz/hillsboro-village.

Joe's Place

BARS | Green Hills isn't a neighborhood known for its dives or holes-in-the-wall, but Joe's Place is a lively antidote to the surrounding area's polished sheen. Stop in for a cold beer or mixed drink, and stay for arcade games, karaoke, TVs, and well-prepared bar fare like pizzas and sandwiches. ⊠ 2227 Bandywood Dr., Green Hills ✛ About 8 miles southwest of Hillsboro Village ☎ 615/383–9115 ⊕ www.facebook.com/joesplacegh.

The Villager Tavern

BARS | Much of Hillsboro Village is hip and manicured, but not The Villager Tavern, which remains one of the neighborhood's longest-running establishments. A true dive, The Villager, which is wildly popular among locals, serves up a limited menu of cheap beer and occasionally has potato chips for when you need something to munch on. The real draws are the front-room jukebox and the back-room dartboards, the latter of which draw serious competitors on any night of the week. ⊠ 1719 21st Ave. S, Hillsboro Village ☎ 615/298–3020 ⊕ www.instagram.com/the_villager_tavern.

The Belcourt Theatre: A Must-See

The Belcourt Theatre has been a Nashville institution for nearly a century, hosting, in turns, the Nashville Children's Theatre and the Grand Ole Opry and serving as the first "twin cinema" theater in middle Tennessee. Since its opening in 1925 as a silent movie house, complete with a Kimball organ, The Belcourt has become Nashville's premier nonprofit film center, where movie lovers can view the latest avant-garde indies, groundbreaking documentaries, and hot new releases. After a $5 million renovation project in 2016, The Belcourt boasts state-of-the-art upgrades, including a newly designed lobby, upstairs classroom space for film education and community outreach, and an additional viewing room for private film screenings. However (and luckily), some things never change: moviegoers can still enjoy a glass of wine or beer with their popcorn, and you can still expect riveting post-film discussions with filmmakers and other experts. The Belcourt has also kept some of its other movie traditions, including Music City Mondays, where music buffs can watch iconic biopics or films with epic soundtracks; Weekend Classics; and seasonal features like Twelve Hours of Terror, an all-night horror marathon.

LIVE MUSIC

★ The Bluebird Cafe

MUSIC | You can't get the full Nashville experience without a visit to The Bluebird Cafe, one of the city's most famous music venues. Catch a show on any given night and you're bound to see some of the world's best songwriters performing new and old material in a truly intimate setting. Be mindful of The Bluebird's reservation policy (online reservations only, seat vs. table reservations), and do your research before you visit. ⊠ *4104 Hillsboro Pike, Green Hills* ⊹ *About 8 minutes southwest of Hillsboro Village* ☎ *615/383–1461* ⊕ *bluebirdcafe.com.*

🎭 Performing Arts

AB Hillsboro Village

MUSIC | Hillsboro Village was once a hub for live music, but it hasn't had a proper venue in some years. That changes with the addition of AB, an arts venue and event space that plays host to concerts, community gatherings, pop-ups and more. AB also hosts neighborhood-wide events, like 2023's first annual AB Block

Party. ✉ *2111 Belcourt Ave., Unit 101, Hillsboro Village* ☎ *615/866–9545* ⊕ *www.anzieblue.com.*

★ The Belcourt Theatre

FILM | The Belcourt Theatre is Nashville's only independent movie theater, first established in 1925 as the Hillsboro Theater. Reopened after extensive renovations in 2016, the newly updated and expanded Belcourt plays host to new films, old classics, special events, speakers, concerts, and more. The Belcourt has all kinds of snacks and drinks (including alcoholic beverages) available, so come hungry. ✉ *2102 Belcourt Ave., Hillsboro Village* ☎ *615/846–3150* ⊕ *www.belcourt.org.*

Shopping

BOOKS

Parnassus Books

BOOKS | Parnassus Books is best-selling author Ann Patchett's independent bookstore and one of Nashville's greatest literary destinations. Come for the shop's well-stocked curated selection of fiction, nonfiction, and more, and check the online schedule for special events like author signings and family story times. ✉ *3900 Hillsboro Pike, Suite 14, Green Hills* ↔ *About 8 minutes southwest of Hillsboro Village* ☎ *615/953–2243* ⊕ *www.parnassusbooks.net.*

CLOTHING

Molly Green

CLOTHING | Molly Green is a local family-run women's clothing boutique with additional locations Downtown and in Franklin. Visit this shop to find an outfit for just about any occasion, whether it's lounging about your vacation rental in a cozy colorful matching sweatsuit or dressing up in a jumpsuit for a screening at The Belcourt. In addition to clothing, the store is well-stocked with reasonably priced accessories, jewelry, and shoes, ensuring all your sartorial needs are met. ✉ *1721 21st Ave. S, Hillsboro Village* ☎ *615/730–7643* ⊕ *www.shopmollygreen.com.*

United Apparel Liquidators

CLOTHING | If you're looking to score a killer deal on designer clothing, look no further than United Apparel Liquidators (UAL for short). This small Southern chain has locations in 12South and West End, with Hillsboro Village's being the smallest. It still has an excellent selection, though, with up to 90% off retail prices for brands like Marc Jacobs and Theory (stock varies seasonally). ✉ *1814 21st Ave. S, Hillsboro Village* ☎ *615/540–0211* ⊕ *store.shopual.com.*

Wilder

CLOTHING | Pop into Wilder for fresh and fun women's fashion sold at affordable prices. The selection runs the gamut from casual to date night, with an array of accessories to boot, as well as a selection of giftable trinkets and goodies to throw in with your new floral dress and beaded purse. Wilder also carries a "Nashville collection" of clothing and accessories, making it a great spot for souvenirs or gifts for friends back home. ⊠ 1720 21st Ave. S, Hillsboro Village ☎ 615/292–9108 ⊕ www.shop-wilder.com.

GIFTS AND SOUVENIRS

Friedman's Army Navy Outdoor Store

SPECIALTY STORE | Friedman's is far more than a surplus and has been a Hillsboro Village institution since opening in 1972. The store offers plenty of surplus gear, plus camping supplies, outdoor equipment, and all you could possibly need for a last-minute fishing trip at one of Nashville's many beloved watering holes. ⊠ 2101 21st Ave. S, Hillsboro Village ☎ 615/297–3343 ⊕ friedmansarmynavyoutdoorstore.net ☉ Closed Sun.

Hester & Cook

HOUSEWARES | Hester & Cook is known for its tabletop decor, like the shop's colorful marbled place mats and handcrafted rickrack fabric napkins. This shop is far more than table dressing, though, and is a great spot to grab seasonal decor, like ghost-shaped coasters for Halloween and glass candy cane ornaments for Christmas. With stationery, toys, puzzles, and much more, this is one of the best gifting destinations in Hillsboro Village. ⊠ 1708 21st Ave. S, Hillsboro Village ☎ 615/205–2600 Ext. 3 ⊕ hesterandcook.com.

MALLS

The Mall at Green Hills

MALL | If a day at the mall is what the doctor ordered, look no further than The Mall at Green Hills. Located close to Downtown and Hillsboro Village, the Mall at Green Hills is the perfect one-stop shop for high-end clothing, accessories, home furnishings, and more. Don't miss the brand-new Restoration Hardware, which features four stories of decor as well as several restaurants. ⊠ 2126 Abbott Martin Rd., Green Hills ⊕ About 8 minutes southwest of Hillsboro Village ☎ 615/298–5478 ⊕ shopgreenhills.com.

12SOUTH

Updated by
MiChelle Jones

⊙ Sights   🍴 Restaurants   🛏 Hotels   🛍 Shopping   🍸 Nightlife

★☆☆☆☆   ★★★★★   ☆☆☆☆☆   ★★★☆☆   ★★★☆☆

NEIGHBORHOOD SNAPSHOT

TOP EXPERIENCES

■ **People-watching:** This neighborhood attracts an entertaining parade of tourists and locals.

■ **Shopping:** Explore a mix of local originals and brick-and-mortar outposts of national brands.

■ **Treats:** Indulge in donuts, cookies, ice cream, or cereal.

■ **Good Restaurants:** From casual burgers and barbecue places to fine dining, reservations required.

■ **Have a Drink:** Several restaurant bars are good hangouts.

PLANNING YOUR TIME

12South really picks up Friday through Sunday, with visitors in for long weekends. Expect long restaurant lines, crowded sidewalks and shops, and a hunt for parking, but it's all part of the fun. For a quieter experience, come Monday through Wednesday. Be aware that 12th Avenue South is a busy two-lane thoroughfare (most locals avoid it, if at all possible) and there is a lot of construction in this area of desirable real estate, so be mindful of cars and large vehicles. Another safety tip: be as careful and sensible at night as you would anywhere else.

ART IN THE WILD

■ Several murals make this neighborhood even more Insta-ready than the charming shops lining the road. Stop by the *I Believe in Nashville* mural at ⊠ *2702 12th Ave. S* (there's a second one at Marathon Music Works). Look for a bright mural made of artificial flowers on the side of the Bullets and Pearls jewelry store at the seasonal open-air market at ⊠ *2501 12th Ave. S* or pose for a pretty picture on the white garden bench in front of the blue-and-white gingham background on the side of the blue-and-white striped Draper James store. A mural on the side of Serendipity12th (⊠ *2814 12th Ave. S, Suite 102*) depicts wildlife and the Nashville skyline dotted with its latest accessory: construction cranes.

On any given weekend, the compact 12South area might be packed with crowds, scooter riders, and cyclists. The eponymous road is one of several parallel streets forming a major commuter corridor, so it is often congested with traffic. The strip of shops, restaurants, and coffee establishments is smack in the middle of a residential neighborhood that has quickly morphed from one of long-established retirees to young families in newly constructed dwellings.

This neighborhood is a great place to people-watch and stroll. Locals come here for dining; college kids come to hang out; and visitors come to take photos in front of murals. 12South is also a favorite on the bachelorette trail—you'll most definitely spot a bride-to-be with a veil attached to her cowboy hat, her entourage in cowboy boots, all in coordinating outfits, enjoying the day or night with friends.

Shopping at some of the celebrity-owned and-curated shops here is another main draw to 12South. Reese Witherspoon (Draper James) and Holly Williams (White's Mercantile) have shops here, as do designers and stylists who regularly work with singers and other performers (HERO and Judith Bright, for example). Along 12th Avenue South, change is spreading as new retail buildings come online—The 12 South Collection is expected to be completed in early 2024 with stores like rag & bone, PAIGE, and others already open.

Other retail developments include the growth of stores catering to men as well as women, the arrival of more national chains, and a number of pop-up concerns in the retail equivalent of food trucks. An absolutely giant complex, Ashwood 12 South Assemblage is scheduled to open at the end of 2024 with more than 44,000 square feet of retail and dining space.

Not all of the changes around 12South are commercial. Sevier Park, the 20-acre green space at the neighborhood's center, is also undergoing improvements, including the restoration and repurposing of the historic mansion on the grounds. Numerous events are held in the park, from a weekly farmers' market to beer and music festivals; it's also good for a walk or run.

Sights

★ Sevier Park

CITY PARK | FAMILY | A much-loved 20-acre site at one end of the 12South neighborhood, Sevier Park is the site of festivals and a weekly farmers' market on Tuesdays from May through late October. The park opened in 1948 and features trails, a creek, two playgrounds, a shelter, picnic tables, and a historic mansion (currently undergoing renovation). The updated community center was opened in 2014 and offers $3 drop-in fitness classes, including yoga. There are also tennis and basketball courts, as well as bike rentals. It's open from 6 am until dark. ⊠ *3021 Lealand La., 12South* ☎ *615/862–8466* ⊕ *www.nashville.gov/departments/ parks.*

🍴 Restaurants

bartaco

$ | SOUTH AMERICAN | FAMILY | This location of the national chain is both cozy and airy, with woven baskets as light fixtures; it serves upscale bites influenced by the street food and beach cultures of Southern California, Uruguay, and Brazil. Tacos (Bibb lettuce is available instead of flour shells) and rice bowls dominate the menu, as well as fresh-squeezed juice and cocktails; there's also a kids' menu. **Known for:** fresh cocktails; outdoor dining; delicious fresh fish tacos. ⑤ *Average main: $8* ⊠ *2526 12th Ave. S, 12South* ☎ *615/269–8226* ⊕ *bartaco.com/location/nashville-tn* ☞ *No cash accepted.*

Burger Up

$$ | BURGER | FAMILY | Popular with all ages, including young families, this comfortable neighborhood hangout serves—you guessed it—burgers, as well as soups and salads. Beef and other meats are sourced from a local farm and butcher shop. **Known for:** truffle fries; Ramsey Pimento Cheese Burger; well-stocked bar. ⑤ *Average main: $16* ⊠ *2901 12th Ave. S, 12South* ☎ *615/279–3767* ⊕ *www.burger-up.com.*

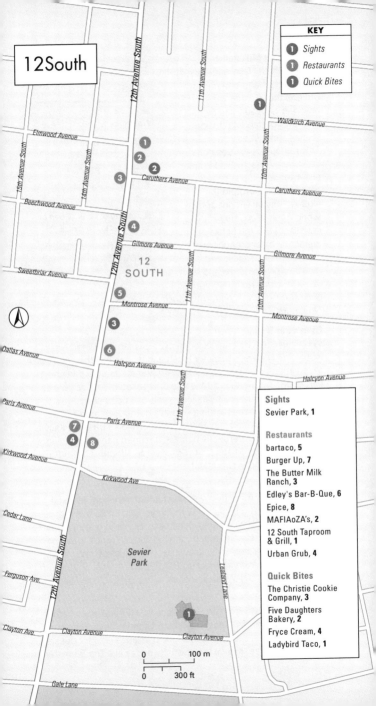

12South

KEY

- ① Sights
- ① Restaurants
- ① Quick Bites

Sights

Sevier Park, **1**

Restaurants

bartaco, **5**

Burger Up, **7**

The Butter Milk Ranch, **3**

Edley's Bar-B-Que, **6**

Epice, **8**

MAFIAoZA's, **2**

12 South Taproom & Grill, **1**

Urban Grub, **4**

Quick Bites

The Christie Cookie Company, **3**

Five Daughters Bakery, **2**

Fryce Cream, **4**

Ladybird Taco, **1**

★ The Butter Milk Ranch

$$ | **AMERICAN** | Come hungry for breakfast and brunch options that include zucchini pie, avocado toast, and unforgettable fluffy and crepe-like blueberry pancakes. This restaurant exudes boho California vibes with its bright airy interior and plant-filled wood accents around the open kitchen. **Known for:** out-of-this world, melt-in-your-mouth croissants like the babka or pistachio; blueberry pancakes; a case full of house-cured meats. $ *Average main: $18* ✉ *2407 12th Ave. S, 12South* ☎ *615/465–8300* ⊕ *buttermilkranch.com* ⊘ *Closed Mon. and Tues. No dinner.*

12South's Must-See Murals

■ *I Believe in Nashville* ✉ *2702 12th Ave. S*

■ *Blue and White Wall at Draper James* ✉ *2608 12th Ave. S*

■ *Flowers* ✉ *2900 12th Ave. S*

■ *Nashville Looks Good on You* ✉ *2511 12th Ave. S*

■ *Just a Few Gents* ✉ *2318 12th Ave. S*

Edley's Bar-B-Que

$$ | **BARBECUE** | The original location of this family-owned Nashville institution is always busy for lunch and dinner, but they don't take reservations, so plan accordingly. Known for its award-winning barbecue, the menu includes lots of smoked meats as well as a number of Southern sides like cornbread bean salad, mac and cheese, and banana pudding—you've got to love a place that includes banana pudding as a side rather than a dessert. **Known for:** brisket tacos; barbecue nachos; whipped banana pudding. $ *Average main: $14* ✉ *2706 12th Ave. S, 12South* ☎ *615/953–2951* ⊕ *www.edleysbbq.com.*

Epice

$$$ | **LEBANESE** | A family-owned restaurant serving traditional Lebanese and Greek dishes with foodie flair, Epice has a large patio where diners can enjoy lunch and dinner in good weather. The popular weekend brunch menu includes French toast, omelets, and special cocktails. **Known for:** olive oil cake; shawarma; egg dishes. $ *Average main: $28* ✉ *2902 12th Ave. S, 12South* ☎ *833/936–3873* ⊕ *www.epicenashville.com* ⊘ *Closed Mon.*

MAFIAoZA's

$$ | **PIZZA** | **FAMILY** | This fun pizza place is where all ages gather for deep-dish pizzas made in an open kitchen. Beyond pizza they serve meatballs, sautéed spinach, and salads—and for dessert, cannoli of course. **Known for:** specialty pizzas like The Teamster

The melt-in-your-mouth croissants at The Butter Milk Ranch are worth waiting in line for.

(bacon, sausage, pepperoni) or The Informant (roasted veggies and pesto cream); The Consigliere meat lasagna; weekly drink specials. $ *Average main: $18* ✉ *2400 12th Ave. S, 12South* ☎ *615/269–4646* ⊕ *www.mafiaozas.com* ⊗ *Closed Mon. No lunch Tues.–Fri.*

12 South Taproom & Grill
$$ | AMERICAN | Part of the 12South scene before there was one, this perennial favorite of families, local college kids, and visitors has a large, covered street-facing patio and small performance space inside. The surprisingly large menu has a seemingly endless list of quesadillas (rib eye!), tacos (tilapia), and salads with vegetarian options, plus there's a kids' menu. **Known for:** extensive beer selection; grass-fed beef; choco-chip banana bread. $ *Average main: $17* ✉ *2318 12th Ave. S, 12South* ☎ *615/463–7552* ⊕ *www. 12southtaproom.com.*

Urban Grub
$$$ | CONTEMPORARY | Located on the site of a former car wash, Urban Grub is now a sophisticated dining space serving seafood and locally sourced meat that's cured in-house. Wait times can soar to two hours, so reservations are strongly encouraged, especially if you're coming with a large group, but there is also seating available at the bar and oyster bar. **Known for:** charcuterie boards; handmade pasta; complimentary valet parking. $ *Average main: $28* ✉ *2506 12th Ave. S, 12South* ☎ *615/679–9342* ⊕ *www. urbangrub.net* ⊗ *Closed Mon. No lunch Tues.–Thurs.*

☕ Coffee and Quick Bites

The Christie Cookie Company

$ | BAKERY | You can't miss the bright red facade or the window where you can order the signature chocolate chip or oatmeal raisin cookies; sometimes there's a tray of samples at the window. This location opened in 2018, but the bakery has been around since 1985. **Known for:** snickerdoodle; white chocolate macadamia nut; cookie of the month (limited editions). $ *Average main: $3* ⊠ *2606 12th Ave. S, 12South* ☎ *615/454–3162* ⊕ *www.christiecookies. com.*

★ Five Daughters Bakery

$ | BAKERY | FAMILY | You know the offerings are good when the hours include a "or till sold out" proviso, and that's the case with this locally-owned bakery located just off 12th Avenue South. Pastries and cookies fill the cases, but the large, beautifully decorated gourmet donuts are what people talk about most (mini versions are also available). **Known for:** Hundred Layer Donut; paleo varieties; choices like King Kong (with bacon and maple glaze). $ *Average main: $4* ⊠ *1110 Caruthers Ave., 12South* ☎ *615/490–6554* ⊕ *fivedaughtersbakery.com.*

Fryce Cream

$ | ICE CREAM | FAMILY | On a hot and humid summer day, this tiny storefront attracts a crowd of locals and tourists alike. Sit outside to people- and pooch-watch while you dip your hot crispy fries into cool soft-serve ice cream—the simple combo is a very good thing. **Known for:** fries and soft serve combo plate; hot crispy fries; creamsicle float. $ *Average main: $10* ⊠ *2905 12th Ave. S, 12South* ⊕ *www.frycecreamnash.com* ☾ *Closed Mon. and Tues. Winter hours may differ.*

Ladybird Taco

$ | SOUTHWESTERN | Inspired by taco culture in Austin, Texas, this bustling eatery specializes in breakfast and lunch tacos—both served all day—featuring brisket, avocado, and other fillings; vegetarian options and a kids' menu are available. The coffee menu has a nice selection of lattes and espresso, and Mexican Coke, Topo Chico, and house-made watermelon agua fresca are also available. **Known for:** brisket tacos; breakfast tacos; churros. $ *Average main: $6* ⊠ *2229 10th Ave. S, 12South* ☎ *615/678–8049* ⊕ *www. ladybirdtaco.com.*

Nightlife

Embers Ski Lodge

BARS | A kitschy hangout with a 1960s après-ski vibe, Embers Ski Lodge serves gastropub fare—burgers, hand-cut Belgian fries—with a hint of the Pacific Northwest and East Asia, as well as a selection of cocktails, beer, and wine. Their large patio is located on a great corner for people-watching. ⊠ *2410 12th Ave. S, 12South* ☎ *615/866–5652* ⊕ *embersskilodge.com.*

🛍 Shopping

ACCESSORIES AND JEWELRY

Judith Bright

JEWELRY & WATCHES | Selling stylish and delicate handmade pieces combining metal with beads, gemstones, or birthstones, a crew of artisans work on-site in this light aqua cottage (one of three Nashville area locations), so stones or other elements can be changed on the spot. Some of Judith Bright's creations have been featured in movies and TV shows. ⊠ *2307 12th Ave. S, 12South* ☎ *615/269–5600* ⊕ *judithbright.com.*

★ Planet Cowboy

SHOES | One of a row of shops on 12th Avenue near Kirkland Avenue, Planet Cowboy stocks a beautiful selection of handmade cowboy boots for men and women in a variety of hues and materials, ranging from traditional Western to more understated styles. The store's namesake brand is made in Mexico; other brands hail from Texas and elsewhere. Cowboy hats are customizable with designs in the crown, for example; there's also a selection of Western-inspired jewelry. The store smells great and looks great, with hide rugs on the floor and a leather settee in the small showroom space. A second location is located at The Factory in Franklin. ⊠ *2905 12th Ave. S, 12South* ☎ *615/730–5789* ⊕ *planet-cowboy.com* ⊙ *Closed Tues.*

CLOTHING

Buck Mason

CLOTHING | Set up to look like a garage—a nice nod to the brand's origins in a California garage and also ironic since this isn't one of the 12South shops housed in a former car-centric building—Buck Mason even has a 1968 Porsche as a giant centerpiece. Stylish comfortable clothes like tees, sweatshirts, and other refined casual pieces are on offer for men and women. ⊠ *1119 Halcyon Ave., 12South* ☎ *615/730–8814* ⊕ *www.buckmason.com.*

Located in the former Granny White Service Station, the flagship location of Nashville's imogene + willie is worth visiting, especially to pick up some denim.

Draper James

CLOTHING | Once you step under the blue-and-white-striped awning, you'll be greeted by friendly sales associates and welcomed into the Southern fantasy of the brand founded by Reese Witherspoon. The charming flagship store sells stylish feminine clothing, pretty home accents, and gifts. There is comfy seating for those who need a break, a good selection of sale items, and a nice assortment of sizes. Don't forget to pose for a selfie in front of the mural on the side of the building. There's a Draper James location in Nashville's ever-expanding airport in case you decide to hunt for a last-minute souvenir. ⊠ *2608 12th Ave. S, 12South* ☎ *615/997–3601* ⊕ *draperjames.com.*

★ Emerson Grace

CLOTHING | This beautifully curated collection of women's clothing features the work of numerous designers and is showcased in a rustic-industrial space matching the casual-chic aesthetic of the apparel. You'll find local and international brands in this shop that's been a neighborhood fixture for a decade. ⊠ *2304 12th Ave. S, 12South* ☎ *615/454–6407* ⊕ *www.emersongracenashville.com.*

HERO

CLOTHING | This is one of three Nashville-area boutiques (each has a different name) owned by Claudia Robertson Fowler, stylist to country music stars such as Faith Hill, Trisha Yearwood, Martina McBride, and Miranda Lambert. The items here have a certain rock-star flair: flowing frocks, fuzzy fur jackets in bright hues, and sparkly tops. The store also stocks hats by Nashville hat makers such as Claire West. ⊠ *2306 12th Ave. S, 12South* ☎ *615/457–1206* ⊕ *hero12s.com.*

imogene + willie

CLOTHING | If you really love denim or indigo, this is your store. Known for handmade jeans, overalls, and other denim wear, as well as small-batch T-shirts and other items, the store is as comfortable as your favorite pair and is worth a look, even if you can't splurge. The building is a former gas station dating from the 1950s, which gives you an idea of how this neighborhood looked in a former incarnation. Another throwback feature: all the clothing is made in the USA. The store hosts occasional music events in the back. ⊠ *2601 12th Ave. S, 12South* ☎ *615/292–5005* ⊕ *imogeneandwillie.com/pages/nashville.*

Marine Layer

CLOTHING | This stand-alone store for the popular brand comes complete with a Mystery Tee Machine, where $20 gets you a surprise shirt (a $40 value, apparently). You'll find stylish comfortable clothing for men and women. The friendly staff will ship your purchases for free—handy if you've run out of space in your luggage. ⊠ *2705 12th Ave. S., 12South* ☎ *615/622–4586* ⊕ *www.marinelayer.com.*

MODA Boutique

CLOTHING | This small shop in a converted cottage offers women's designer clothes, ranging from casual to edgy. Jeans and denim jackets, novelty T-shirts, small gift items, and a jewelry selection that includes pieces made by local designers can all be found here. ⊠ *2511 12th Ave. S, 12South* ☎ *615/298–2271* ⊕ *www.modanashville.com.*

Vinnie Louise

CLOTHING | Named after the owner's grandmother, this boutique stocks casual trendy women's clothing at accessible prices along with a small selection of footwear and jewelry. Greeting cards, candles, and a few other gift items are available. The store's earthy vibe is enhanced by its worn brick floor. This is one of four locations in Nashville, with an additional one in Franklin. ⊠ *2301 12th Ave. S, Suite 2430, 12South* ☎ *615/730–8253* ⊕ *www.vinnielouise.com.*

GIFTS AND SOUVENIRS

Made in TN

SOUVENIRS | One of four locations in Nashville, this little shop is absolutely packed with potential presents for the folks back home: candles, puzzles, jewelry, food products, and more from a number of Nashville and/or Tennessee enterprises. Thistle Farms, an organization dedicated to helping women survivors of abuse and addiction, is well represented here, as is Loveless Cafe, Bongo Java coffee, and Sweet Tea Candle Company. There's a good selection of items for little ones, too. No room? No problem, you can arrange free shipping when you check out. ✉ *2905 12th Ave. S, Suite 102, 12South* ☎ *615/337–2517* ⊕ *shopmadeintn.com.*

★ Ranger Station

SPECIALTY STORE | You can find Ranger Station's candles all over Nashville—including in a few stores in 12South—but why not stop in the flagship store? The aesthetic is clean and rustic, with small black and white tiles on the floor and walls lined with small wooden cubby holes for the candles. At the factory in Wedgehood-Houston, each heavenly scented candle is poured in its own reusable cocktail glass adorned with the ranger hat logo; purchase one and you'll also get a cocktail recipe and a box of matches. Try the Nashville candle, whose fragrance combines magnolia, dogwood, amber, and musk. The shop also carries unisex perfumes, room sprays, and body products. ✉ *2095 12th Ave. S, Suite 106, 12South* ⊕ *rangerstation.co.*

Serendipity12th

SOUVENIRS | **FAMILY** | Located in its current location since 2021, Serendipity has been a 12South staple since 2001. You'll still find lots and lots of gifts for everyone. Travel games, novelty items, little books, and locally made candles with scents such as "Nashville" (whiskey and leather) abound. This store also stocks women's clothing and accessories and has quite a collection of children's books, games, and more. ✉ *2814 12th Ave. S, 12South* ☎ *615/279–5570* ⊕ *serendipity12th.com.*

★ White's Mercantile

SPECIALTY STORE | The flagship location of singer-songwriter Holly Williams's shop stocks shirts and tees for men and women; gifts and greeting cards; and a quirky collection of housewares. This is a great stop for Nashville- or Southern-themed gifts. Beautiful leather totes, shoulder bags, and more from Nashville-based ABLE can be found, and they do an impressive job of gift-wrapping purchases. There are now four Nashville-area locations of this updated take on a general store. To immerse yourself further into the lifestyle, you can stay at a White's Mercantile Room and Board property in neighboring counties. ✉ *2908 12th Ave. S, 12South* ☎ *615/750–5379* ⊕ *whitesmercantile.com.*

MELROSE AND BERRY HILL

Updated by
Chris Chamberlain

◉ Sights 🍴 Restaurants 🛏 Hotels 🛍 Shopping 🍸 Nightlife
★☆☆☆☆ ★★★★☆ ☆☆☆☆☆ ★☆☆☆☆ ★☆☆☆☆

NEIGHBORHOOD SNAPSHOT

TOP EXPERIENCES

■ **Low-Key Atmosphere:** Unlike other parts of Nashville, people actually live here—and have for their entire lives.

■ **Casual Dining:** The eating and drinking spots in these two neighborhoods are decidedly casual and invite you to come as you are.

■ **Hidden History:** A striking statue commemorating the Battle of Nashville is tucked away on a hill in Battlemont Park. It's worth seeking out.

■ **Woodlawn Memorial Cemetery:** Many famous country musicians are interred in the lovely rolling green hills that take up much of the center of Berry Hill.

PLANNING YOUR TIME

While some neighborhoods in Nashville are best avoided right after church lets out on Sundays because of the congestion, there aren't many places of worship in Melrose and Berry Hill, making it a brunch-lovers paradise. Since much of the area is residential, commuter traffic can be a bit rough during morning and evening rush hours.

PAUSE HERE

While the giant limestone reservoir looming over Melrose is inaccessible to the public (it's an active water supply for the city), the park that surrounds it is a lovely place to stroll and think of how in 1912, a wall collapsed and sent 25 million gallons of water flooding into the neighborhood below. Don't worry—they fixed it!

OFF THE BEATEN PATH

■ Nashville has one of the country's fastest-growing immigrant populations, especially in the neighborhoods of South Nashville and Woodbine, which border Berry Hill to the east. This diversity has made the area's main thoroughfare, Nolensville Pike, the city's epicenter of delicious international food: in addition to its famed taco trucks, there's Turkish food, multiple Thai options, and a food court with Mexican and Latin American options called Plaza Mariachi.

GETTING HERE

■ Berry Hill and Melrose are south of Downtown, clustered around the bottom of the Downtown Interstate Loop. A car is recommended to get around as city bus service is sparse.

Melrose and Berry Hill used to represent the outskirts of Nashville, before urban sprawl pushed all the way out from Downtown to the farms and suburbs south of the city. Now, these two neighborhoods still exhibit some of the residential charm from the time before 1962, when Nashville adopted a metropolitan form of government that combined the urban core with the rest of the countryside under the auspices of a single mayor and city council.

Even after the consolidation, Berry Hill maintained its status as a satellite city. With its own city hall, police force, and welcome sign, Berry Hill still depends on the Metro government for fire protection and trash collection, but the neighborhood's independent spirit shines through with a collection of fun boutiques, jewelry stores, and souvenir shops that don't take themselves or their neighbors Downtown too seriously. Convivial coffee shops, bars, and a large brewery taproom are gathering spots for residents and for visitors who want to check out the vibe.

Melrose is to the northwest of Berry Hill, a little closer to the urban core. There is a more distinct division between the neighborhoods of windy streets lined with early 20th-century bungalows and the much more commercial strip that runs along 8th Avenue. Residents still walk the sidewalks of the Historic Waverly portion on Melrose, but 8th Avenue has not caught up with the rest of the city's desire for safe pedestrian travel. That doesn't stop some intrepid tourists from riding rental scooters all the way from Downtown to the popular bars and restaurants at the far end of Melrose, but it's not the recommended manner of travel unless you're a daredevil. Besides, how are you going to carry all the vintage finds you discover at clothing shops and antiques stores around Melrose if you're riding on just two wheels? After an enjoyable evening spent sampling pints of regional brews at a neighborhood haunt like M.L.Rose Craft Beer & Burgers or taking advantage of the voluminous rare whiskey list at the upstairs bar at Sinema, even four-wheel travel probably isn't the best idea.

Avail yourself of the ample availability of rideshares to get around town, and everyone will be a whole lot safer.

Both Melrose and Berry Hill are primarily residential and commercial neighborhoods, without many lodging options. The best bet is to search for a short-term rental option or make the short trip back and forth from Downtown hotels to visit these intriguing enclaves.

Melrose

The Melrose neighborhood sits where 8th Avenue changes to Franklin Pike, a nod to the early days of Nashville when this was the main road that connected the farms and homes of Franklin to the markets Downtown. Later, a streetcar route ran down the old trading road to some of Nashville's original suburbs. This primarily residential community was known as Waverly—you'll still see that designation on some maps today—while the commercial center is referred to as Melrose.

8th Avenue is lined with restaurants, vintage shops, cafés, and other business amenities that residents require, including grocery stores, auto-repair shops, and convenience marts. It's an interesting place to visit to see where town and country meet on the outskirts of Nashville.

Sights

Browns Creek Greenway at Battlemont Park

CITY PARK | Tucked behind an apartment complex, the Browns Creek Greenway is a 0.65-mile trail in Battlemont Park. Occupying a space that was cleared of houses after the 2010 Nashville Flood, the repurposed area features a dog-friendly paved loop that is shaded by mature trees. The Battle of Nashville Monument stands nearby in Battlemont Park to commemorate soldiers from both sides of the Civil War who fought in an important battle in this portion of the city in 1864. ⊠ *816 Park Terr., Berry Hill* ⊕ *greenwaysfornashville.org* ⊠ *Free.*

 Restaurants

Fenwick's 300

$$ | DINER | FAMILY | Bright and airy, this diner-style restaurant features a stand-alone coffee bar within the dining room, where Bongo Java's coffee and signature drinks are paired with thoughtful and hearty brunch selections and breakfast cocktails. The large center bar is topped with a bowling lane, a nod to the building's

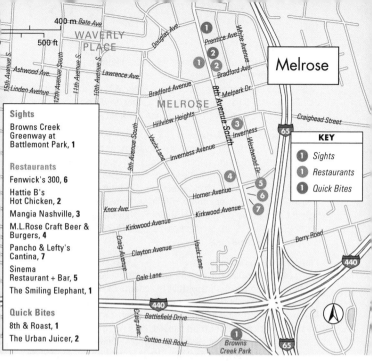

past life and the source of the restaurant's name since the kitchen tries to roll a perfect game every time. **Known for:** upscale coffee bar; open design concept; breakfast tacos and bagels. ⑤ *Average main: $13* ⌖ *2600 8th Ave. S, Suite 103, Melrose* ☎ *615/840–6462* ⊕ *www.fenwicks300.com* ⊗ *No dinner.*

★ Hattie B's Hot Chicken

$ | SOUTHERN | One of four Nashville Hattie B's locations, the Melrose Hattie B's provides the hot chicken hookup, often with less of a line than at the other outposts. Enjoy hot chicken of varying heat levels, wash it down with a sweet tea or craft brew, and finish off your meal with a delicious Southern-inspired side or two like Southern greens, bacon-cheddar grits, or pimento mac and cheese. **Known for:** hot chicken; expansive covered patio; yard games. ⑤ *Average main: $10* ⌖ *2222 8th Ave. S, Melrose* ☎ *615/722–4700* ⊕ *www.hattieb.com/sub-locations/melrose.*

Mangia Nashville

$$$$ | ITALIAN | FAMILY | Authentic New York–style Italian food is the name of the game at Mangia Nashville, and they bring it to a new level with their reservation-only weekend Italian Feasts. With multiple courses served family-style to the table and lively Italian music playing in the background, don't be surprised if guests push back their chairs between courses to dance and sing along—spontaneous conga lines have been known to break out. **Known for:** family-style feasts; Italian favorites with a New York twist; gluten-free options. $ *Average main: $70* ✉ *701 Craighead St., Melrose* ☎ *615/750–5233* ⊕ *mangianashville.com* 🕑 *Closed Sun.–Thurs. No lunch* ☞ *Reservations required.*

★ M.L.Rose Craft Beer & Burgers

$ | **BURGER** | This bustling brewpub serves more than 90 varieties of craft beer, focusing on local and regional brews and seasonal flavors in a warm setting featuring an ivy-covered back patio with picnic tables. Their food is simple pub food done well, with a focus on juicy burgers and waffle fries. **Known for:** broad beer selection; creative burgers; trivia night. $ *Average main: $12* ✉ *2535 8th Ave. S, Suite 107, Melrose* ☎ *615/712–8160* ⊕ *mlrose. com/locations/#melrose.*

Pancho & Lefty's Cantina

$$ | **MEXICAN FUSION** | The interior of this attractive "Nash-Mex" cantina welcomes guests with bold accents of color and warm exposed brick walls to create a cozy environment. The menu features comfort food as well, with inventive tacos stuffed with Nashville hot chicken or fried pickles, plus more traditional Mexican fillings like adobo chicken and carnitas. **Known for:** popular specialty margaritas and cocktails; large plattters of grilled fajitas; Nashville-style Mexican food. $ *Average main: $15* ✉ *2600 8th Ave. S, Suite 109, Melrose* ☎ *615/538–8906* ⊕ *www.pancho-andleftys.com/melrose.*

Sinema Restaurant + Bar

$$$ | **MODERN AMERICAN** | With upscale American dining featuring elevated entrées, inventive cocktails, and a bottomless brunch, Sinema is housed in the stylish setting of a former movie theater, with screens inside that still play classic movies. The design of the dining room, lounge, and even the restrooms is eclectic yet elegant, much like the menu. **Known for:** bottomless brunch; Southern-inspired entrées; Instagrammable ambience. $ *Average main: $35* ✉ *2600 8th Ave. S, Suite 102, Melrose* ☎ *615/942–7746* ⊕ *www.sinemanashville.com.*

The Smiling Elephant

$$ | **THAI** | Arguably Nashville's most popular Thai restaurant, The Smiling Elephant serves classic Thai dishes featuring a daily rotating curry menu in a quirky cottage-like environment. Given its popularity and no-reservations policy, expect a moderate wait, especially at peak mealtimes. **Known for:** authentic Thai dishes; ample portions; health-conscious preparation. $ *Average main: $15* ✉ *2213 8th Ave. S, Melrose* ☎ *615/891–4488* ⊕ *www.the-smilingelephant.com* 🕑 *Closed Sun. and Mon.*

☕ Coffee and Quick Bites

★ 8th & Roast

$ | CAFÉ | The original location of this growing local coffee roaster serves ethically sourced coffee roasted in-house, plus seasonal treats, breakfast sandwiches, and lunch items. Lined with exposed brick, the bright space is industrial yet cozy, featuring seating for both individuals and larger groups. **Known for:** in-house coffee bean roasting; slow-style pour-over coffee; quick service. ⓢ *Average main: $10* ✉ *2108 8th Ave. S, Waverly* ☎ *615/730–8074* ⊕ *www.8thandroast.com.*

The Urban Juicer

$ | CAFÉ | Fresh locally sourced ingredients are front and center at The Urban Juicer, which focuses on fresh juices, smoothies, and superfood-laden bowls. Whether grabbing a breakfast sandwich and made-to-order juice or signing on for a cleanse, the helpful staff will guide you through their health-food options. **Known for:** made-to-order juices; vegan options; meal-replacement smoothies. ⓢ *Average main: $10* ✉ *2206 8th Ave. S, Melrose* ☎ *855/905–8423* ⊕ *theurbanjuicer.com/locations/8th-ave-s.*

🍸 Nightlife

Melrose Billiard Parlor

GATHERING PLACE | Originally opened in 1944 but recently reimagined under new ownership, Melrose Billiard Parlor is a classic dive where you can play pool, ping-pong, darts, and shuffleboard in a subterranean lair. A ban on indoor smoking may have changed the ambience a bit, but it has certainly improved the "atmosphere." Patrons fuel up for indoor sports on draft beer, a full bar, and pizza slices. ✉ *2600 8th Ave. S, Suite 109, Melrose* ☎ *615/678–5489* ⊕ *www.dirtymelrose.com.*

🎭 Performing Arts

ZANIES Comedy Night Club

THEATER | As Nashville's oldest comedy club, many of the biggest stars of the genre have graced the stage and had their faces enshrined on the mural on the side of the building. The intimate setting of ZANIES is shared between big-name touring acts and local talent. Shows typically have a two-drink or food-item minimum from the bar's menu, but the venue's up-close seating is a plus for many comedy fans. ✉ *2025 8th Ave. S, Waverly* ☎ *615/269–0221* ⊕ *nashville.zanies.com.*

Shopping

Cosmic Connections

SPECIALTY STORE | A self-described "woo woo store," Cosmic Connections is a one-stop shop for all things mystical. Multiple rooms are filled with bins of gems and crystals, shelves of books, jewelry, tarot and oracle cards, hanging tapestries, and aromatic candles and incense. Stalls in the back of the store are available for private appointments with intuitive readers. ⊠ *2117 8th Ave S., Melrose* ☎ *615/463–7677* ⊕ *yourcosmicconnections.com.*

Gruhn Guitars

MUSIC | This long-standing destination sells rare and vintage guitars, banjos, mandolins, and more. Music fans will be in awe of their extensive inventory and knowledgeable staff. Many famous musicians take advantage of Gruhn's instrument repair services, so you know that they are among the best. ⊠ *2120 8th Ave. S, Waverly* ☎ *615/256–2033* ⊕ *guitars.com* ☾ *Closed Sun.*

Must-See Murals

- *ZANIES Comedy Legends* ⊠ *2025 8th Ave. S*
- *Life Can Be Sweet* ⊠ *1512 8th Ave. S*

Berry Hill

Berry Hill is the rare Nashville commercial zone that still feels like a neighborhood. In fact, many of the most interesting restaurants and boutiques scattered around the charming Bransford Avenue shopping district are in cozy converted houses and can be discovered as part of an easy walk along the neighborhood's sidewalks. Tucked in among these retail locations are more than 40 music publishing businesses and recording studios operating out of 1940s-era cottages and bungalows, making Nashville's smallest satellite city a hidden industry gem.

 Sights

Travellers Rest Historic House and Museum

HISTORIC HOME | Berry Hill and the surrounding areas are rich in early Tennessee state history, full of key markers for the battle lines during the Battle of Nashville and housing homesteads like Judge John Overton's, which has been preserved as Travellers Rest Plantation. With archaeological finds and Civil War significance,

At the Paddywax Candle Bar, hour-long classes are available for people to make custom candles. There's another location in The Gulch.

the plantation is a museum and is a popular stop for history buffs. ⊠ *636 Farrell Pkwy., Battlemont* ☎ *615/832–8197* ⊕ *www.travellersrestplantation.org* 🗺 *$15 for tours* 🕓 *Closed Sun. and Mon.*

Paddywax Candle Bar

OTHER ATTRACTION | Perfect for groups, this candle shop and creator space offers hour-long classes by appointment where guests can select the vessel and scent to make their own custom candles. Since these creations take three hours to cool, you can arrange to have them shipped, wait on them at the fully-stocked bar, or explore the neighborhood and come back later. There's another location in The Gulch that offers more of a "pop in and pour" experience. ⊠ *2934 Sidco Dr., Suite 140, Berry Hill* ☎ *615/630–7135* ⊕ *thecandlebar.co* 🗺 *$45 for custom candle workshops* 🕓 *Closed Mon.*

Woodlawn Memorial Park Cemetery

CEMETERY | The 133 lush green acres of Woodlawn Memorial Park have served as the final resting space for generations of Nashvillians, including many major country music stars whose grave sites are open for visits from tour groups or individuals. Among those buried in Woodlawn are George Jones, Tammy Wynette, Felice and Boudleaux Bryant, Little Jimmy Dickens, Jerry Reed, Webb Pierce, Johnny Paycheck, Marty Robbins, and Porter Wagoner. The beautiful Lynn Anderson Rose Garden pays homage to the late-great songstress and her greatest hit. ⊠ *660 Thompson La., Berry Hill* ☎ *383–4754* ⊕ *www.dignitymemorial.com/funeral-homes/tennessee/nashville/*

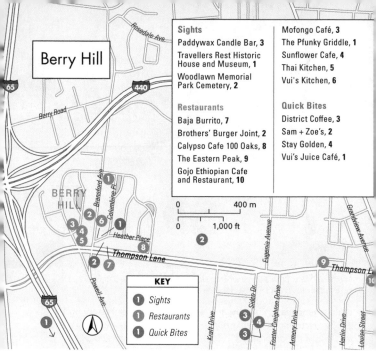

woodlawn-roesch-patton-funeral-home-memorial-park/4881
🎟 Free.

🍴 Restaurants

★ Baja Burrito
$ | MEXICAN FUSION | This colorful neighborhood staple is a locally owned Baja Californian–style Mexican food restaurant, with build-your-own counter service featuring local meats, handmade salsas, and delicious fruit teas. In addition to their namesake burritos, they offer plentiful taco and salad options, all in generous portions, making this funky and fun spot a local favorite. **Known for:** colorful atmosphere; quick counter service; pineapple salsa made in-house. ⑤ *Average main: $7* ✉ *722 Thompson La., Berry Hill* ☎ *615/383–2252* ⊕ *www.bajaburrito.com* ⊗ *Closed Sun.*

Brothers' Burger Joint
$$ | BURGER | Twin brothers joined forces to start up a food truck before moving their operation to a permanent location in this converted house with an expansive patio. The atmosphere is buoyant as diners scarf down gourmet burgers that are more than a handful or po'boy sandwiches overstuffed with fried seafood or chicken. **Known for:** craft beer selection; creole and Cajun

influences; gourmet griddle-smashed hamburgers. $ *Average main: $16* ✉ *2821 Bransford Ave., Berry Hill* ☎ *615/712–7607* ⊕ *brothersburgerjoint.com.*

★ Calypso Cafe 100 Oaks

$ | **CARIBBEAN** | Casual healthy dining that is easy on the wallet is Calypso Cafe's focus, making it a popular laid-back lunch spot. The menu features Caribbean influences, with an emphasis on chicken and fresh produce, creating tropical flavor combinations like their Lucayan salad and famed corn muffins that easily satisfy nutrition-focused eaters and those with dietary restrictions. **Known for:** budget-friendly; light lunch fare; vegetarian and vegan options. $ *Average main: $10* ✉ *700 Thompson La., Berry Hill* ☎ *615/297–3888* ⊕ *calypsocafe.com* ⊘ *Closed Sun.*

The Eastern Peak

$$ | **THAI** | Asian fusion entrées, Thai curries, and sushi come together in a stylish setting at The Eastern Peak. Enjoy well-priced lunch specials on the covered porch, or pair a cocktail with a sushi combo for happy hour. **Known for:** chic finishes; Thai favorites made fresh; porch seating. $ *Average main: $15* ✉ *536 Thompson La., Berry Hill* ☎ *615/610–4888* ⊕ *www.theeasternpeak.com.*

Gojo Ethiopian Cafe and Restaurant

$$ | **ETHIOPIAN** | A standout in the pocket of international eateries clustered around Nolensville Pike, Gojo Ethiopian Cafe serves authentic dishes in a cozy brightly colored building. The lunch buffet is a favorite of both vegetarians and meat-eaters. **Known for:** traditional Ethiopian coffee service; abundant injera (sourdough flatbread); good for Ethiopian food rookies. $ *Average main: $16* ✉ *415 W. Thompson La., Berry Hill* ☎ *615/332–0710* ⊕ *www. gojoethiopiancafetogo.com* ⊘ *Closed Tues.*

Mofongo Café

$$ | **CARIBBEAN** | Focusing on Dominican, Puerto Rican, and Cuban cuisine, Mofongo Café is a popular destination for diners seeking the flavors of the Caribbean. There aren't many restaurants in town where you can find goat and oxtail, but Mofongo Café is known for those succulent meat dishes along with a long list of varieties of empanadas, tostones, mofongos, and seafood from the menu or off the buffet. **Known for:** a wide array of Carribean specialty dishes; Cuban coffee drinks; buffet or à la carte options. $ *Average main: $15* ✉ *654 W. Iris Dr., Berry Hill* ☎ *615/915–3642* ⊕ *mofongocafenashville.com.*

The Pfunky Griddle

$ | **AMERICAN** | **FAMILY** | One of the city's most inventive brunch experiences puts you in control of your pancakes and more with an in-table griddle set up for a DIY menu. In addition to creative toppings for the all-you-can-eat pancakes, you can also griddle-cook your own grilled cheese sandwich or order from the kitchen if you aren't up for the task of making your own. **Known for:** cook-your-own brunch experience; pancakes with many toppings; family-friendly. $ *Average main: $11* ⊠ *2800 Bransford Ave., Berry Hill* ☎ *615/298–2088* ⊕ *www.thepfunkygriddle.com* ☉ *Closed Mon. No dinner.*

Sunflower Cafe

$ | **VEGETARIAN** | Welcoming and straightforward, Sunflower Cafe feeds the vegans, vegetarians, and gluten-free eaters of Nashville with mouthwatering veggie burger options, vegan barbecue, ample salads, potato bowls, and enticing daily specials. The menu features both Southern staples and international-inspired flavors, providing many options for diners who are used to feeling restricted by other menus. **Known for:** daily specials; ample seating; helpful staff. $ *Average main: $10* ⊠ *2834 Azalea Pl., Berry Hill* ☎ *615/457–2568* ⊕ *www.sunflowercafenashville.com* ☉ *Closed Sun.*

Thai Kitchen

$$ | **THAI** | Don't let the spartan appearance of this hole-in-the-wall Thai restaurant trick you: their authentic dishes are anything but plain. With an extensive curry menu, multiple dishes featuring duck, and a range of sushi choices, your taste buds and wallet will be pleased. **Known for:** cheap eats; abundant portions; no-frills atmosphere. $ *Average main: $16* ⊠ *738 Thompson La., Berry Hill* ☎ *615/385–9854* ⊕ *www.thaikitchennashville.com* ☉ *Closed Mon.*

★ Vui's Kitchen

$ | **VIETNAMESE** | Chic yet inviting, the fresh Vietnamese fare at Vui's Kitchen includes favorite dishes like pho and dumplings garnished with local greens, as well as a seasonal selection of local beer and wine. The kitchen sources seasonal local produce whenever possible. **Known for:** fresh noodle bowls; ample outdoor seating; vegan options. $ *Average main: $10* ⊠ *2832 Bransford Ave., Berry Hill* ☎ *615/241–8847* ⊕ *www.vuiskitchen.com.*

Coffee and Quick Bites

District Coffee

$ | **CAFÉ** | With its quiet vibe and speedy free Wi-Fi, District Coffee welcomes remote workers along with anyone who enjoys a good cup of coffee or espresso made using locally roasted beans. An eclectic menu of pastries, bagels, and New Zealand–style savory hand pies offers food choices while you work and sip. **Known**

for: remote worker–friendly atmosphere; specialty coffee drinks brewed with locally-roasted beans from 8th & Roast; offers pastries and small lunch items from Nashville purveyors. $ *Average main: $7* ⊠ *2927 Sidco Dr., Berry Hill* ☎ *615/922–2910* ⊕ *districtcoffeetn.com* ☾ *No dinner.*

Sam + Zoe's

$ | **CAFÉ** | This pleasantly low-key coffee shop is decorated with quirky local art and is typically quiet, making it a relaxing place to work or chat. In addition to coffee, Sam + Zoe's offers tea, breakfast food, salads, sandwiches, smoothies, and desserts. **Known for:** large porch; all-day breakfast; creative latte art. $ *Average main: $8* ⊠ *525 Heather Pl., Berry Hill* ☎ *615/385–2676* ⊕ *samandzoes.com* ☾ *No dinner.*

Stay Golden

$ | **CAFÉ** | Founded by veterans of the Nashville coffee scene, Stay Golden is a stylish and sophisticated spot to sip on single-origin coffee and teas, try a craft cocktail, or check out local brews on draft; there's even a prosecco bar to get the day off to a festive start. In addition to their beverages, seasonally inspired breakfast and lunch options are available. **Known for:** high-quality coffee beverages; knowledgeable staff; well-styled interior. $ *Average main: $12* ⊠ *2934 Sidco Dr., Suite 130, Berry Hill* ☎ *615/241–5105* ⊕ *www.stay-golden.com* ☾ *No dinner.*

★ Vui's Juice Café

$ | **VIETNAMESE** | Utilizing products from local farmers and producers, this bright and airy café caters a healthy menu of all-day breakfast and lunch dishes, ranging from berry bowls, smoothies, and breakfast sandwiches to pad Thai noodle bowls and housemade hummus. Grab-and-go options include wellness shots, juice cleanses, boba tea, and specialty coffee drinks. **Known for:** fresh juice drinks and cleanse programs; fruits and vegetable bowls; cozy atmosphere where remote workers are welcome. $ *Average main: $10* ⊠ *522 Heather Pl., Berry Hill* ☎ *615/241–8847* ⊕ *vuisjuicecafe.com* ☾ *No dinner.*

Nightlife

★ The Black Abbey Brewing Company

BREWPUBS | While Black Abbey beers can be found on tap throughout Nashville, a visit to their monastery-themed brewery in Berry Hill is an experience all its own. Enjoy a brewery tour, then sample their flavorful beers in the Fellowship Hall located in the middle of the working brewhouse. The brewery also hosts food trucks most nights along with trivia nights and vinyl pop-up parties, where the staff spin their favorite records. ✉ *2952 Sidco Dr., Berry Hill* ☎ *615/755–0070* ⊕ *blackabbeybrewing.com.*

Rosie's Twin Kegs

BARS | The sign touts popular local hangout Twin Kegs as internationally famous, and once you try one of their juicy burgers you'll understand why. This classic dive features cheap beer, karaoke, a pinball machine, shuffleboard, inventive Burgers of the Month, and occasional live music. ✉ *413 Thompson La., Berry Hill* ☎ *615/832–3167* ⊕ *rosiestwinkegs.com.*

 # Shopping

★ GasLamp Antiques

ANTIQUES & COLLECTIBLES | Gas Lamp Antiques features more than 300 vendor booths that stock furniture, vintage jewelry, and pop culture memorabilia. More items are available at the nearby GasLamp Too (✉ *128 Powell Pl.*). ✉ *100 Powell Pl., Suite 200, Berry Hill* ☎ *615/297–2224* ⊕ *gaslampantiques.com.*

Land of Odds—Be Dazzled Beads

CRAFTS | For more than three decades, this strip mall shop has acted like "a hardware store for jewelry designers," stocking hundreds of different sizes and styles of beads, stringing materials, clasps, and crafting tools. The store also offers jewelry-repair services and weekend instructional classes. ✉ *918 Thompson La., Suite 123, Berry Hill* ☎ *615/292–0610* ⊕ *landofodds.com* ☉ *Closed Sun.*

Nadeau

FURNITURE | Not your average furniture store, Nadeau features quirky furnishings, often with bright colors and an international twist. Their bold selections are fairly priced and always rotating, making it a fun stop in Nashville's Design District. ✉ *647 Thompson La., Berry Hill* ☎ *615/298–2474* ⊕ *www.furniturewithasoul. com/nashville.*

Southeastern Salvage

FURNITURE | Eclectic furniture and unbeatable closeout deals are the hallmarks of Southeastern Salvage, a large warehouse store for both home renovators and decorators. The ever-rotating stock of home furnishings, housewares, lawn and garden accessories, and more make for a treasure hunt at discount prices. ✉ *2728 Eugenia Ave., Berry Hill* ☎ *615/244–1001* ⊕ *southeasternsalvage. com/Nashville.php.*

Chapter 11

WEDGEWOOD-HOUSTON

Updated by
MiChelle Jones

● Sights   🍴 Restaurants   🛏 Hotels   ● Shopping   ● Nightlife

★☆☆☆☆   ★★★☆☆   ★★★☆☆   ★★☆☆☆   ★★☆☆☆

NEIGHBORHOOD SNAPSHOT

TOP EXPERIENCES

- **Arts Scene:** Join the First Saturday Art Crawl and visit galleries, pop-ups, and artist happenings.

- **Wet Your Whistle:** Cocktails, whiskey, cider and alcohol-free spirits are on offer.

- **Gooooal!:** Don navy and yellow and cheer on Nashville SC soccer team at GEODIS Park or a neighborhood bar.

- **Look Out:** Take a hike around historic Fort Negley and be rewarded with expansive views of Downtown.

- **Grab a Bite:** Enjoy a fantastic meal at one of the numerous new restaurants.

GETTING HERE

The best way to get to Wedgewood-Houston is via car or bike. If you're coming via interstate, take I–65. Take Exit 81 and turn onto Wedgewood Avenue (left if coming from I–65 South, right if coming from I–65 North). Turn left from Wedgewood onto Martin Street to get to the heart of the neighborhood.

PLANNING YOUR TIME

During weekdays, the narrow streets are crowded, as cars navigate around construction and delivery vehicles. Restaurants and bars come alive in the evenings. On a random weekend day, the area can feel a bit deserted. On Nashville SC game days, it's packed with fans bedecked in the soccer team's blue-and-yellow kit, and various parking lots become parking areas for those heading to the GEODIS Park.

BIG TICKETS MURAL

- This clever homage to Nashville's varied music history is located just past the Nashville City Cemetery along 4th Avenue approaching Chestnut Avenue at the Nashville Warehouse Company. Created by Adventurous Journeys, Studio Delger, and Eastside Mural, the design features 62 oversized ticket stubs highlighting actual performances at venues around the city.

GIANT GUITAR SIGN

- Once the scoreboard for the Nashville Sounds, the giant guitar is now a focal point of a tiny green space at the mixed-use Nashville Warehouse Company (✉ *410 Chestnut St.*). One side of the refurbished sign is painted to resemble an acoustic guitar.

A look around Wedgewood-Houston shows you Nashville's past, present, and future. Old buildings—many of them industrial spaces like warehouses and textile mills—are being repurposed, renovated, and in some cases torn down and replaced with eateries, distilleries, and residences.

Most of the converted spaces have kept reminders of their rough origins, like the garage doors at the back of galleries on Hagan Street that hint at the building's former life as a truck repair shop. Across the street from this cluster, the one remaining building from a sausage-making factory is now The Packing Plant, home to pop-up art spaces. Houston Station, whose buildings date as far back as 1885, houses eateries and shops. Meanwhile, the sprawling former May Hosiery Mills complex is now home to Soho House Nashville, an elegant members' hotel and club.

Urban renewal is also spreading to the other end of the neighborhood, where GEODIS Park, home to Nashville's pro soccer club, was built as part of a revitalization of the Nashville Fairgrounds. New high-end apartments are being constructed next to the stadium, but the impact of Nashville SC extends beyond real estate. Watch parties and tailgating have become popular activities, further boosting the neighborhood's restaurants and bars.

The pace of change in Wedgewood-Houston is astounding, with new businesses opening constantly. This trend should continue as developments like the multi-acre Nashville Warehouse Company—home to LiveNation's offices, a small park, and the iconic guitar sign—progress and the neighborhood's borders expand. Adjacent Chestnut Hill, until recently considered as unfashionable as Wedgewood-Houston used to be, is now seeing newly opened restaurants and businesses. The area is now referred to as WeHo–Chestnut Hill, or simply WeHo proper.

 Sights

★ Adventure Science Center

SCIENCE MUSEUM | FAMILY | Yes, this is a space designed with kids in mind, but there are also several elements that adults can enjoy, such as virtual reality stations, planetarium and laser shows, and the Max Flight: Full Motion simulator. Popular Way Late Play Dates are after-hours events exclusively for adults 21 and older. The Adventure Science Center sits on a bluff with good views of Downtown. ⊠ *800 Fort Negley Blvd., Wedgewood-Houston* ☎ *615/862–5160* ⊕ *www. adventuresci.org* 🖃 *$22; $9 for planetarium shows; $1 for laser shows; $10 for Max Flight simulator* ⊘ *Closed Tues. and Wed.*

WeHo's Must-See Murals

- *Big Tickets* ⊠ *4th Ave. S*
- *Loading Dock* ⊠ *2028A Lindell Ave.*
- *Look on the Bright Cider Life* at Diskin Cider ⊠ *1235 Martin St.*
- *A New Anthem* ⊠ *462 Humphreys St.*
- *Love Y'all* ⊠ *2020 Lindell Ave.*

Corsair Distillery

DISTILLERY | Corsair's second location opened in 2016 and serves as the headquarters for this creator of small-batch whiskeys and other spirits. The hour-long tour includes a 45-minute history of the distillery that ends with a five-spirit tasting. Tastings are available without tours, and cocktail classes are also available. Dogs are welcome on the large patio. There's another location in Marathon Village. ⊠ *601 Merritt Ave., Wedgewood-Houston* ☎ *615/200–0320* ⊕ *www.corsairdistillery.com* 🖃 *$20 for tours; $10 for nondrinkers* ⊘ *Closed Mon.–Wed.*

David Lusk Gallery

ART GALLERY | David Lusk's Memphis gallery has been around since 1995; the Nashville location opened in 2014 and features paintings, photography, and sculpture by regional and national artists. The gallery takes part in the Wedgewood-Houston art crawls and also hosts receptions and other events. ⊠ *516 Hagan St., Wedgewood-Houston* ☎ *615/780–9990* ⊕ *www.davidluskgallery.com* ⊘ *Closed Sun. and Mon.*

Diskin Cider

BREWERY | The 8,000-square-foot facility includes a tasting room and patio with a menu that features ciders (all gluten-free and hand-pressed), cocktails, and food provided by Cabin Attic. Regular events include pregame parties on Nashville SC game days, outdoor movie screenings, and a monthly drag brunch (18+). The large patio has multiple firepits, and dogs are welcome. ⊠ *1235 Martin St., Wedgewood-Houston* ☎ *615/248–8000* ⊕ *www.diskincider.com* ⊘ *Closed Mon.–Wed.*

Home of the Major League Soccer club Nashville SC, GEODIS Park is the largest soccer-specific stadium in the United States and Canada.

Fair Park

CITY PARK | A place to play for humans and dogs, this green space has paved walking paths, sports fields, restrooms, and a dog park. The Bransford Avenue and Craighead Street entrance is a good spot to enter the park. ⊠ *300 Raines Ave., Wedgewood-Houston* ☎ *615/862–8400* ⊕ *www.nashville.gov/departments/parks* 🎫 *Free.*

Fort Negley Visitors Center Park

HISTORIC SIGHT | The history of this Civil War–era fort is told through videos in the visitor center and panels along outdoor pathways. Veterans events take place throughout the year, and there's a gift shop and great views of the Nashville skyline. Revitalization plans for the park include adding 1½ to 2 miles of trails and additional interpretations to highlight African-American history from the Civil War to the civil rights era. Sheep are sometimes used for natural landscaping, watched over by a so-called livestock guardian dog. Be advised: you may also come across a deer on the grounds. ⊠ *1100 Fort Negley Blvd., Wedgewood-Houston* ☎ *615/862–8470* ⊕ *www.nashville.gov/departments/parks/historic-sites/fort-negley* ⊙ *Visitor center closed Sun. and Mon.*

GEODIS Park

SPORTS VENUE | **FAMILY** | Home to the Major League Soccer club Nashville SC, this 30,000-seat stadium is the largest soccer-specific stadium in the United States and Canada. The venue opened in May 2022 and has quickly become a towering feature of the neighborhood, both literally and figuratively. Single game tickets run about $20 to $30. Concerts and other events are staged here

KEY

1 Sights
1 Restaurants
1 Quick Bites
1 Hotels

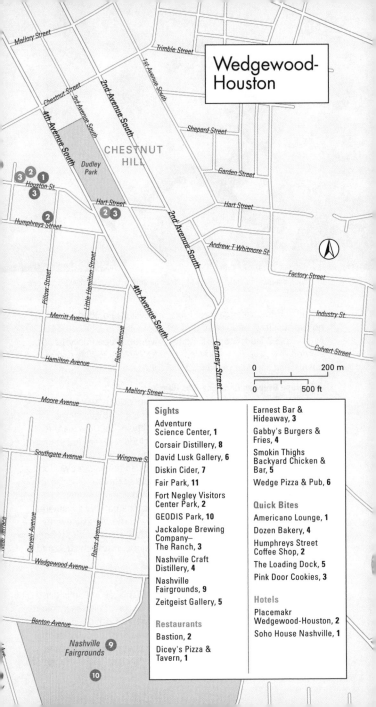

Wedgewood-Houston

CHESTNUT HILL

Dudley Park

Sights

Adventure Science Center, **1**

Corsair Distillery, **8**

David Lusk Gallery, **6**

Diskin Cider, **7**

Fair Park, **11**

Fort Negley Visitors Center Park, **2**

GEODIS Park, **10**

Jackalope Brewing Company– The Ranch, **3**

Nashville Craft Distillery, **4**

Nashville Fairgrounds, **9**

Zeitgeist Gallery, **5**

Restaurants

Bastion, **2**

Dicey's Pizza & Tavern, **1**

Earnest Bar & Hideaway, **3**

Gabby's Burgers & Fries, **4**

Smokin Thighs Backyard Chicken & Bar, **5**

Wedge Pizza & Pub, **6**

Quick Bites

Americano Lounge, **1**

Dozen Bakery, **4**

Humphreys Street Coffee Shop, **2**

The Loading Dock, **5**

Pink Door Cookies, **3**

Hotels

Placemakr Wedgewood-Houston, **2**

Soho House Nashville, **1**

0   200 m

0   500 ft

Nashville Fairgrounds

The contemporary Zeitgeist Gallery has been an anchor of the Nashville art scene since 1994.

in addition to soccer games. Tours are available on Fridays when no events are scheduled and must be booked in advance. The Nashville SC Team Store off Benton Avenue is open daily. ⊠ *501 Benton Ave., Wedgewood-Houston* ☎ *615/701–2500* ⊕ *www. nashvillesc.com/geodispark* ✉ *$20 for tours.*

Jackalope Brewing Company–The Ranch

BREWERY | This popular small-batch brewery outgrew its first location, so "The Ranch" is now its sole outpost. Housing a taproom, event space, and brewing facility in 15,000 square feet, it doesn't disappoint. Available beers include a year-round standard selection, along with seasonal brews and special selections. The taproom serves a limited menu, but you can bring your own food and food trucks are typically on-site. Tours of the brewing facility, which typically last 45 minutes, are available and are open to children at a discount and with reservations. The patio is considered one of the best in town and dogs are welcome. Weekly events include trivia nights and group jogs. ⊠ *429B Houston St., Wedgewood-Houston* ☎ *615/873–4313* ⊕ *jackalopebrew.com* ✉ *$20 for tours* ⊙ *Closed Mon.*

Nashville Craft Distillery

DISTILLERY | Part of the official Tennessee Whiskey Trail, this distillery is known for small-batch spirits with clever names inspired by Nashville, such as Naked Biscuit Sorghum Spirit and Crane City Gin. Tastings, cocktails, and bottle sales are available during operating hours, but tours that include tastings are only offered Thursday through Sunday for those 21 and older. ⊠ *514 Hagan St.,*

Wedgewood-Houston ☎ *615/457–3036* ⊕ *www.nashvillecraft.com* ✉ *$20 for tours* ☉ *Closed Mon. No tours Tues. and Wed.*

Nashville Fairgrounds

FAIRGROUND | **FAMILY** | There's something going on at the fairgrounds almost any time of the year. The 117-acre site hosts auto races at the Speedway, craft fairs, monthly flea markets, the annual Christmas Village holiday market, concerts, and other special events throughout the year. It's also where you'll find GEODIS Park, Nashville's soccer stadium. The newest event is the 10-day Nashville Fair held every September. ✉ *625 Smith Ave., Wedgewood-Houston* ⊹ *Entrance location varies with event* ☎ *615/862–8980* ⊕ *thefairgrounds.com.*

Zeitgeist Gallery

ART GALLERY | The anchor of the Wedgewood-Houston art scene, this gallery shares space with an architectural studio responsible for designing several of Nashville's most stylish popular spaces. Zeitgeist shows artists who explore daring concepts through intelligent sophisticated work. The gallery's receptions draw a large knowledgeable crowd of local art insiders. ✉ *516 Hagan St., Suite 100, Wedgewood-Houston* ☎ *615/256–4805* ⊕ *zeitgeist-art. com* ☉ *Closed Sun.–Wed.*

 Restaurants

Bastion

$$$$ | **AMERICAN** | This is one of Nashville's most exclusive dining options, a 24-seat restaurant where reservations are both required and difficult to get. The reward is a chef's choice multicourse meal that features dishes like swordfish served with pumpkin and marigold, and cocao beef tongue served with vaquero beans. **Known for:** chef's choice gourmet menu; hard to get reservation; restaurant and bar are 21-and-over establishments. ⑤ *Average main: $125* ✉ *434 Houston St., Wedgewood-Houston* ☎ *615/490–8434* ⊕ *www.bastionnashville.com* ☉ *Restaurant closed Sun.–Tues.*

Dicey's Pizza & Tavern

$$ | **PIZZA** | **FAMILY** | This place looks and feels like it's been here for ages—and it has, but not as a pizza restaurant that now serves thin-crust pizzas cut into small squares, a selection of subs, and a few salads. In a short time it has become a neighborhood hangout where, depending on the time of day, you'll find families with babies in strollers meeting with out-of-town friends or fans tailgating or settling in to watch the soccer match. **Known for:** square-cut pizzas; sub sandwiches; fried pickles and peppers.

⑤ *Average main: $14* ✉ *425 Chestnut St., Wedgewood-Houston* ☎ *615/964–7022* ⊕ *www.diceystavern.com.*

Earnest Bar & Hideaway

$$$ | **AMERICAN** | Inspired by a literary giant (guess which one) this restaurant exudes rustic elegance—rough brick walls, rich hardwood floors—found throughout Houston Station. A hearty menu (pork rib eye and poutine) and an extensive drinks menu complement the vintage decor. **Known for:** pork rib eye with Georgia peaches; poutine with braised short rib and duck fat French fries; brunch Friday–Sunday. ⑤ *Average main: $35* ✉ *438 Houston St., Wedgewood-Houston* ☎ *615/915–1715* ⊕ *earnestbarandhideaway. com* ⊗ *Closed Mon. No lunch Tues.–Thurs.*

★ Gabby's Burgers & Fries

$ | **BURGER** | **FAMILY** | Gabby's is where locals go for really good burgers (grass-fed beef or vegan) and addictive sweet potato fries. The ever-present line moves quickly; eat at the tables or small counter overlooking the grill, or grab and go; just remember the portions are HUGE! **Known for:** huge portions; shakes made with house-made syrups; sweet potato fries. ⑤ *Average main: $10* ✉ *493 Humphreys St., Wedgewood-Houston* ☎ *615/733–3119* ⊕ *www.gabbysburgersandfries.com* ⊗ *Closed Sun. No dinner.*

Smokin Thighs Backyard Chicken & Bar

$$ | **AMERICAN** | **FAMILY** | Chicken has become kind of a thing in Nashville, and Smokin Thighs has lots of it on its menu—wings, quarters, and, of course, thighs—all smoked or grilled using a signature applewood blend. There's also salads, chicken burgers, and tacos available, as well as pimento mac and cheese. **Known for:** crowded spot at lunch and on Nashville SC game days; smoked or grilled chicken in all its forms; menu of rubs, sauces, and seasoning to choose from. ⑤ *Average main: $14* ✉ *611 Wedgewood Ave., Wedgewood-Houston* ☎ *615/601–2582* ⊕ *www.smokinthighs. com.*

Wedge Pizza & Pub

$$ | **PIZZA** | Follow the gravel drive to the back of the Wedge building and you'll see a large covered deck and a huge mural of a pizza slice—the pizza here is delicious. The space inside is both cavernous and cozy, with comfy seating areas and a reading area stocked with books, which are great places to enjoy salads, wings, and other typical pizza-restaurant fare such as breadsticks, dessert wedges, and New York–style cheesecake. **Known for:** Nashville hot chicken pizza; cauliflower-crust pizza; dart tournaments. ⑤ *Average main: $18* ✉ *2026 Lindell Ave., Wedgewood-Houston* ☎ *615/679–9428* ⊕ *bethewedge.com.*

☕ Coffee and Quick Bites

Americano Lounge

$ | CAFÉ | Since opening in 2018, this eatery has dropped "coffee" from its name but certainly not from its menu, which includes coffee, coffee cocktails (espresso martini!), dessert cocktails, and an extensive list of traditional cocktails. The atmosphere is that of a European café with a menu to match: pastries, panini, and desserts that are both delicious and gorgeous. **Known for:** coffee cocktails; cozy atmosphere; lemon-berry torte with mascarpone. ⑤ *Average main: $8 ⊠ 434 Houston St., Suite 120, Wedgewood-Houston ☎ 629/203–6991 ⊕ americanolounge.com.*

Dozen Bakery

$ | BAKERY | This small space is airy and bright, and it maintains a bit of its pop-up-shop origins. Serving breakfast and lunch items—including soups and sandwiches, some seasonal—the best options are the cookies and pastries made on-site and also sold at a number of Nashville eateries. **Known for:** artisanal breads; cupcakes; pumpkin pie. ⑤ *Average main: $5 ⊠ 516 Hagan St., Suite 103, Wedgewood-Houston ☎ 615/712–8150 ⊕ www. dozen-nashville.com.*

★ Humphreys Street Coffee Shop

$ | CAFÉ | The nonprofit enterprise that runs this bright pleasant shop was established in 2008 to train and mentor students. In addition to prepared coffees and teas, the shop sells the beans, soaps and scrubs made by the students, and mugs and T-shirts bearing the coffeehouse's logo. **Known for:** 100% of profits support students; great atmosphere; good tea menu. ⑤ *Average main: $5 ⊠ 424 Humphreys St., Wedgewood-Houston ⊹ Look for the entrance on Pillow St. ☎ 615/647–7554 ⊕ humphreysstreet.com.*

The Loading Dock

$ | CAFÉ | Once you turn onto Lindell Avenue, look for picnic tables and a brightly colored mural on the white Wedge Building and you'll find this local gem whose Grumpy Hour (8 to 10 am) gets you a free coffee with any breakfast order. The salads are huge, the sandwiches are delicious, and the staff are super nice. **Known for:** classic avocado toast; huge salads; Grumpy Hour (free coffee with any breakfast order). ⑤ *Average main: $7 ⊠ 2028A Lindell Ave., Wedgewood-Houston ☎ 615/651–8154 ⊕ loadingdocknashville.com ☉ Closed Sun. No dinner.*

★ Pink Door Cookies

$ | BAKERY | Place your order for "fancy and whimsical" cookies at the window of this teensy space that produces small batches of large cookies that are big on flavor and inspiration. Current offerings are indicated by photos taped to the wall, with notes on flavors and vibe or inspiration; some cookies are mini works of art, like the optimistic Rainbow Brownie, a beautiful cookie covered in chocolate frosting, mini chocolate chips, and "bits of rainbow." Meanwhile, the backstory of this little cookie place is magical: the brand was born during lockdown when pastry chef Matthew Rice found himself at a crossroads. **Known for:** yummy cookies; nostalgic flavors like PB&J with peanut butter chips and a grape glaze; oatmeal butterscotch. ⑤ *Average main: $4* ⊠ *321 Hart St., Suite 309, Wedgewood-Houston* ☏ *615/882–1227* ⊕ *pinkdoorcookies. com* ⊘ *Closed Mon. and Tues.*

Hotels

Placemakr Wedgewood-Houston
$ | APARTMENT | This space opened as a hotel in 2023, offering a range of accommodations from micro-studios with communal living and kitchen spaces to two-bedroom, two-bath apartments. **Pros:** apartment spaces; lots of privacy; balconies in every unit. **Cons:** limited on-site dining options; odd location (unless you like railroad tracks); could feel isolated. ⑤ *Rooms from: $180* ⊠ *321 Hart St., Wedgewood-Houston* ☏ *629/231–4001* ⊕ *www.place-makr.com/locations/nashville/wedgewood-houston* ⌲ *87 units* ⍒ *No Meals.*

Soho House Nashville
$$$ | HOTEL | Rooms at Soho House range from cozy (300 square feet) to big+ (600 square feet), and each space is uniquely furnished and decorated; local designers and artists were tapped for the decor. **Pros:** unique experience; privacy; Wedgewood-Houston location. **Cons:** might be too exclusive for some; nonmembers don't have access to pool, gym, etc.; restrictions on where laptops and phones can be used and photos can be taken (some might find this a pro). ⑤ *Rooms from: $450* ⊠ *500 Houston St., Wedgewood-Houston* ☏ *615/551–8100* ⊕ *www.sohohouse.com/en-us/houses/soho-house-nashville* ⌲ *47 units* ⍒ *No Meals* ⌕ *Room rates vary depending on room size, membership status, and availability.*

Nightlife

The Basement
LIVE MUSIC | This small venue, which seats 100 people, hosts indie acts, emerging talent, and holiday events. It's one of two venues under the Basement umbrella (their other venue is The Basement East in East Nashville, close to Little Five Points). Entry

is generally affordable, ranging from free to $20. ⊠ *1604 8th Ave. S, Suite 330, Wedgewood-Houston* ☎ *615/645–9174* ⊕ *www. thebasementnashville.com.*

Flamingo Cocktail Club

GATHERING PLACE | Drawing inspiration from Miami clubs of the 1950s and '60s, this space has a large open area and minimalist seating. They host theme parties (disco, for example), live jazz, workshops for makers and creatives, and other special events, including yoga and sound baths. ⊠ *509 Houston St., Wedgewood-Houston* ☎ *786/942–8279* ⊕ *www.flamingococktailclub.com* ⊗ *Closed Tues.*

Santa's Pub

BARS | A kitschy dive bar—that's cash-only—with a holiday twist, Santa's is located in a double-wide trailer decorated with vintage and retro Christmas decorations, including a faux flickering fireplace. This karaoke spot is loved by all sorts, including Ed Sheeran, who hung out there after a summer 2023 record-breaking show at Nashville's Nissan Stadium. Open until the wee hours with cheap beer (no liquor is served), the pub is also located within walking distance of GEODIS Park. ⊠ *2225 Bransford Ave., Wedgewood-Houston* ☎ *615/593–1872* ⊕ *www.santaspub.com* ⊗ *Closed Mon. and Tues.*

🎭 Performing Arts

Nashville Repertory Theatre

THEATER | Commonly referred to as Nashville Rep or simply The Rep, this regional company performs original and well-known plays and musicals. The company's Ingram New Works Project fosters new works via a season-long fellowship for playwrights. Nashville Rep's performances are usually at TPAC (The Tennessee Performing Arts Center) Downtown, with occasional shows in other venues like the company's home base in the Nashville Public Television building in Wedgewood-Houston. ⊠ *161 Rains Ave., Wedgewood-Houston* ☎ *615/244–4878* ⊕ *nashvillerep.org.*

The Nashville Shakespeare Festival

THEATER | FAMILY | This beloved Nashville-based theater company specializes in Shakespeare but also performs modern works. Summer Shakespeare shows in Nashville and neighboring Franklin are popular with all ages; preshow entertainment includes live music and a lecture series. Bring a blanket or lawn chair, or find a seat in the bleachers for these free performances. Food and drinks are available from food trucks, or you can pack your own snacks. The company also stages and/or presents winter and spring productions. ✉ *161 Rains Ave., Wedgewood-Houston* ☎ *615/255–2273* ⊕ *www.nashvilleshakes.org* 🎫 *Free; $10 suggested donation.*

Shopping

Fork's Drum Closet

MUSIC | Fork's has been around since 1982, though they've only been in their location near Wedgewood-Houston since 2018. They carry a full stock of new and used items to keep percussionists happy, covering everything from sticks and mallets to drumheads and cases. ✉ *308 Chestnut St., Wedgewood-Houston* ☎ *615/383–8343* ⊕ *www.forksdrumcloset.com* 🕒 *Closed Sun.*

FORTS

CLOTHING | Hanging out in this small super-chill store is like spending time in a sneakerhead's well-appointed closet where shoes, T-shirts, and more are tastefully displayed. In addition to a quite nice selection of sneakers, this menswear store carries watches and streetwear (including vintage items), along with a smattering of housewares like candles. Design books for sale include volumes on Basquiat, Charles and Ray Eames, and, of course, sneakers. ✉ *325 Hart St., Suite 122, Wedgewood-Houston* ☎ *615/933–9911* ⊕ *forts.co.*

Killjoy

WINE/SPIRITS | The concept behind this tiny shop is to give non-drinkers sophisticated options beyond club soda. Alcohol-free or zero-proof beer, wine, and spirits with the flavors of whiskeys, tequila, etc. are available, and there's a small selection of greeting cards, magnets, and—in keeping with the theme of faux "vices"—candy cigarettes. Killjoy sometimes hosts happy hours with popular breakfast and lunch spot The Loading Dock. ✉ *2020 Lindell Ave., Wedgewood-Houston* ☎ *615/669–0704* ⊕ *www.killjoyclub.com* 🕒 *Closed Mon.*

Nashville SC Team Store

SOUVENIRS | The team store for Nashville's professional soccer team has lots of cool merch for everyone from infants to adults, including scarves, hats, T-shirts, onesies, and team kits. There are also plush soccer balls, key chains, etc. If you're not able to catch a game or show, you can at least get a peek at the inside of the stadium through the double doors inside the store. ✉ *501 Benton Ave., Wedgewood-Houston* ☎ *615/701–2464* ⊕ *www.nashvillesc.com/geodispark/store.*

EAST NASHVILLE

Updated by
Brittney McKenna

○ Sights   🍴 Restaurants   🛏 Hotels   ○ Shopping   🍸 Nightlife
★★☆☆☆   ★★★★★   ★★☆☆☆   ★★★★☆   ★★★★☆

NEIGHBORHOOD SNAPSHOT

TOP EXPERIENCES

■ **Grab a Cocktail:** Great drinks can be had at places like the Fox Bar And Cocktail Club or the LGBT-friendly The Lipstick Lounge.

■ **Shop 'Til You Drop:** Visit locally owned shops like Gift Horse for gifts and souvenirs or The Bookshop to grab a read for your flight home.

■ **Get Outside:** Shelby Park has a wide variety of outdoor offerings, including walking trails and a nature center. On the banks of the Cumberland River you'll find water activities like kayaking and boat tours.

■ **Good Eats:** East Nashville has every type of dining you could imagine, from casual tacos to French-inspired Southern fare and thoughtfully prepared Mediterranean.

■ **For Music Lovers:** Grimey's New and Preloved Music is a must-visit for music fans of all stripes. Stop in to grab an LP and stay for one of the shop's many in-store events.

■ **Grab a Brew:** There's no shortage of breweries in East Nashville, including Southern Grist Brewing and East Nashville Beer Works.

GETTING HERE

East Nashville hub Five Points is easily accessible via bus, particularly for visitors traveling from the Downtown area. Once in Five Points, visitors will find adjacent neighborhoods easily accessible by a short walk, ride share, or additional bus trip. The majority of East Nashville's neighborhoods have sidewalks and bike lanes and are very friendly to pedestrians and cyclists.

VIEWFINDER

■ Tiki bar Pearl Diver has all kinds of colorful nooks and crannies, perfect for eye-popping photos. Shelby Park is the perfect spot for those who prefer to take their photos in nature, and there are plenty of eye-catching murals along Gallatin Pike.

PLANNING YOUR TIME

■ There's plenty to do in East Nashville regardless of time of day. Most bars and restaurants stay open late, while some— like Cafe Roze and Redheaded Stranger—open for breakfast. Most parking is either free on-street parking or in paid lots, though many businesses have at least a handful of free spots available for customers. Much of East Nashville is walkable, too, especially the popular Five Points area.

Located on the east side of the Cumberland River, East Nashville is one of the city's hippest enclaves. Made up of several smaller neighborhoods, it is home to some of the city's best local dining and nightlife, as well as unique local shopping, scenic views, and beloved small and midsize music venues. It's also where you'll find Nissan Stadium, home to the NFL's Tennessee Titans, along with a number of other big events.

East Nashville epicenter Five Points boasts numerous local favorite watering holes like The 5 Spot, while adjacent neighborhoods like Lockeland Springs and Cleveland Park are home to many excellent restaurants, including Lockeland Table and Folk, respectively. Running along the eastern edge of East Nashville is Shelby Park, a 1,000-acre urban green space with playgrounds, a dog park, a golf course, and hiking and biking trails.

There aren't many hotel options in East Nashville, but there are plenty of homes and apartments available for rent, which let visitors live like locals.

Give yourself plenty of time to explore—there are charming pockets of businesses and attractions tucked away across the area, and you never know what delicious bites or must-have buys you'll stumble across next.

Sights

Cumberland Park

CITY PARK | FAMILY | This park on the east bank of the Cumberland River at the foot of the Shelby Street Pedestrian Bridge was designed with kids and families in mind. Sandboxes, a playground, an obstacle course, a climbing wall, and trails (one designed to attract butterflies) are among the offerings for kids; there's also a picnic area and 1,200-seat amphitheater. You can also enjoy great views of the river with the Nashville skyline just beyond the bank. ⊠ 592 S. 1st St., Downtown ☎ 615/862–8508 ⊕ www.nashville. gov/departments/parks/parks/cumberland-park.

East Nashville's Sub-Neighborhoods

While East Nashville is itself a neighborhood, it also has numerous sub-neighborhoods within it that we cover in this chapter. To try to alleviate some geographical confusion that might arise, below is a list of all the sub-neighborhoods covered in this chapter.

- Five Points
- Riverside Village
- Inglewood
- Cleveland Park
- Lockeland Springs
- McFerrin Park
- East Bank
- Historic Edgefield
- Eastwood

Nissan Stadium

SPORTS VENUE | Home to the NFL's Tennessee Titans, this stadium has played host to CMA Fest, Tennessee State University's home football games, and more recently, three record-breaking nights in May 2023 for Taylor Swift's Eras tour. Plans for a new stadium are in the works, but private tours of the current stadium can be scheduled for groups of 20 or less. The on-site Pro Shop is open daily. ⊠ *1 Titans Way, East Nashville* ☎ *615/565–4300* ⊕ *nissanstadium.com.*

Shelby Park

CITY PARK | Shelby Park (as well as the connecting Shelby Bottoms and Cornelia Fort Airpark) is an East Nashville gem. With more than 336 acres of park land, hiking trails, public recreational facilities, and bike/pedestrian paths, Shelby offers a wide variety of free outdoor activities to locals and visitors alike. There's a public 18-hole golf course, too, so bring your clubs. ⊠ *401 S. 20th St., East Nashville* ⊕ *www.nashville.gov/departments/parks/parks/shelby-park.*

Restaurants

Bolton's Famous Hot Chicken and Fish

$ | **SOUTHERN** | Breaded and fried to a golden brown, fried catfish is a classic Southern dish that can be found all over the city, but take it a step further with Bolton's hot fish. This is a Nashville mainstay for a reason—they make hot chicken and fish better than anyone else. **Known for:** fried catfish; hot chicken; friendly staff. ⑤ *Average main: $8* ⊠ *624 Main St., East Nashville* ☎ *615/254–8015* ⊕ *www.facebook.com/BoltonsSpicyChickenandFish* ☺ *Closed Mon.*

The 1,300-acre Shelby Park has 10 miles of paved trails, free outdoor activities, and a golf course.

Butcher and Bee

$$ | ECLECTIC | Though it only opened in 2015, Butcher and Bee is already a Nashville culinary mainstay. The restaurant is convenient both to Downtown and to East Nashville's Five Points, and offers guests a variety of dining options, from a casual weekend brunch to an elegant dinner of small shared plates, all of which find the middle ground between Middle Eastern and Southern American influences. **Known for:** shareable small plates; large lively space; Middle Eastern influences. $ *Average main: $14* ⊠ *902 Main St., East Nashville* ☎ *615/229–5019* ⊕ *www.butcherandbee.com.*

Cafe Roze

$$ | ECLECTIC | This bright and bustling all-day restaurant fulfills all of your breakfast, brunch, lunch, and dinner needs with a menu that spans a number of healthy options that utilize fresh seasonal ingredients. There are more indulgent items on offer, too, like the perfectly griddled smash burger or the paprika chicken. **Known for:** creative coffee drinks; lively neighborhood feel; all-day service. $ *Average main: $18* ⊠ *1115 Porter Rd., East Nashville* ☎ *615/645–9100* ⊕ *www.caferoze.com.*

Edley's Bar-B-Que

$ | BARBECUE | At Edley's it's first come, first served for their mouthwatering brisket. If you miss the brisket, there are plenty of other delectable Southern barbecue favorites, quickly made to order and enjoy on polished-wood picnic tables inside or on the large patio; you can wash it down with a local craft beer or their signature Bushwacker, a chocolate rum milkshake. **Known**

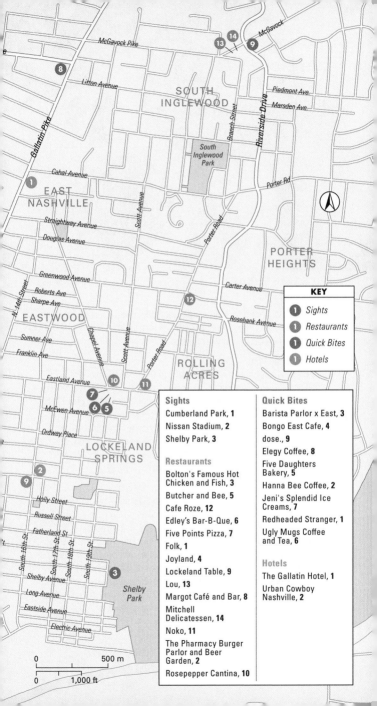

KEY

- **1** Sights
- **1** Restaurants
- **1** Quick Bites
- **1** Hotels

Sights
Cumberland Park, **1**
Nissan Stadium, **2**
Shelby Park, **3**

Restaurants
Bolton's Famous Hot Chicken and Fish, **3**
Butcher and Bee, **5**
Cafe Roze, **12**
Edley's Bar-B-Que, **6**
Five Points Pizza, **7**
Folk, **1**
Joyland, **4**
Lockeland Table, **9**
Lou, **13**
Margot Café and Bar, **8**
Mitchell Delicatessen, **14**
Noko, **11**
The Pharmacy Burger Parlor and Beer Garden, **2**
Rosepepper Cantina, **10**

Quick Bites
Barista Parlor x East, **3**
Bongo East Cafe, **4**
dose., **9**
Elegy Coffee, **8**
Five Daughters Bakery, **5**
Hanna Bee Coffee, **2**
Jeni's Splendid Ice Creams, **7**
Redheaded Stranger, **1**
Ugly Mugs Coffee and Tea, **6**

Hotels
The Gallatin Hotel, **1**
Urban Cowboy Nashville, **2**

Folk, located in East Nashville's Cleveland Park neighborhood, is a great dinner spot for large groups.

for: house-smoked barbecue; delectable sides; extensive beer list. *⑤ Average main: $12 ⊠ 1004 Woodland St., East Nashville ☎ 615/873–4085 ⊕ www.edleysbbq.com.*

★ Five Points Pizza

$ | **PIZZA** | A lively strip of bars wouldn't be complete without a pizza joint, and Five Points Pizza fills that void in the Five Points neighborhood, slinging slices, pies, and brews to the crowds heading to nearby Duke's or The 5 Spot. For the late-night set, Five Points offers a walk-up window for ordering slices to go. **Known for:** fresh fast pizza; lively neighborhood feel; local craft beer. *⑤ Average main: $9 ⊠ 1012 Woodland St., East Nashville ☎ 615/915–4174 ⊕ fivepointspizza.com.*

★ Folk

$$ | **ECLECTIC** | Chef Philip Krajeck's first Nashville restaurant Rolf & Daughters has been a runaway success since opening in 2012, and he has another success on his hands with new spot Folk, situated in East Nashville's Cleveland Park neighborhood. Seasonal salads and small plates round out a well-balanced menu of wood-fired pizzas, locally sourced proteins, and vegetable-forward dishes. **Known for:** wood-fired pizza; fresh seasonal ingredients; hip artsy interior. *⑤ Average main: $20 ⊠ 823 Meridian St., East Nashville ☎ 615/610–2595 ⊕ www.goodasfolk.com ☉ Closed Wed. No lunch.*

Joyland

$ | **BURGER** | Sean Brock's culinary influence is all over Nashville, but nowhere is the famed chef's playfulness more evident than at Joyland, his friendly colorful spot for quick and easy comfort food. Relish a bit of nostalgia while enjoying a JoyBurger, a no-frills burger reminiscent of fast food fare but far more delicious (and available in a vegetarian option). **Known for:** walkable location; comfort food by Sean Brock; griddled JoyBurgers. ⑤ *Average main: $12* ⊠ *901 Woodland St., East Nashville* ☎ *615/922–4934* ⊕ *www. eatjoyland.com.*

Lockeland Table

$$ | **ECLECTIC** | Equipped with a wood-burning stove, a smoker, and a garden of fresh vegetables, Chef Hal Holden-Bache gets down to business preparing some serious down-home cooking at his popular neighborhood restaurant, which serves comfort-gourmet food in a relaxed setting. Don't miss their cocktail menu, which features seasonal-inspired mixed drinks. **Known for:** creative comfort food; thoughtful beverage program; neighborhood atmosphere. ⑤ *Average main: $22* ⊠ *1520 Woodland St., East Nashville* ☎ *615/228–4864* ⊕ *www.lockelandtable.com* ۞ *Closed Sun.*

Lou

$$ | **AMERICAN** | Find Lou tucked into a repurposed house in Riverside Village, a dining and shopping destination in the Inglewood neighborhood of East Nashville. Grab a cozy dinner of fresh seasonal vegetables and creatively prepared protein, or enjoy a chocolate and maple buckwheat pancake during weekend brunch service. **Known for:** weekend brunch; natural wine program; friendly neighborhood feel. ⑤ *Average main: $22* ⊠ *1304 McGavock Pike, East Nashville* ☎ *615/499–4495* ⊕ *lounashville.com* ۞ *Closed Mon.*

What is that 👁 Structure?

If you've walked along the Cumberland River on the Downtown side or gazed out from one of the city's numerous rooftop bars, you may have wondered, "What is that roller-coaster-looking thing by the river?" and you wouldn't be alone. Officially called *Ghost Ballet for the East Bank Machineworks*, the sculpture was created in 2007 by Alice Aycock, who wanted to portray the area's transformation from industrial to recreational. The East Bank Greenway has several other pieces of art including *Threshold* by Joe Sorci, which is closer to Nissan Stadium.

Margot Café and Bar

$$ | ECLECTIC | In 2001, when Nashville native Margot McCormack brought her Culinary Institute of America/New York City café–pedigree back home to establish Margot Café, she sparked a food revolution that has since swept through East Nashville. Her local dining institution consistently offers a delightfully inconsistent menu, with Southern-influenced rustic Italian and French dishes served daily. **Known for:** locally sourced ingredients; creatively prepared comfort food; intimate atmosphere. $ *Average main: $22* ✉ *1017 Woodland St., East Nashville* ☎ *615/227–4668* ⊕ *www. margotcafe.com* ☾ *Closed Mon.*

★ Mitchell Delicatessen

$ | SANDWICHES | Mitchell Delicatessen is one of the pillars of East Nashville's Riverside Village neighborhood; having relocated from across the street to a larger space in 2014, it's one of the more spacious delis in town (with a large covered patio, to boot). Come for classics like the Turkey Avocado, and come back for Mitchell creations like the Turkey Brie and Asian Flank Steak. **Known for:** creative and traditional sandwiches; generous portions; gluten-free and vegetarian options. $ *Average main: $7* ✉ *1306 McGavock Pike, East Nashville* ☎ *615/262–9862* ⊕ *mitchelldeli. com* ☾ *No dinner Sun.*

★ Noko

$$$ | ASIAN FUSION | Occupying the space left by longtime Italian restaurant Pomodoro East, Noko serves creative, Asian-inspired wood-fired dishes, bringing an array of new flavors to the east side. Outfitted in sleek decor with wood accents, Noko also has a lively beverage program, including expertly made and supremely refreshing traditional Japanese highballs. **Known for:** wood-fired cuisine; Japanese cooking techniques; expertly made whiskey highballs. $ *Average main: $25* ✉ *701 Porter Rd., East Nashville* ☎ *615/712–6894* ⊕ *www.nokonashville.com* ☾ *Closed Mon. No lunch Tues.–Sat.*

★ The Pharmacy Burger Parlor and Beer Garden

$ | BURGER | If you have a hankering for good burgers and good beer, look no further than The Pharmacy to cure what ails you. The outdoor beer garden is hard to beat for both its size and ambience, and the food itself is fresh, locally sourced, and thoughtfully served. **Known for:** house-made phosphates (sodas) and milkshakes; hard-to-find beers; large outdoor dining space. $ *Average main: $10* ✉ *731 McFerrin Ave., East Nashville* ☎ *615/712–9517* ⊕ *thepharmacynashville.com.*

Rosepepper Cantina

$$ | MEXICAN | Even if you haven't been to Rosepepper, it's possible you've seen a photo of the restaurant's front sign, which features humorous comments like, "We love margaritas as much as Kanye loves Kanye." Luckily for guests, the food and drinks—which span classic Mexican fare like tacos as well as Americanized hybrids like the Mexican Caesar salad—are as good as the restaurant's sense of humor. They have a great outdoor space, too, so visit when the weather's nice. **Known for:** strong flavorful margaritas; vegetarian options; Instagram-worthy sign and great outdoor seating space. $ *Average main: $13* ✉ *1907 Eastland Ave., East Nashville* ☎ *615/227–4777* ⊕ *rosepepper.com.*

☕ Coffee and Quick Bites

Barista Parlor x East

$ | AMERICAN | The East Nashville location is the spot that started it all for this growing local coffee chain. Barista Parlor is known for paying almost an excruciating level of detail to its coffee beverages, so you know you're getting a quality cup every time you visit. **Known for:** carefully made coffee drinks; hip trendy setting; knowledgeable staff. $ *Average main: $5* ✉ *519 Gallatin Ave., Suite B, East Nashville* ☎ *615/712–9766* ⊕ *baristaparlor.com.*

Bongo East Cafe

$ | AMERICAN | The eastern outpost of the local Bongo Java empire, this location is in East Nashville's bustling Five Points neighborhood. Stop in for coffee, tea, pastries, sandwiches, and more, served up in a refreshingly unpretentious environment by a friendly knowledgeable staff. **Known for:** ethically sourced coffee; locally sourced food; friendly staff. $ *Average main: $5* ✉ *107 S. 11th St., East Nashville* ☎ *615/777–3278* ⊕ *www.bongojava.com/pages/bongo-east.*

dose.

$ | AMERICAN | Located in East Nashville's Riverside Village neighborhood, this café serves up some of the city's finest espresso drinks. In addition to a caffeine fix, you'll find a full food menu, baked goods, beer, wine, and cocktails, making it the perfect one-stop-shop for exploring the neighborhood. **Known for:** breakfast and lunch options; beer, wine, and cocktails; specialty coffee. $ *Average main: $10* ✉ *1400 McGavock Pike, East Nashville* ☎ *615/730–8625* ⊕ *dosenashville.com/riverside.*

Elegy Coffee

$ | CAFÉ | A coffee concept by the owners of The Fox Bar & Cocktail Club, Elegy is a tiny shop with bold flavors on offer. Pop in for a

East Nashville's Must-See Murals

- *Dolly Parton* ✉ *1006 Forrest Ave.*

- *Dragon* ✉ *1224 Meridian St.*

- *Flower Balm* ✉ *2909 Gallatin Pike*

- *I Say Tomato* ✉ *701 Porter Rd.*

- *What Lifts You - Hot Air Balloon* ✉ *1034 West Eastland Ave.*

- *The Red Rose at Hunter's* ✉ *975 Main St.*

- *East Nashville text* ✉ *311 Gallatin Ave.*

seasonal latte or one of several rotating burritos, like the autumnal Witching Hour burrito with black forest ham and Havarti. **Known for:** Honey Bear cold brew; seasonal burritos; hip space. ⑤ *Average main: $6* ✉ *2909A Gallatin Pike, East Nashville* ⊕ *www. elegycoffee.com/pages/east-nashville?ref=site-nav* ⊙ *No dinner.*

Five Daughters Bakery

$ | **BAKERY** | A donut wonderland right in the middle of bustling East Nashville, Five Daughters Bakery is known for its Hundred Layer Donut, a doughnut/croissant hybrid stuffed with various flavors and creams. Popular donuts sell out quickly so go early in the day. **Known for:** Hundred Layer Donut; seasonal flavors; vegan and gluten-free options. ⑤ *Average main: $5* ✉ *1900 Eastland Ave., Suite 101, East Nashville* ☎ *615/891–1293* ⊕ *fivedaughters-bakery.com.*

Hanna Bee Coffee

$ | **CAFÉ** | Pop into this bright friendly space to satisfy your munchies, get a caffeine fix—or better yet, do both. The woman- and family-owned shop boasts a wide array of specialty coffee drinks, going out of their way to cater to visitors with food sensitivities by including menu items like gluten-free bread, alternative milks, and optional plant-based cold foam. **Known for:** plant-based cold foam and gluten-free bread; next to indie bookstore; airy vibey interior. ⑤ *Average main: $7* ✉ *1035 W. Eastland Ave., Suite 1045, East Nashville* ⊕ *www.hannabeecoffee.com.*

Jeni's Splendid Ice Creams

$ | **ICE CREAM** | Jeni's has become such a popular presence in Nashville that many people—locals included—forget the string of ice-cream shops is actually based in Ohio. No matter, though, as the colorful shop and its artful flavors of ice cream and sorbet fit right in here in Music City, particularly in East Nashville. **Known for:** fresh ingredients; creative flavors; modern minimal atmosphere.

⑤ *Average main: $5* ⊠ *1892 Eastland Ave., East Nashville*
☎ *615/262–8611* ⊕ *jenis.com/blogs/scoop-shops/nashville-tn.*

Redheaded Stranger

$ | MEXICAN | At this all-day Mexican diner in East Nashville's
Cleveland Park neighborhood, expect a variety of tacos on offer,
including breakfast tacos, homemade Crunchwraps, and a green
chile cheeseburger that is not to be missed. There's ample indoor
and outdoor seating, though it's a popular spot so expect to wait
in line during peak hours. **Known for:** homemade Crunchwraps;
array of housemade salsas; boozy slushies. ⑤ *Average main: $8*
⊠ *305 Arrington St., East Nashville* ☎ *615/544–8226* ⊕ *redheaded-
strangertacos.com.*

Ugly Mugs Coffee and Tea

$ | AMERICAN | Ugly Mugs is a neighborhood coffee shop on the
edge of East Nashville's Lockeland Springs neighborhood. For
those staying in the area, it's a great spot to grab coffee, breakfast, or a simple lunch or dinner. **Known for:** well-crafted espresso
drinks; fresh locally sourced food; friendly comfortable atmosphere. ⑤ *Average main: $5* ⊠ *1886 Eastland Ave., East Nashville*
☎ *615/915–0675* ⊕ *www.uglymugsnashville.com.*

Hotels

The Gallatin Hotel

$$$ | HOTEL | One of East Nashville's newer hotel offerings, The
Gallatin is housed in a repurposed church just steps from many
popular bars and restaurants. **Pros:** proceeds benefit charity; colorful funky decor; beautifully repurposed church. **Cons:** no on-site
staff; limited room availability; louder area. ⑤ *Rooms from: $450*
⊠ *2510 Gallatin Ave., East Nashville* ☎ *615/861–1634* ⊕ *thegallatin-
hotel.com* ⇆ *25 rooms* ⑩ *No Meals.*

Urban Cowboy Nashville

$ | B&B/INN | This intimate revamped Victorian bed-and-breakfast in
the famously hip Lockeland Springs neighborhood of East Nashville provides refuge from the crowds, though it's still situated
within walking distance of popular establishments like Lockeland
Table. **Pros:** Instagrammable setting; on-site cocktail bar; luxe
decor. **Cons:** limited room availability; not for traditional hotel
lovers; not for families, as rooms are 21+. ⑤ *Rooms from: $250*
⊠ *1603 Woodland St., East Nashville* ☎ *347/840–0525* ⊕ *www.
urbancowboy.com/nashville* ⇆ *8 rooms* ⑩ *No Meals.*

Nightlife

BARS AND PUBS

★ Dino's

BARS | Billed as Nashville's oldest dive bar, Dino's has maintained its charm by changing little over the years. The bar stocks a handful of cheap beer selections and can make simple cocktails, while the kitchen serves up hot chicken, Frito pie, and sneakily delicious burgers. On the weekends, Dino's serves one of the best brunches in town, with offerings like hot chicken French toast. ⊠ *411 Gallatin Ave., East Nashville* ☎ *615/226–3566* ⊕ *www.dinosnashville.com.*

Mickey's Tavern

BARS | Located in East Hill in a small strip with like-minded bars and restaurants, Mickey's Tavern is a no-frills dive with a neighborhood vibe. Serving local beer and simple mixed drinks to a diverse mix of patrons, Mickey's offers darts, foosball, and outdoor seating options. Big bonus points to Mickey's for allowing patrons to bring over a meal from next-door local Italian establishment Nicoletto's Italian Kitchen. ⊠ *2907 Gallatin Pike, East Nashville* ☎ *615/852–5228* ⊕ *mickeystavernnashville.com.*

Pearl Diver

BARS | East Nashville bar Pearl Diver is an island vacation in bar form. From the tropical decor to the extensive list of tiki drinks, no detail at Pearl Diver was left unconsidered. The drink menu features island classics like daiquiris and mai tais, as well as new signature drinks whipped up by Pearl Diver's bartenders. They also serve small bites like dumplings and skewers. Charge your phone before hitting Pearl Diver—it's one big photo op. ⊠ *1008 Gallatin Ave., East Nashville* ☎ *615/988–2265* ⊕ *www.pearldivernashville.com* ☾ *Closed Sun.*

Village Pub and Beer Garden

BEER GARDENS | East Nashville neighborhood Riverside Village is one of the few remaining stretches in town that has managed to retain a true community feel. Part of the reason is Village Pub, a friendly neighborhood bar serving up craft beer and specialty mule cocktails alongside a menu heavy on soft pretzels and pretzel sandwiches. ⊠ *1308 McGavock Pike, East Nashville* ☎ *615/942–5880* ⊕ *www.riversidevillagepub.com.*

BREWERIES

East Nashville Beer Works

BREWPUBS | This neighborhood gem serves up beers like Miro Miel blonde ale, as well as an eclectic menu of pizza, salads, and appetizers. The brewery and taproom's back patio is dog-friendly

East Nashville Brewery Crawl ⓨ

Nashville has become a major craft beer destination in recent years, with breweries like Yazoo and Jackalope achieving national recognition. And while there are worthwhile craft brewers scattered throughout the city, East Nashville has some of the best. Here are the breweries worth checking off your list during an East Nashville beer crawl. All of them offer great food options as well.

Start at **East Nashville Beer Works** (⊠ *320 E. Trinity La.*). Try one of the five "core" beers on tap—a hazy IPA, a Citra IPA, a sour beer, a honey blonde ale, and a golden light ale—or one of the many seasonal beers on the back patio. Next, head to **Southern Grist Brewing** (⊠ *754 Douglas Ave.*), which is a must for adventurous beer lovers; all offerings are seasonal and vary depending on availability. Your last stop is **Smith and Lentz Brewing** (⊠ *903 Main St.*), one of Nashville's more acclaimed craft brewers. Favorites include the Mosaic IPA and German Pils, but you can't go wrong with their rotating seasonal offerings, either.

and great for families with young kids. ⊠ *320 E. Trinity La., East Nashville* ☎ *615/891–3108* ⊕ *eastnashbeerworks.com.*

★ Smith and Lentz Brewing

BREWPUBS | A host of craft breweries have opened in Nashville over the last few years, and Smith and Lentz ranks among the best of them. Conveniently located to Five Points, they offer a number of house and rotating brews, as well as an array of housemade pizzas, salads, and small plates, with flavors and ingredients far more elevated than your typical brewery fare. ⊠ *903 Main St., East Nashville* ☎ *615/649–8761* ⊕ *www.smithandlentz.com.*

Southern Grist Brewing

BREWPUBS | For lovers of adventurous varieties of beer, Southern Grist is a must-visit. Check out inventive brews like the Money Moves milk stout and the BroCoNut coconut IPA (note that all offerings are seasonal and vary depending on availability). For a great in-house meal, stop by the inventive and surprising Lauter. ⊠ *754 Douglas Ave., East Nashville* ☎ *629/203–7159* ⊕ *www. southerngristbrewing.com/taprooms/east-nashville.*

COCKTAIL LOUNGES

The Fox Bar & Cocktail Club

COCKTAIL BARS | Enjoy some of the best cocktails in Nashville at this cozy hideaway tucked beneath Nicoletto's Italian Kitchen.

Drinks are creative and fun, like the rotating selection of old fashioneds, with levels of adventurousness listed on the menu. The Fox is committed to sustainability, taking great pains to use local and seasonal ingredients. You'll likely want a reservation, as the small space fills up quickly most evenings. ⊠ *2905B Gallatin Pike, East Nashville* ⊕ *www.thefoxnashville.com.*

The Lipstick Lounge

COCKTAIL BARS | Tucked away in East Nashville's Lockeland Springs neighborhood, this long-standing queer bar with a friendly community feel has all of your standard options, plus excellent brunch offerings like Bloody Marys on the weekend. Don't sleep on the food, which is better than your typical bar fare and has a Tex-Mex influence. Karaoke lovers, rejoice: The Lipstick Lounge offers up some of the best in town. ⊠ *1400 Woodland St., East Nashville* ☎ *615/226–6343* ⊕ *thelipsticklounge.com.*

Urban Cowboy Public House

COCKTAIL BARS | Adjacent to the Urban Cowboy bed-and-breakfast, Urban Cowboy Public House is one of East Nashville's trendiest cocktail bars. Serving up high-end libations and a thoughtfully designed food menu in a cozy backyard setting, Urban Cowboy caters to hip younger crowds. Most seating is outdoors, so plan accordingly. ⊠ *103 N. 16th St., East Nashville* ☎ *347/840–0525* ⊕ *www.urbancowboybnb.com.*

LIVE MUSIC

The Basement East

MUSIC | Affectionately known as "the Beast," The Basement East is an East Nashville offshoot of the long-popular Basement venue located across the river. The midsize venue draws an eclectic array of local bands and national touring acts, hosting shows in an intimate environment convenient to Five Points. ⊠ *917 Woodland St., East Nashville* ☎ *615/645–9174* ⊕ *www.thebasementnashville.com.*

The Cobra

MUSIC | While The Cobra is open on non-show nights, too, this East Nashville bar/venue is especially known for its live music. If your tastes venture outside country and Americana, you'll be pleased with the variety of music represented in the nightly lineups, which often include local and national rock acts. The Cobra is also a lively spot for a drink or a quick bite, so stop in early to enjoy the divey atmosphere. ⊠ *2511 Gallatin Ave., East Nashville* ☎ *629/800–2515* ⊕ *cobranashville.com.*

Eastside Bowl

MUSIC | Eastside Bowl is your one-stop shop for music, activities and good eats on the east side. Stop in for a round of bowling and the popular shepherd's pie, or check out the calendar and grab tickets to see local and national touring acts. There's also an arcade on-site, making Eastside Bowl a great spot for fun for all ages. ✉ *1508A Gallatin Pike S, East Nashville* ☎ *615/636–9093* ⊕ *eastsidebowl.com.*

★ The 5 Spot

MUSIC | Five Points favorite The 5 Spot is a great place to grab a quick drink and an even better spot to catch a show or cut a rug. The venue/bar hosts a bevy of local musical talent, as well as a number of weekly dance nights, including the wildly popular Motown Mondays, which features—you guessed it—a danceable selection of soul and R&B classics. ✉ *1006 Forrest Ave., East Nashville* ☎ *615/650–9333* ⊕ *the5spot.club.*

Shopping

GIFTS AND SOUVENIRS

Apple and Oak

HOUSEWARES | Located close to the restaurants and coffee shops on Eastland Avenue, Apple and Oak is a haven for lovers of good design. You'll find art, rugs, and home decor galore in this locally owned boutique, as well as clothing, accessories, and small gifts. Their greeting card selection is tough to beat, too, making it a one-stop shop for all your gifting needs. ✉ *717 Porter Rd., East Nashville* ☎ *615/568–8633* ⊕ *appleandoaknash.com.*

The Bookshop

BOOKS | The Bookshop is the place to shop for all things literary in East Nashville. Though it's tucked into a small space, the shop has an expertly curated assortment of books, ranging from literary fiction to art to cooking. It's connected to Hanna Bee Coffee, making for the perfect leisurely browsing experience. The shop also plays hosts to bookish events, so check the calendar to join the fun. ✉ *1043 W. Eastland Ave., East Nashville* ☎ *615/485–5420* ⊕ *thebookshopnashville.com.*

Colts Chocolates

CHOCOLATE | Founded by a former cast member of the popular country music variety show *Hee Haw*, this charming little chocolate shop serves up seriously sweet treats like whiskey caramel brownies, their signature chocolate–peanut butter cups with roasted almonds, and a variety of samplers and gift baskets. This is a great stop to make before you board your flight back home. ✉ *3611 Gallatin Pike, East Nashville* ☎ *615/251–0100* ⊕ *coltschocolates.com* ☉ *Closed Sun.*

Gift Horse

STATIONERY | If you can't check gifts off your list at Gift Horse, you must not be looking hard enough. The small friendly shop is chock-full of unique and clever goodies, like a wide array of notebooks and stationery, funny graphic T-shirts and bumper stickers galore. For those looking for Nashville- and Tennessee-inspired gifts, head around the corner to Tenn Gallon Hat, Gift Horse's outpost for local souvenirs. ⊠ *1006 Fatherland St., Suite 301, East Nashville* ☎ *615/727–4404* ⊕ *gifthorsenashville.com.*

Olive & Sinclair Chocolate Company

CHOCOLATE | Olive & Sinclair has been producing small-batch chocolate since 2007, but they've had their factory space since 2014. Tours of the factory ($8) are offered on Saturdays and last about 40 minutes; they must be booked in advance. ⊠ *1628 Fatherland St., East Nashville* ☎ *615/262–3007* ⊕ *www.oliveandsinclair.com* ☿ *Closed Sun.*

MUSIC

Fanny's House of Music

MUSIC | If your trip to Nashville has you itching to make music of your own, stop by Fanny's House of Music to pick out the guitar of your dreams. Situated in East Nashville's Five Points neighborhood, the mom-and-pop shop boasts a wide variety of new and vintage instruments, many of which are unusual or hard to find. The store also sells music accessories, so you'll find everything you need to plug in and rock out. ⊠ *1101 Holly St., East Nashville* ☎ *615/750–5746* ⊕ *www.fannyshouseofmusic.com.*

★ Grimey's New and Preloved Music

MUSIC | A purveyor of new and used music as well as music-geek accessories, Grimey's is a Nashville institution and a must-visit for music fans touring Nashville. Before you visit, check the store's in-store events calendar—there's a good chance you'll catch some great music while browsing the vinyl crates. ⊠ *1060 E. Trinity La., East Nashville* ☎ *615/226–3811* ⊕ *www.grimeys.com.*

VINTAGE

★ Old Made Good

HOUSEWARES | Located in East Nashville's Inglewood neighborhood, Old Made Good is your one-stop shop for all things vintage and fun. From old-school band T-shirts to the perfect mid-century modern side table, everything is carefully curated and stocked by the store's staff. In addition to vintage items, Old Made Good also stocks locally made candles, crafts, jewelry, and gifts. ⊠ *3701B Gallatin Pike, East Nashville* ☎ *615/432–2882* ⊕ *oldmadegood-nashville.bigcartel.com.*

OPRYLAND AND MUSIC VALLEY

Updated by
Chris Chamberlain

◉ Sights	🍴 Restaurants	🛏 Hotels	◉ Shopping	🍸 Nightlife
★★★★☆	★★★★★	★★★★★	★★★☆☆	★★★☆☆

NEIGHBORHOOD SNAPSHOT

TOP EXPERIENCES

■ **Gaylord Opryland Resort:** Set aside some time to walk around this cavernous hotel, with its plant-filled glass-ceilinged atriums and running river.

■ **Opry Mills Mall:** This massive mall is a great place to beat the heat or escape the cold while getting some retail therapy.

■ **Grand Ole Opry House:** Home to the iconic Grand Ole Opry, country music's heroes and next big stars perform here regularly.

■ **Music Valley Drive:** Family-friendly activities abound, from miniature golf and go-kart racing to souvenir shops and restaurants.

GETTING HERE

Less than a 15-minute drive from Downtown, Opry Mills and Gaylord Opryland Resort have their own exits off of Briley Parkway. Parking at Gaylord is expensive, so leave your car in the north lot at Opry Mills and walk across to Gaylord. An hourly WeGo public transit bus runs from the main Music City Central bus station Downtown to the mall.

PLANNING YOUR TIME

Thanks to the hundreds of guests normally staying at Gaylord Opryland Resort and the thousands of shoppers at Opry Mills Mall, this area stays pretty crowded from noon until late. The attractions around Music Valley Drive are pretty sparsely attended until sunset, so the chance to listen at an uncrowded honky-tonk can be a rare treat.

VIEWFINDER

■ Hop on the greenway at the parking lot of the Two Rivers Skatepark (⊠ 2320 Two Rivers Pkwy.) and take a short downhill stroll to the foot of the Cumberland River Pedestrian Bridge for sweeping views up and down the river to Downtown. It's a great spot for nature shots of wetlands and creatures like egrets and herons that make their homes along the riverbank and in Shelby Bottoms on the other side of the bridge. Lucky visitors may see The General Jackson Showboat or industrial barges cruising on the Cumberland. Keep an eye out for speeding cyclists, who also use the pedestrian walkway as a connector between Shelby Park and the Opryland/ Music Valley Drive neighborhood.

Named for the closed, but still beloved, Opryland USA theme park that shuttered in 1997, the Opryland area and adjacent Music Valley neighborhood still revolve around the music and entertainment options that made the former tourist attraction a standout in a world of amusement parks. Gaylord Opryland Resort shows off the more refined world of country and western, with its music-themed decor and beautiful soaring glass pavilions filled with flora. Music Valley Drive is home to the more soulful roots of traditional and outlaw country, still performed in showrooms, honky-tonks, and tiny bars.

After Opryland closed, the site became home to Opry Mills Mall as another way to keep resort guests entertained and conduct commerce in between meetings. It's true that most of these things were built to accommodate the Opry's tourism runoff, and much of Music Valley still accommodates this crowd today. But there's an earnestness to Music Valley's offerings that you won't find on Lower Broadway or Music Row, where country music can be a loud, expensive, neon caricature of itself. Music Valley has resisted the influence of new Nashville trends the way that classic country has resisted the influence of pop, and you can still hear steel guitars accompanying the house bands, a rarity Downtown.

Frankly, this isn't the part of town you come to if you want to wait in line to take an Instagram picture in front of a hip mural. This is where you come if you want to listen to real country music while you take a minute to slow down, stop trying to impress every-one, and eat a fried bologna sandwich, probably next to a retired couple in cowboy boots.

There's no better neighborhood to shop for souvenirs, ranging from kitschy T-shirts to actual vintage memorabilia, than in thrift shops along Music Valley Drive. In addition to the resort and the attractive lower-cost Inn at Opryland, many more affordable chain hotels have outposts along Music Valley Drive, conveniently visible from Briley Parkway. The neighborhood is also popular with the camping and RV set, thanks to a few clean and comfortable campgrounds at the curve of Pennington Bend, near the Cumberland River.

Sights

Cooter's

SPECIALTY MUSEUM | A must-visit for fans of the early '80s TV sitcom *The Dukes of Hazzard*, Cooter's offers a plethora of collectibles and Duke Boys ephemera. After seven seasons portraying the amiable mechanic Cooter on the show, Ben Jones served four years as a U.S. congressman representing Georgia's 4th District. After retiring from public service, Jones opened this museum and gift shop filled with memorabilia, props, and autographed items from the show. Some are for sale and others are too rare for Jones to part with, but they all tell the story of the fictional Hazzard County. Visitors can even get a photo in the General Lee for an added cost. ⊠ *Music Valley Village, 2613 McGavock Pike, Opryland/Music Valley* ☎ *615/872–8358* ⊕ *cootersplace.com* ⌨ *Free.*

Gaylord Opryland Resort and Convention Center

HOTEL | Technically the Gaylord Opryland Resort is a hotel and convention center, but it's worth a visit even if you aren't staying the night. For one thing, there are 9 acres of gardens inside, all laced with walking paths, fountains, and rivers. These gardens feature more than 50,000 tropical plants, contained within a soaring glass ceiling that lets the sun shine through during the day and reflects a thousand warm twinkle lights at night (particularly at Christmas). Even the locals can't resist an occasional walk through the immaculately tended branches and waterfalls of the Cascade Atrium—especially when you consider that you can do it with a beer, cocktail, or cup of gelato in hand. There are almost 20 restaurants to choose from if you get hungry, and plenty of kitschy shops if you're in the market for souvenirs. To avoid the hefty parking fee, it's recommended that you park next door at the mall and walk over. ⊠ *2800 Opryland Dr., Opryland/Music Valley* ☎ *615/889–1000* ⊕ *www.marriott.com* ⌨ *Free.*

Grand Ole Opry House

PERFORMANCE VENUE | The enormously popular radio show, the Grand Ole Opry, has been performed in the Opry House since 1925. You can see superstars, legends, and up-and-coming stars on this stage. The Opry has been in its current location since 1974, when then-President Richard Nixon played a song on the

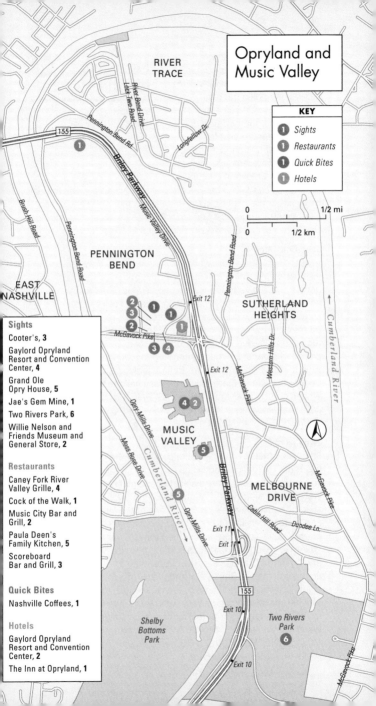

Opryland and Music Valley

RIVER TRACE

River Bend Drive
Lock Two Road
Pennington Bend Rd.
Longfellow Dr.

Briley Parkway
Music Valley Drive

PENNINGTON BEND

Brush Hill Road
Pennington Bend Road

EAST NASHVILLE

Pennington Bend Road

KEY

- ① Sights
- ① Restaurants
- ① Quick Bites
- ① Hotels

0 ——— 1/2 mi
0 ——— 1/2 km

SUTHERLAND HEIGHTS

Cumberland River

Exit 12

McGavock Pike

② ③ ① ① ②

McGavock Pike ② ③ ④

Exit 12

Western Hills Dr.

Opry Mills Drive
Moss Rose Drive
Cumberland River

MUSIC VALLEY

④ ②
⑤

Briley Parkway
Opry Mills Drive

MELBOURNE DRIVE

Cabin Hill Road
Dandee Ln.
McGavock Pike

⑤

Exit 11
Exit 11

155

Exit 10

Shelby Bottoms Park

Two Rivers Park

⑥

Exit 10

McGavock Pike

Sights

Cooter's, **3**

Gaylord Opryland Resort and Convention Center, **4**

Grand Ole Opry House, **5**

Jae's Gem Mine, **1**

Two Rivers Park, **6**

Willie Nelson and Friends Museum and General Store, **2**

Restaurants

Caney Fork River Valley Grille, **4**

Cock of the Walk, **1**

Music City Bar and Grill, **2**

Paula Deen's Family Kitchen, **5**

Scoreboard Bar and Grill, **3**

Quick Bites

Nashville Coffees, **1**

Hotels

Gaylord Opryland Resort and Convention Center, **2**

The Inn at Opryland, **1**

house piano on opening night, and as such it's the epicenter around which the rest of Music Valley has rippled out over the years. Even if you aren't a huge fan of country music, it's definitely worth a visit for the spectacle of it all. And if attending a live show isn't enough to satisfy your love of country music, you can take a backstage tour seven days a week to hear more about the history, stars, and stories that make the Grand Ole Opry truly grand. ⊠ *600 Opry Mills Dr., Opryland/Music Valley* ☎ *615/871–6779* ⊕ *www.opry.com* ⊡ *$45.85 for tours.*

Must-See Mural

■ *Electric Dolly* ⊠ *2611 Music Valley Dr.*

Jae's Gem Mine

OTHER ATTRACTION | **FAMILY** | For something really down to earth, visit Jae's Gem Mine to learn about the minerals, fossils, and gemstones native to Tennessee and beyond. Their mission is more scientific than metaphysical, though they do sell crystals—as well as gems and minerals presented through an interactive simulated mining experience. In addition to retail, they're a full-service rock shop, offering everything from lapidary services (cutting and polishing stones) and geode cracking to rockhounding classes and trips that take you into nature to find geological treasures of your own. While you're there, be sure to say hello to the shop dog, whose name is (obviously) Rocky. ⊠ *2416 Music Valley Dr., Suite 102, Opryland/Music Valley* ☎ *615/481–7909* ⊕ *jaesgemmine.com* ⊙ *Closed Tues. and Wed.*

Two Rivers Park

CITY PARK | **FAMILY** | This 374-acre park along the Cumberland River has more recreational activities than any other park in Nashville. To name just a few, there's a skate park, golf course, and small water park called Wave Country, featuring a wave pool and several slides. The Two Rivers Dog Park is one of the largest in the city, and there's a walking track around the perimeter so you can jog or walk while your dog frolics. The Stones River Greenway is a 10.2-mile paved trail that runs straight through Two Rivers Park, ending in the Cumberland River Pedestrian Bridge that leads east across the river to Shelby Bottoms Park. In addition to the natural sights provided by leafy green Tennessee, you may pass a beautiful Italianate mansion on your walk. That's Two Rivers Mansion, an 1859 plantation home that's now used as a private venue for weddings and events. ⊠ *3150 McGavock Pike, Opryland/Music Valley* ☎ *615/862–8400* ⊕ *www.nashville.gov/departments/parks/parks/two-rivers-park* ⊡ *Free.*

The Gaylord Opryland Resort and Convention Center has 9 acres of gardens that feature more than 50,000 tropical plants and cascading waterfalls.

Willie Nelson and Friends Museum and General Store

SPECIALTY MUSEUM | All the Nashville classics are amassed here at the Willie Nelson and Friends Museum and General Store: fringe leather goods, zebra print flasks, cowboy hats, fudge, Goo Goo Clusters, and Donald Trump voodoo dolls. At the back of the general store, buy a ticket and go through the door on your right into the 5,000-square-foot museum. There you'll find instruments, awards, photos, costumes, and other Willie Nelson memorabilia on display. Even if you're not a huge Willie Nelson fan, the "and Friends" part of the Willie Nelson and Friends Museum may entice you. There's also memorabilia from the likes of Waylon Jennings, Patsy Cline, Dolly Parton, Porter Wagoner, and dozens of other country music superstars. ⌧ *Music Valley Village, 2613A McGavock Pike, Opryland/Music Valley* ☎ *615/885–1515* ⊕ *willienelsonmuseum.com* ⌧ *$12.95.*

🍴 Restaurants

Caney Fork River Valley Grille

$$$ | SOUTHERN | FAMILY | Though the Caney Fork River Valley Grille is best known for its ribs and catfish, the wild-game menu is a must-try for those with a taste for adventure—this is truly the only place in Nashville where you'll find gator chili, wild elk sliders, or a venison sausage Philly (think classic cheesesteak sandwich but with sausage). There's live music every Friday and Saturday against a backdrop of taxidermy possums, bears, deer, wolves, bobcats, and much more. **Known for:** wild-game menu; sweet and savory barbecue ribs; golden fried catfish. $ *Average main: $27* ✉ *2400 Music Valley Dr., Opryland/Music Valley* ☏ *615/724–1200* ⊕ *www.caneyforkrestaurant.com* ⊗ *No lunch Mon.–Thurs.*

Cock of the Walk

$$ | SOUTHERN | FAMILY | From the rustic wood-paneled walls and the rows of rocking chairs to the shrine of signed headshots from country music legends, this catfish surf-and-turf restaurant has been turning out traditional Tennessee cooking in a laid-back family atmosphere for decades. Beyond the obvious steak, catfish, and shrimp mains, they also offer several standout sides like coleslaw, hush puppies, and fried pickles. **Known for:** fried catfish fillets; crisp and pillowy hush puppies; tangy fried pickles. $ *Average main: $20* ✉ *2624 Music Valley Dr., Opryland/Music Valley* ☏ *615/889–1930* ⊕ *www.cockofthewalkrestaurant.com* ⊗ *Closed Mon. No lunch Tues.–Thurs.*

Music City Bar and Grill

$ | SOUTHERN | With multiple bars ringing the dance floor and stage area, this is more of a "beer-and-a-shot" place where the focus is on the music. Enjoy bar bites while listening to old-school country from singer-songwriters and bands who play in the afternoons and evenings. **Known for:** live music; cold beer; bar bites like wings, burgers, and pizzas. $ *Average main: $12* ✉ *2416 Music Valley Dr., Opryland/Music Valley* ☏ *615/883–2367* ⊕ *www.facebook.com/ musiccitybar.*

Paula Deen's Family Kitchen

$$$ | SOUTHERN | FAMILY | Celebrity television chef Paula Deen brought her country cooking to Nashville with this all-you-can-eat restaurant where meals are served family-style to your table. Choose from two to four classic Southern main dishes, like fried chicken, pork chops, or chicken and dumplings, along with four side dishes that would be at home on any Southern grandma's table, like green beans, broccoli casserole, and baked mac and cheese. **Known for:** all-you-can-eat Southern food; casual Southern decor; gift shop filled with cookbooks and kitchen gear. $ *Average main: $30* ✉ *Opry Mills Mall, 575 Opry Mills Dr., Opryland/Music Valley* ☏ *615/492–6500* ⊕ *pauladeensfamilykitchen.com.*

Scoreboard Bar and Grill

$$ | BURGER | Good drink specials, hot chicken, and chill karaoke characterize this sports bar and restaurant. There's a rustic/ modern dissonance here, with old-timey features like log-cabin-style booths and a cigarette vending machine (although smoking indoors is now banned) right next to more updated fixtures like pool tables, televisions, and a virtual golfing game. **Known for:** some of the city's best hot chicken; daily live music in an open-air room separate from the restaurant; an outdoor patio for yard games and seasonal seafood boils. ⑤ *Average main: $15* ⊠ *2408 Music Valley Dr., Opryland/Music Valley* ✛ *Across from Gaylord Opryland Resort* ☎ *615/883–3866* ⊕ *www.scoreboardopry.com.*

Coffee and Quick Bites

Nashville Coffees
$ | CAFÉ | This cozy family-owned coffee shop is much more charming than its strip mall locale might imply. The walls of the bright interior space are adorned with country music stars' promotional headshots and other bits of memorabilia to peruse while enjoying specialty coffee drinks made using locally roasted beans, bagels and croissants, or more substantial sandwiches during the lunch hour. **Known for:** specialty coffee drinks; quick breakfast bites; local art on the walls. ⑤ *Average main: $6* ⊠ *2416 Music Valley Dr., Suite 143, Opryland/Music Valley* ☎ *615/970–7337* ⊕ *www. nashvillecoffees.com.*

🛏 Hotels

★ Gaylord Opryland Resort and Convention Center
$$ | RESORT | FAMILY | This sprawling complex, now part of the Marriott group, is a fantastic urban getaway with a spa, indoor and outdoor pool, a riverboat ride, a waterfall, 17 restaurants ranging from casual to fine dining, and numerous shops. **Pros:** a worthy tourist destination even if you're not staying there; shuttles available; multiple dining options. **Cons:** distances within the complex can be long; expensive parking; traffic in the area can be a nuisance. ⑤ *Rooms from: $399* ⊠ *2800 Opryland Dr., Opryland/ Music Valley* ☎ *615/889–1000* ⊕ *www.marriott.com* ➯ *2,882 rooms* ⦿ *No Meals.*

The Inn at Opryland
$ | HOTEL | Just across the street from its partner property, Gaylord Opryland Resort, The Inn at Opryland offers comfortable rooms and elevated amenities at a more budget-friendly price for frugal travelers. **Pros:** close to Gaylord Opryland Resort without the crowds; free parking as opposed to steep charges at Gaylord Opryland; live entertainment at the Opry Backstage Grill, including singing servers. **Cons:** not many activities for children of guests; events at the resort necessitate walking or taking a shuttle; no covered parking. ⑤ *Rooms from: $250* ⊠ *2401 Music Valley Dr., Opryland/Music Valley* ☎ *615/889–0800* ⊕ *www.marriott.com* ➯ *303 rooms* ⦿ *No Meals.*

The Victorian-style *General Jackson* riverboat cruise offers dinner and a show on their cruises down the Cumberland River.

Nightlife

★ Nashville Palace

LIVE MUSIC | If you're a classic country music fan whose tastes lean more towards Waylon, Merle, and Willie than Luke and Luke (Bryan and Combs), get yourself to the Nashville Palace as quickly as you can. This bar and venue is a country music legend and one of the few places in town that showcases classic country exclusively. They have live music from open to close, and you can order a fried bologna sandwich whenever your heart desires. In the back is a huge dance floor where they have special events and concerts (usually ticketed) on weekends, but it isn't uncommon to see a little line dancing or two-stepping on the smaller dance floor in the front room either. ⌧ *2611 McGavock Pike, Opryland/Music Valley* ☎ *615/889–1541* ⊕ *www.thefamousnashvillepalace.com.*

 Performing Arts

The *General Jackson* Showboat

MUSIC | **FAMILY** | The *General Jackson* is a Victorian-style riverboat that cruises down the Cumberland River up to twice a day. On board, there's a two-story theater that showcases a couple of flashy, choreographed, cheesy but fun contemporary country productions—the Tennessee Legends show, which plays during the midday cruise, and the Rollin' on the River show, which takes place as the sun is setting. Special holiday-themed shows are also quite popular. Each show comes with the option to purchase a meal; after the show, you can roam the different decks outside, including a rooftop bar from which you can enjoy views of the sparkling Downtown skyline. ⊠ *2812 Opryland Dr., Opryland/ Music Valley* ☎ *615/458–3900* ⊕ *generaljackson.com* 🎫 *From $45.*

★ The Grand Ole Opry

MUSIC | The Grand Ole Opry is the most famous country music show in the world—in fact, it's the show that made country music famous. They've been broadcasting their concerts every week since 1925, making it the longest-running radio broadcast in the United States, and there isn't a country, bluegrass, or Americana icon who hasn't performed here. The Opry continues to be a major part of the soundtrack of the region and a destination for country fans and performers alike. ⊠ *600 Opry Mills Dr., Opryland/ Music Valley* ☎ *615/871–6779* ⊕ *www.opry.com* 🎫 *From $49.*

Nashville Night Life Dinner Theater

MUSIC | This is a perfect antidote for when ultra-cool New Nashville starts to take itself too seriously. This place is just unpretentious, good-hearted country music fun. Join 300 of your closest friends for a buffet-style dinner and an hour and a half of some of Nashville's most seasoned musicians putting on the best country music variety show in town. The band performs country music through the ages, from Hank Williams to Toby Keith, and you better believe there's fruit cobbler for dessert. Touring country tribute acts sometimes make stops for special performances, so check the music calendar. ⊠ *2416 Music Valley Dr., Opryland/Music Valley* ☎ *615/885–4747* ⊕ *www.nashvillenightlife.com* 🎫 *$57.95 with dinner.*

Shopping

Dashwood Vintage & Flora

ANTIQUES & COLLECTIBLES | This amazingly curated boutique specializes in the two things essential to every fashionable home: mid-century furniture and beautiful plants. The offerings here are more vintage than antique—couches, chairs, lamps, tables, and other one-of-a-kind statement pieces from the '50s, '60s, and '70s, all perfectly preserved and irresistibly cool. There are some new items for sale, too, all of which are ethically produced (either American made or, if they're imported, fair trade). And yes—for any literary buffs who were wondering, the name is in fact a reference to Jane Austen's *Sense and Sensibility*. ⊠ *2416 Music Valley Dr., Suite 115, Opryland/Music Valley* ☎ *615/712–7091* ⊕ *www. dashwoodtn.com* ☉ *Closed Mon. and Tues.*

Music Valley Antiques & Marketplace

ANTIQUES & COLLECTIBLES | A treasure trove of brass, porcelain, and wood awaits you in this sunny antiques store. Music Valley Antiques & Marketplace combines the selective inventory of a high-end vintage boutique with the prices of a dig-until-you-hit-the-bottom flea market. With books, art, records, clothes, furniture, dishes, vintage toys, exquisite tea sets, and (of course) instruments from more than 30 vendors, you're sure to find at least one thing you didn't know you couldn't live without. ✉ *Village Shopping Center, 2416 Music Valley Dr., Suite 126, Opryland/Music Valley* ☎ *615/557–6560* ⊕ *musicvalleyantiques.antiquetrail.com* ☾ *Closed Tues.*

Opry Mills

SHOPPING CENTER | **FAMILY** | Opry Mills is the be-all end-all of malls in Tennessee. In fact, it's so gigantic that it has its own exit off of Briley Parkway. There are more than 200 stores inside, both outlet and retail, covering every corner of the shopping landscape: shoes, clothes, sporting goods, hunting gear, handbags, and multiple vendors who sell nothing but cowboy boots. And the brands cover just as wide a spectrum, from Coach to rue21. The layout is a huge oval, so there are no shortcuts as you make a full lap around this hall of commerce. When you've reached your shopping limit, catch a movie at the Regal Opry Mills IMAX & RPX and enjoy a bottle of Nashville craft beer. For food, Chuy's Mexican Food is the best pick for both flavor and value, and Aquarium Restaurant is an excellent choice if you're willing to shell out a little more for the dreamy experience of dining surrounded by a 200,000-gallon saltwater aquarium. ✉ *433 Opry Mills Dr., Opryland/Music Valley* ☎ *615/514–1000* ⊕ *www.simon.com/mall/opry-mills.*

DAY TRIPS FROM NASHVILLE

Updated by
Brittney McKenna

⊙ Sights   🍴 Restaurants   🏨 Hotels   🛍 Shopping   🍸 Nightlife

★★★★☆   ★★★★★   ★★★★★   ★★★☆☆   ★★★☆☆

WELCOME TO DAY TRIPS FROM NASHVILLE

1 Airport, Donelson, and Hermitage. Here you'll find the airport, outposts of some of the city's best eateries, and Andrew Jackson's Hermitage.

2 Franklin. This charming town filled with shops and good food is also home to lots of Civil War history.

3 Bellevue. Home to the botanical garden and art museum Cheekwood Estate and Gardens, as well as the beginning of the Natchez Trace Parkway driving and cycling route.

4 Belle Meade. The Belle Meade Historic Site & Winery is just 10 miles southwest of the Music City.

5 Lynchburg. Seventy-five miles southeast of Nashville is the famous Jack Daniel's Distillery.

6 Arrington Vineyards. Charming vineyard just 40 minutes south of Nashville.

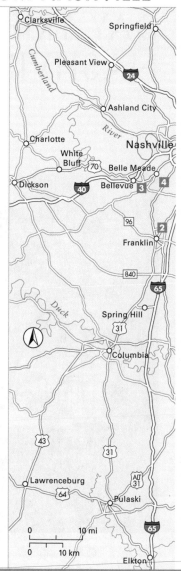

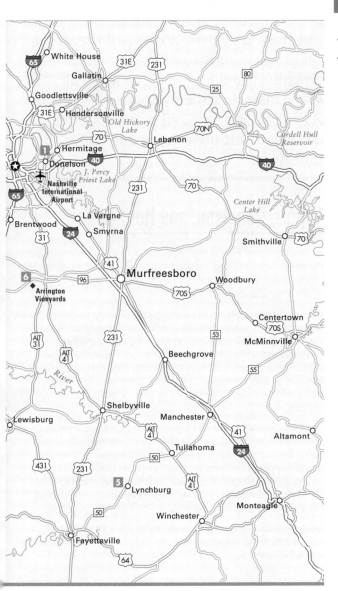

The middle Tennessee area surrounding Nashville is a pocket of gently rolling Cumberland Mountain foothills and bluegrass meadows. It is one of the state's richest farming areas. Small towns like Lynchburg and Franklin, the latter of which historian Shelby Foote calls one of the nation's top Civil War sites, offer wonderful antiques shops and crafts boutiques.

Airport, Donelson, and Hermitage

15 miles east of Nashville via I–40.

Donelson and Hermitage are less-talked-about areas of Nashville, but that doesn't mean that these neighborhoods don't have exciting attractions to offer travelers.

Donelson is one of Nashville's more rapidly growing neighborhoods, offering a bevy of local restaurants and attractions a short drive from Downtown. Several popular Nashville restaurants have outposts in the area, like hot chicken purveyors Party Fowl and barbecue favorites Edley's. Grab a cold beer at Homegrown Taproom, or if you're feeling health-conscious, stop at Nectar Urban Cantina for a freshly made smoothie or delicious coffee concoction.

The Hermitage neighborhood is famously home to Andrew Jackson's Hermitage, the seventh president's former home and final resting place. In addition to boasting beautiful grounds, The Hermitage includes a historical museum and offers several tours. You can make an afternoon of your visit, too, by eating at the on-site restaurant, FKS Kitchen. The Hermitage is also home to Natchez Hills Winery, if you prefer your history with a nice glass of red.

The greater area is also home to Nashville International Airport, making it convenient for travelers looking for a last-minute activity before flying home.

The Lane Motor Museum has more than 550 vehicles in its collection, but only about 150 are displayed at a time.

Sights

The Hermitage

HISTORIC SIGHT | **FAMILY** | The life and times of Andrew Jackson, known as Old Hickory, are reflected with great care at this house and museum. Jackson built the mansion on 600 acres for his wife, Rachel, for whose honor he fought and won a duel; both are buried here in the family graveyard. By the 1840s, more than 140 enslaved people lived and worked on the Hermitage Plantation, and archaeological digs uncovered the remains of many slave dwellings. The Andrew Jackson Center, a 28,000-square-foot museum, visitor center, and education center, contains many Jackson artifacts never before exhibited. Mansion tours are led by costumed guides, while audio tours of the grounds are self-guided. Optional activities include wagon tours (April through October) and tours of Tulip Grove, home of the niece who served as Jackson's White House hostess and her husband, Jackson's presidential secretary. ⊠ *4580 Rachel's La., Nashville* ✛ *12 miles east of Nashville. Take I–40E to Exit 221A (Hermitage exit). From I–65 North, take Exit 92 (Old Hickory Boulevard South exit)* ☎ *615/889–2941* ⊕ *thehermitage.com* ✉ *$20.*

Lane Motor Museum

SPECIALTY MUSEUM | **FAMILY** | One man's passion for automobiles (and motorcycles) led to this collection of mostly European vehicles of all shapes and sizes, from mini cars (including a Smartcar) to an amphibious car—one vehicle for almost every letter of the alphabet. The museum also includes a children's area, art gallery, and gift shop. ✉ *702 Murfreesboro Pike, Nashville* ☎ *615/742–7445* 🌐 *www.lanemotormuseum.org* 🎫 *$12* 🕒 *Closed Tues. and Wed.*

Nashville Shores

WATER PARK | FAMILY | Nashville Shores is a fun water park and marina on Percy Priest Lake with a 25,000-square-foot wave pool, a 1,000-foot-long lazy river float experience, and other splashy activities. You can air-dry in the Shores' Treetop Adventure Park where there are ziplines, cargo nets, suspended bridges, and other challenges. Private guide service is also available. ✉ *4001 Bell Rd., Hermitage* ✥ *10 miles east of Downtown* ☎ *615/889–7050* 🌐 *www.nashvilleshores.com* 🎫 *$50 for water park; $50 for Treetop* 🕒 *Water park closed Sept.–mid-May; Treetop closed Dec.–Feb.*

Restaurants

McNamara's Irish Pub

$$ | IRISH | FAMILY | It's impossible to overstate how cozy this Irish pub is. There's live music every night of the week, but on Friday and Saturday, you can catch the owner himself performing traditional Irish tunes with his band, Nosey Flynn. **Known for:** live music; steak-and-Guinness pie; full Irish breakfast. $ *Average main: $15* ✉ *2740 Old Lebanon Rd., Donelson* ✥ *2 miles north of the Nashville International Airport* ☎ *615/885–7262* 🌐 *www.mcnamarasirishpub.com* 🕒 *Closed Sun. and Mon.*

Nadeen's Hermitage Haven

$$ | DINER | FAMILY | For a neighborhood joint that takes diner fare to the next level, Nadeen's balance of folksy and classy won't disappoint. The rolls for their Philly cheesesteaks actually come from Philadelphia, and their biscuits are made fresh every morning. **Known for:** poutine; fried pies; chicken and waffles. $ *Average main: $15* ✉ *3410 Lebanon Pike, Hermitage* ☎ *615/873–1184* 🌐 *www.nadeensinhermitage.com* 🕒 *Closed Mon. and Tues.*

Coffee and Quick Bites

Nectar Urban Cantina

$$ | MODERN MEXICAN | Half café (pressed juices, coffee, and wraps) and half restaurant (tacos, burrito bowls, and a full bar), Nectar Urban Cantina is great whether you're in a hurry or have more time to kill. Inside an updated Tudor-style house, they offer fresh Mexican-inspired cuisine in a bright casual space. **Known for:** tacos; fresh-pressed juice; fried plantains. $ *Average main: $13* ✉ *206 McGavock Pike, Donelson* ☎ *615/454–2277* 🌐 *www.nectarcantina.com.*

Franklin has been called the "number one small town in Tennessee."

Phat Bites

$ | SANDWICHES | Maybe it's the graffitied walls, maybe it's the local bee-pollen honey, but this crunchy sandwich shop inside a converted garage is undeniably cool. Come any time, morning or night, and you'll find a goat cheese–smothered waffle, a hummus-stuffed veggie wrap, or a late-night cocktail that will suit your needs. **Known for:** hummus; funky atmosphere; sandwiches. ⑤ *Average main: $8* ✉ *2730 Lebanon Pike, Suite B, Donelson* ☎ *615/871–4055* ⊕ *www.phatbites.com.*

Franklin

22 miles south of Nashville via I–65.

Turning off the interstate, a simple sign welcomes visitors to the "number one small town in Tennessee." Strictly speaking, Franklin, Tennessee, is closer to a city than a small town: more than 78,000 people now live there, which is more than six times the number of people who lived there as recently as 1980. But through all its growth, Franklin hasn't forgotten its small-town manners. From its founding in 1799 until the Civil War, Franklin was a rural but wealthy community of tobacco, hemp, and livestock farmers, as well as the many Black Americans who were brought to Franklin as slaves. In 1864 the Civil War devastated Franklin; when slavery was abolished, Franklin's plantation economy collapsed. In the years since, Franklin has experienced a slow

Tennessee Antebellum Trail

The Tennessee Antebellum Trail (⊕ *antebellumtrail.com*), which includes more than 54 historic sites, plantations, and Civil War battlefields, is a 90-mile loop tour that begins south of Nashville in Franklin and continues through historic Maury and Williamson counties. Nine sites are open to the public daily. The official website includes downloads of a detailed brochure and map.

climb back to prosperity. However, today it's one of the wealthiest cities in one of the wealthiest counties in the country. You can still find huge rolling tracts of Tennessee greenery throughout Franklin, dotted with antebellum and Victorian homes and Civil War battlegrounds. Downtown Franklin is the quintessential picture of small-town charm, packed with shops, restaurants, and quaint cafés, all crowded into historic redbrick storefronts around narrow lamp-lit streets.

GETTING HERE AND AROUND
If you're staying in Nashville, you'll need a car for a day trip to Franklin. Renting a car or bringing your own is best; the ride-share fare will be pretty hefty, and there's no public transportation between Nashville and Franklin. However, once you reach Franklin's city center, it's easy to find street parking Downtown and most places will be walkable from there.

VISITOR INFORMATION
CONTACTS Visit Franklin. ⊠ *400 Main St., Suite 130, Franklin* ☎ *615/591–8514* ⊕ *visitfranklin.com.*

Sights

Carnton
HISTORIC SIGHT | FAMILY | This antebellum home was converted to a field hospital after the Battle of Franklin in 1864. Today, the property offers several different tours, including a 90-minute Behind the Scenes Tour of the house and the 90-minute Slavery & the Enslaved Tour focusing on the individuals enslaved at Carnton and how emancipation changed their lives; check the online schedule before visiting. Be sure to explore the grounds after your visit. In addition to the house, there are gardens, several outbuildings, and a Civil War cemetery. Combination tickets are available with Carter House and Rippa Villa. ⊠ *1345 Eastern Flank Circle, Franklin* ☎ *615/794–0903* ⊕ *boft.org/carnton* ⊠ *$20 for Classic House Tour;*

$27 for Slavery & the Enslaved Tour; $27 for Behind the Scenes Tour ☞ Last guided tour of the day begins at 4 pm.

Carter House

HISTORIC HOME | FAMILY | On the morning of November 30, 1864, General Jacob D. Cox seized the Carter family's home and made it the Federal Army's headquarters for the Battle of Franklin. Today you can tour this one-and-a-half-story brick house and hear how the Civil War changed the lives of one family in particular, the country at large, and the enslaved people who also lived here. Combination tickets are available with Carnton and Rippa Villa. ⊠ *1140 Columbia Ave., Franklin* ☎ *615/791–1861* ⊕ *boft.org/carter-house* ☒ *$20 for Classic House Tour; $27 for Slavery & the Enslaved Tour ☞ Last guided tour of the day begins at 4 pm.*

The Factory at Franklin

STORE/MALL | FAMILY | You'll find boutiques, antiques, restaurants, a guitar shop, and a theater in this airy brick complex of late 1920s-era buildings. Once home to a stoveworks, it's now listed on the National Register of Historic Places. ⊠ *230 Franklin Rd., Franklin* ☎ *615/791–1777* ⊕ *factoryatfranklin.com.*

Fort Granger

MILITARY SIGHT | FAMILY | Fort Granger was an earthwork fort created by the Union troops during the Civil War. Today, it's a park along the Harpeth River with a self-guided walking tour through the Franklin Battlefield. Start at the beginning of the path and follow the placards to learn the history of the Battle of Franklin. If you follow the path all the way to the end, it will lead you to Pinkerton Park. ⊠ *113 Fort Granger Dr., Franklin* ☎ *615/794–2103* ⊕ *www.franklintn.gov/government/departments-k-z/parks/park-locations/fort-granger* ☒ *Free.*

Lotz House

COLLEGE | FAMILY | Built in 1858, this grand house in Downtown Franklin was home to a family of German immigrants during the years surrounding the Civil War. Even those who don't care for Civil War history will enjoy touring this house. It contains one of the best antique collections in Tennessee, as well as the art of Matilda Lotz, who became a world-renowned painter of animals after the war. ⊠ *1111 Columbia Ave., Franklin* ☎ *615/790–7190* ⊕ *www.lotzhouse.com* ☒ *$14 ☞ Last guided tour of the day begins 1 hr before closing.*

Pinkerton Park

CITY PARK | FAMILY | This park has not one but two playgrounds for little ones to explore. For older kids, there are ping-pong tables, plenty of green space, and a paved 1-mile walking trail around the

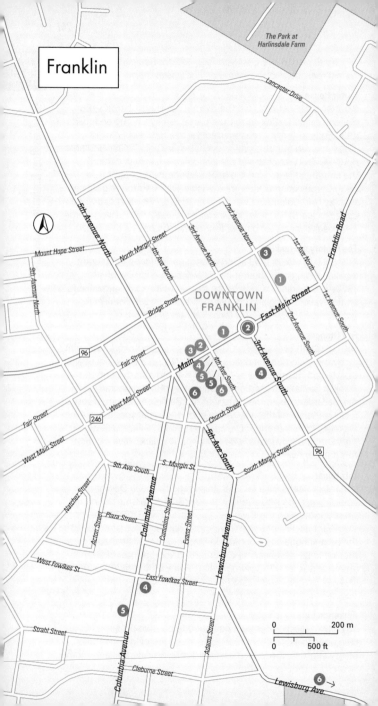

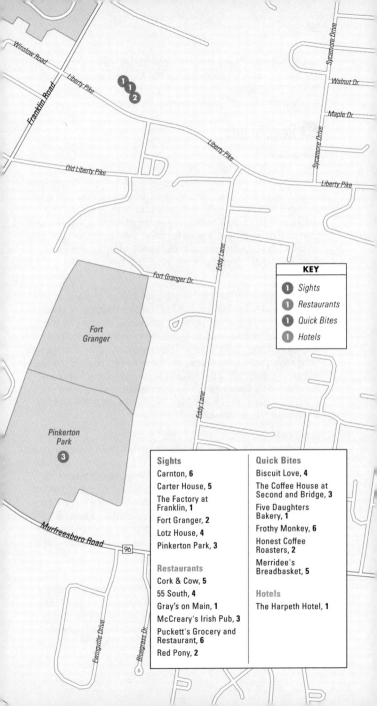

KEY

- 1 *Sights*
- 1 *Restaurants*
- 1 *Quick Bites*
- 1 *Hotels*

Sights

Carnton, **6**

Carter House, **5**

The Factory at Franklin, **1**

Fort Granger, **2**

Lotz House, **4**

Pinkerton Park, **3**

Restaurants

Cork & Cow, **5**

55 South, **4**

Gray's on Main, **1**

McCreary's Irish Pub, **3**

Puckett's Grocery and Restaurant, **6**

Red Pony, **2**

Quick Bites

Biscuit Love, **4**

The Coffee House at Second and Bridge, **3**

Five Daughters Bakery, **1**

Frothy Monkey, **6**

Honest Coffee Roasters, **2**

Merridee's Breadbasket, **5**

Hotels

The Harpeth Hotel, **1**

park's perimeter. There are also picnic tables, pavilions, and grills if the weather calls for barbecue. ✉ *405 Murfreesboro Rd., Franklin* ☎ *615/794–2103* ⊕ *www.franklintn.gov/government/depart-ments-k-z/parks/park-locations/pinkerton-park* 🖅 *Free.*

 Restaurants

Cork & Cow

$$$$ | **STEAK HOUSE** | This steak house has major chops: if an exquisite cut of beef isn't epicurean enough for you, you can pair your steak with lobster, crab, scallops, or shrimp. And with a long luxurious cocktail menu and plenty of aperitifs, desserts, and even a port flight, your meal can drag on all evening, with no end to indulgences in sight. **Known for:** great steak; creative cocktails; swanky vibe. ⑤ *Average main: $50* ✉ *403 Main St., Franklin* ☎ *615/538–6021* ⊕ *corkandcow.com* ⊘ *No lunch.*

55 South

$$ | **CAJUN** | Named for I–55, which cuts through the Mississippi Delta toward New Orleans, this Gulf-inspired restaurant pulls out all the stops: gumbo, po'boys, jambalaya, shrimp and grits, oysters (char-grilled, fried, or in the shell), and even fried green tomato and shrimp rémoulade. Tables are first come, first served, but it's worth the wait—especially for weekend brunch: their build-your-own-Bloody-Mary bar has all the fixings for the hair of just about any dog. **Known for:** boozy brunch; oysters; Cajun classics. ⑤ *Average main: $15* ✉ *403 Main St., Franklin* ☎ *615/538–6001* ⊕ *www.eat55.com/franklin.*

Gray's on Main

$$$ | **SOUTHERN** | Before Gray's signature neon sign signaled innova-tive cocktails and comfort food, it was the sign for the pharmacy that occupied that space for 72 years. When Gray's the restau-rant moved into the building in 2012, they kept all the discarded memorabilia from the pharmacy and decorated the place with handwritten prescriptions and vintage pill bottles. **Known for:** innovative cocktails; historic building; upscale Southern dining. ⑤ *Average main: $30* ✉ *332 Main St., Franklin* ☎ *615/435–3603* ⊕ *www.graysonmain.com.*

McCreary's Irish Pub

$ | **IRISH** | **FAMILY** | If you need some place snug to get out of the rain, stop into McCreary's for shepherd's pie and a pint of Harp. Their selection of seafood fare, like the Galway fish sandwich, will give you that Irish coastal feeling even as far inland as Tennessee. **Known for:** fish-and-chips; shepherd's pie; Irish beer and whiskey.

Bonnaroo

Set on a 700-acre farm in Manchester, Tennessee, Bonnaroo Music & Arts Festival (⊕ www.bonnaroo.com) is about one hour southeast of Nashville. Paul McCartney, Stevie Wonder, and Bob Dylan are among the giants who have headlined, but many of today's top artists have also received a huge bump in recognition with iconic performances on the Bonnaroo stage. Witness local and regional acts become the next big thing at this career-launching musical event.

Ⓢ *Average main: $12* ⊠ *414 Main St., Franklin* ☏ *615/591–3197* ⊕ *www.mccrearyspub.com* ⊙ *No breakfast weekdays.*

Puckett's Grocery and Restaurant

$$ | SOUTHERN | FAMILY | If SunDrop and fried chicken set your heart aflutter, this Southern grocery store/restaurant combo is not to be missed. The cherrywood smoker out back churns out piles of pork, chicken, and brisket every day, and you can buy their signature barbecue rub and sauce at the register. **Known for:** barbecue pork, chicken, and brisket; Puckett's To Go packs (2 pounds of meat, 2 quart sides, and choice of bread); cobbler of the day. Ⓢ *Average main: $20* ⊠ *120 4th Ave. S, Franklin* ☏ *615/794–5527* ⊕ *puckettsgro.com/franklin.*

Red Pony

$$$ | SOUTHERN | This sophisticated eatery serves innovative Southern cuisine in an upscale environment for a dining experience that's elegant without compromising on fun. The menu changes six times a year to keep up with the freshest ingredients, and their award-winning wine menu shouldn't be overlooked. **Known for:** Southern cuisine; great wine list; shrimp and grits. Ⓢ *Average main: $30* ⊠ *408 Main St., Franklin* ☏ *615/595–7669* ⊕ *www.redponyrestaurant.com* ⊙ *Closed Sun. No lunch.*

☕ Coffee and Quick Bites

Biscuit Love

$$ | SOUTHERN | FAMILY | What goes better with buttermilk biscuits than a historical Queen Anne Victorian home? This one, affectionately known as the Corn House (after the Corn family who lived there from 1920 to 1980), is home to some of the best Southern brunch around, from the traditional (biscuits and sausage gravy with a side of cheese grits) to the unconventional (a biscuit burger with pimento cheese and tomato jam). **Known for:** cheese grits; historic location; gourmet biscuits. $ *Average main: $13* ⊠ *132 3rd Ave. S, Franklin* ☎ *615/905–0386* ⊕ *www.biscuitlove.com.*

The Coffee House at Second and Bridge

$ | **CAFÉ** | **FAMILY** | This coffeehouse is in a literal house, built in 1904 in Downtown Franklin, and during a good mid-morning lull, you can curl up with a cinnamon toast crepe in one of the sitting rooms and listen to a record or read a book. The library room is an especially good spot to pass a rainy afternoon with hot soup and a grown-up grilled cheese sandwich. **Known for:** crepes; sandwiches; cozy vibe. $ *Average main: $9* ⊠ *144 2nd Ave. N, Franklin* ☎ *615/465–6362* ⊕ *www.thecoffeehousefranklinshop.com.*

Five Daughters Bakery

$ | **BAKERY** | **FAMILY** | Located inside The Factory, this dreamy bakery seems to glow with soft pink light. They specialize in donuts, but not just any old donuts—these are 100-layer croissant-donut hybrids, cream-filled and glazed in flavors like chocolate–sea salt and maple-bacon (they also have a wide selection of paleo and vegan donuts). **Known for:** Hundred Layer Donuts; classic pastries; vegan and paleo donuts. $ *Average main: $5* ⊠ *230 Franklin Rd., Suite 11J, Franklin* ⌖ *Inside Bldg. 11* ☎ *615/933–9332* ⊕ *fivedaughtersbakery.com.*

Frothy Monkey

$ | **CAFÉ** | **FAMILY** | This coffeehouse opens first thing in the morning and stays open through breakfast, lunch, and dinner. There's plenty of porch space to enjoy your rosemary-honey latte outside, and in the evening they expand their drink menu to include craft beer and wine. **Known for:** locally roasted coffee; craft beer; comfort food. $ *Average main: $11* ⊠ *125 5th Ave. S, Franklin* ☎ *615/600–4756 Ext. 3* ⊕ *frothymonkey.com/locations/downtown-franklin.*

Honest Coffee Roasters

$ | **CAFÉ** | Franklin's first coffee-roasting company is an honest-to-goodness great place to get a cup of coffee. Located inside The Factory, Franklin's converted industrial shopping complex, it's also a great place to get an honest day's work done on your laptop. **Known for:** locally roasted coffee; excellent espresso; friendly service. $ *Average main: $5* ⊠ *230 Franklin Rd., Suite 11AB, Franklin* ⌖ *Inside Bldg. 11* ☎ *615/807–1726* ⊕ *www.honest.coffee.*

Meridee's Breadbasket

$ | **BAKERY** | **FAMILY** | As soon as you squeeze through the front door of Meridee's Breadbasket, you'll feel at home. The shelves are stocked with fresh-baked bread, and the cabinets are full of peanut butter pie and butterscotch bars. **Known for:** Viking bread;

chicken salad; pastries. $ *Average main: $7* ✉ *110 4th Ave. S, Franklin* ☎ *615/790–3755* ⊕ *www.merridees.com* ✆ *Closed Sun. No dinner.*

 Hotels

The Harpeth Hotel

$$ | HOTEL | Book your stay at The Harpeth Hotel to enjoy a beautiful historic space just steps away from the shopping and dining in Downtown Franklin. **Pros:** historic building; on-site dining and beverages; steps to Downtown Franklin. **Cons:** rooms book quickly; suites are pricey; could be loud during peak seasons. $ *Rooms from: $400* ✉ *130 2nd Ave. N, Franklin* ☎ *615/206–7510* ⊕ *harpeth-hotel.com* ⇥ *119 rooms* �’◉❜ *No Meals.*

 Nightlife

The Bunganut Pig

PUB | Franklin's oldest bar is an English-style pub known by locals as simply "the Pig." Downstairs, the stained glass–adorned door leads you into a dark Victorian-style bar, complete with a Beefeater statue, fireplace, and stuffed boar's head. Upstairs is a bit more modern, with pool tables and darts, as well as a second bar. On a nice day, the café-style seating outside feels especially old-world. ✉ *1143 Columbia Ave., Franklin* ☎ *615/794–4777* ⊕ *bunganutpig-franklin.com.*

JJ's Wine Bar

WINE BAR | This historic-home-turned-wine-bar in the heart of Downtown Franklin is overflowing with charm, inside and out, with countless cozy hideaways within and a wraparound porch with picturesque views of Main Street. Add soft music and even softer lighting, and it's the perfect spot to share intimate conversation and good wine. The center hallway is lined with wine-dispensing machines that offer 1-ounce, 5-ounce, and 8-ounce pours of 28 different wines. There's also a full bar if you'd rather order a whole bottle of wine, small plates, or cocktails. ✉ *206 E. Main St., Franklin* ☎ *615/942–5033* ⊕ *www.jjswinebar.com* ✆ *Closed Sun. and Mon.*

The Legendary Kimbro's Pickin' Parlor

LIVE MUSIC | Broken jukeboxes, dusty lamps, countless hand-scribbled mementos thumbtacked to the walls—and, of course, some of the best live music in Franklin. This legendary restaurant, bar, and music venue puts on a show every night of the week; expect to pay a cover to watch the band. Sundays are open-stage: just bring an instrument, and they'll rotate the players. For great

Opened in 1937, the Franklin Theatre offers concerts, live theater performances, and movies.

food, local beer, and a genuine everybody-knows-your-name vibe, Kimbro's is one of a kind. ✉ *214 S. Margin St., Franklin* ☎ *615/567–3877* ⊕ *www.legendarykimbros.com.*

O' Be Joyful

BARS | This bar serves up essential American staples every night of the week: hamburgers, hot dogs, beer, and whiskey. They don't get too inventive with their menu, preferring instead to perfect timeless classics like a black-and-bleu burger with an old-fashioned. And with one of Franklin's largest whiskey collections, you'll never have to order the same Sazerac twice. ✉ *328 Main St., Franklin* ⊕ *objfranklin.com.*

 Performing Arts

The Franklin Theatre

CONCERTS | FAMILY | The Franklin Theatre's iconic neon sign is the centerpiece of Downtown Franklin. Opened in 1937 and refurbished in 2011, the theater now offers an ongoing lineup of concerts, live theater performances, and movies (mostly second-run and classics). You can purchase beer and wine at the concession stand, as well as Showtime chocolate bars, created exclusively for The Franklin by local chocolatier, Schakolad. ✉ *419 Main St., Franklin* ☎ *615/538–2076* ⊕ *www.franklintheatre.com.*

Pull-Tight Players Theater

PERFORMANCE VENUES | FAMILY | The Pull-Tight Players formed in 1968 and set up shop in their current location in 1985. They produce six main-stage shows each year in their intimate theater on 2nd Avenue, which in years past has been everything from a church to a grocery store. Between the small size of the theater and the popularity of the productions, it's best to get tickets in advance. ✉ *112 2nd Ave. S, Franklin* ☎ *615/791–5007* ⊕ *www. pull-tight.com.*

 # Shopping

Carpe Diem

ANTIQUES & COLLECTIBLES | This small but mighty record store offers an impressive collection of vintage vinyls, antique doodads, and art. Run by the same folks as Kimbro's Pickin' Parlor next door, it definitely has a similar vibe: curated junk, gritty rock and roll, and down-home family lovin'. ✉ *212 S. Margin St., Franklin* ☎ *615/429– 0157* ⊕ *www.carpediem212.com* ☾ *Closed Sun. and Mon.*

Johnnie Q

JEWELRY & WATCHES | No, you haven't died and gone to earring heaven. You've just stepped into Johnnie Q, a shop with so many beautiful pieces of handmade jewelry and vintage accessories, you may briefly feel transported to a higher sartorial plane. Featuring the designs of jewelry makers from across the United States and Canada (including five local designers), every piece is totally unique and certifiably eye-popping. ✉ *317 Main St., Franklin* ☎ *615/794–2763* ⊕ *www.johnnieq.com.*

Landmark Booksellers

BOOKS | FAMILY | There are so many rows of bookshelves filling out this snug bookstore, you'll feel like you're burrowing through tunnels of leather-bound volumes. Landmark Booksellers specializes in old, out-of-print, and rare books, but they have some new books, as well. You'll find plenty of Southern Americana here, as well as books that focus on regional history, culture, and literature. And all 35,000 books are nestled inside the oldest standing commercial building in Franklin (built in 1808). It's a bibliophile's dream. ✉ *114 E. Main St., Franklin* ☎ *615/791–6400* ⊕ *www.landmark- booksellers.com.*

Rare Prints Gallery

ANTIQUES & COLLECTIBLES | For rare botanical prints, vintage maps, and lithographs dating back to the 1500s, Rare Prints Gallery is second to none. Don't be too intimidated by the art-gallery-meets-museum air of the place. From medieval lynx prints to *Vanity Fair* covers from 1871, they have something for every price range. ✉ *420 Main St., Franklin* ☎ *615/472–1980* ⊕ *rareprintsgal- lery.com* ☾ *Closed Sun. and Mon.*

White's Mercantile

GENERAL STORE | FAMILY | This folksy-chic boutique has the feel of an upscale general store. Owned and curated by country singer/songwriter Holly Williams (daughter of Hank Williams Jr.), every item reflects her style. There are decanter sets with deer and geese on them, candles scented like leather and tobacco, and flannel throw pillows fit for any frontiersman with taste. ⊠ *345 Main St., Franklin* ☎ *615/721–8028* ⊕ *whitesmercantile.com.*

Bellevue

13 miles southwest of Nashville via I–40.

Head to Bellevue, southwest of Downtown, to get some fresh air and enjoy some wide-open country spaces.

The Bellevue area is home to a number of natural offerings, including the botanical garden and art museum Cheekwood Estate and Gardens, as well as the beginning of the Natchez Trace Parkway driving and cycling route—follow it to its end and you'll find yourself in Natchez, Mississippi, 444 miles away.

A trip to Bellevue wouldn't be complete without a stop at the famous Loveless Cafe, one of the best and most celebrated Southern restaurants in the Nashville area. The Loveless is particularly famous for its biscuits, which the establishment serves with an assortment of homemade jams and jellies. No matter your tastes, there's sure to be something to satisfy your appetite, perhaps after an afternoon spent treasure hunting at nearby used-media mecca, McKay's.

GETTING HERE AND AROUND

Bellevue sits about 13 miles southwest of Downtown Nashville. Public transit options are limited, so your best bet for visiting Bellevue is driving or using a rideshare. Once there, most destinations are spread out and it will be necessary to drive from place to place, so keep that in mind if using rideshares, as fees may add up quickly.

Sights

Cheekwood Estate and Gardens

GARDEN | FAMILY | At the center of this sprawling 55-acre botanical garden is a Georgian-style limestone mansion-turned-art gallery, enclosed by clipped lawns, terraced gardens, and an ancient-looking reflection pool. In addition to the collection of paintings and photographs inside the mansion, the Carell Woodland Sculpture

The Cheekwood Estate and Gardens in Bellevue offers seasonal garden displays ranging from thousands of tulips in the spring to Cheekwood Harvest in the fall.

Trail takes you down a 0.9-mile path of outdoor art pieces. There are seasonal garden displays, as well—including 150,000 blooming tulip bulbs in the spring and 5,000 chrysanthemums in the fall—so there's always something new to enjoy no matter what time of year you visit. ✉ *1200 Forrest Park Dr., Bellevue* ☎ *615/356–8000* ⊕ *cheekwood.org* 🖼 *$26 for gardens; $29 for gardens and mansion* 🕙 *Closed Mon.*

🍴 Restaurants

The Loveless Cafe
$ | **SOUTHERN** | **FAMILY** | Southwest of Nashville on Highway 100, The Loveless Cafe serves up its famous scratch-made biscuits and country ham every day of the week. Long waits for a table are typical, so be prepared to do some shopping and play a round of cornhole while you wait. **Known for:** biscuits; country ham; fried chicken. 💲 *Average main: $12* ✉ *8400 Hwy. 100, Bellevue* ☎ *615/646–9700* ⊕ *lovelesscafe.com.*

🛍 Shopping

McKay's Nashville
MUSIC | **FAMILY** | This two-story warehouse is the used-media mecca of the South. You can buy, sell, or trade everything from books to movies, CDs, records, games, electronics, and even instruments. If you're overwhelmed by the sheer number of aisles to explore, start with the bookshelf next to the stairs. That's where

you'll find new releases that are up for grabs. ✉ *636 Old Hickory Blvd., Bellevue* ☎ *615/353–2595* ⊕ *www.mckaybooks.com.*

Activities

Ford Ice Center

ICE SKATING | If you're a sports fan on a budget, the Nashville Predators' practice sessions at the ice center are open to the public; the Predators also practice at the Centennial Sportsplex near Centennial Park. Dates vary but are posted on their website as they become available. ✉ *7638B Hwy 70 S, Bellevue* ☎ *615/744–6640* ⊕ *www.fordicecenter.com.*

Belle Meade

10 miles southwest of Nashville via I–40.

Head southwest of Nashville and you'll encounter Belle Meade, a tony neighborhood home to some of the area's wealthiest residents. Some of that pedigree can be traced back to the Belle Meade Mansion, a historic home now part of the Belle Meade Historic Site & Winery. Visit the site for various educational tours of the mansion, and enjoy a glass of wine as you digest what you've learned.

After your visit, drive around to marvel at the many estates and mansions, some of which are the largest in the area.

GETTING HERE

Belle Meade sits on the southeast edge of Nashville city limits and is about 10 miles from Downtown. You'll want to drive or take a rideshare to get there, as public transit in the area is particularly limited. Once there, you'll likely drive from destination to destination, as much of Belle Meade is not pedestrian-friendly. Visitors to more involved destinations like Belle Meade Historic Site & Winery can easily spend an afternoon in one spot, though.

Sights

Belle Meade Historic Site & Winery

HISTORIC SIGHT | FAMILY | The tall limestone pillars of Belle Meade are markers of a bygone era. Today, this historic mansion is a museum at the center of 30 acres of smooth green pastures west of Nashville. In addition to the Greek Revival–style mansion, the property includes a winery and more than 10 outbuildings.

General tours are available, or you can take a themed tour like The Journey to Jubilee, which tells the stories of the people who were enslaved at Belle Meade Plantation. A complimentary wine tasting is offered at the end of your tour, or you can book a private tasting separately. ✉ *110 Leake Ave., Belle Meade* ☎ *615/356–0501* ⊕ *visitbellemeade.com* 🎫 *From $28 for mansion tour; from $25 for Journey to Jubilee Tour* ⊙ *Last tour at 4 pm daily.*

Warner Park Nature Center

NATURE PRESERVE | If you want to get down and dirty and learn about birds, insects, and trees, head to the more than 3,100 acres that make up the Warner Parks. Here you'll find picnic spots, a dog park, hiking and biking trails, an equestrian center, golf courses, and the Nature Center, which hosts numerous activities—many of which are free—like guided bird walks, group meditation classes, and holiday-themed events. ✉ *7311 Hwy. 100, Belle Meade* ⊹ *9 miles southwest of downtown Nashville* ☎ *615/862–8555* ⊕ *www.nashville.gov/departments/parks/parks/warner-parks.*

Lynchburg

75 miles southeast of Nashville.

If you're looking to leave the hustle and bustle of Nashville for the day, a quick and scenic drive to Lynchburg is a great way to experience Tennessee culture and take in some beautiful natural sights.

Visitors flock to Lynchburg to tour the famous Jack Daniel's Distillery, a holy site for whiskey lovers. Visitors can enjoy an educational walking tour of the distillery grounds, which includes a stop in Jack Daniel's office.

The surrounding town is small and quaint, with a small town square playing host to shops and restaurants. If you're looking for souvenirs, head this way—the distillery itself offers little for sale. Once you've worked up a sweat on your walking tour, dine at Miss Mary Bobo's Restaurant for some authentic Southern eats.

GETTING HERE

Lynchburg is 75 miles southeast of Nashville, making for a nearly 1½-hour drive. If you don't have a car, you'll want to rent one, as ride-share fees would be quite costly. Once in Lynchburg, much of the town is walkable, so you'll be able to park in one spot and take in the sights without needing to drive around very much.

Sights

★ Jack Daniel's Distillery

DISTILLERY | This quaint town is home to the Jack Daniel's Distillery, the oldest registered distillery in the country, where you can observe every step of the art of making sour-mash whiskey. Tours are lively and informative and involve a lot of walking throughout the beautiful grounds (including the spring that continues to source the whiskey) with stops at several buildings—among them Jack Daniel's office. Some tour options include sampling flights of different whiskeys. Note that even though Lynchburg is a dry town, you can buy a personalized bottle at the distillery's shop, and the whiskey inside it is considered "free," a loophole in the law. ⊠ *182 Lynchburg Hwy., Lynchburg* ✛ *Off Rte. 55* ☎ *931/759–4221* ⊕ *www.jackdaniels. com* 🖾 *Free.*

> ## Don't Open That Bottle! 🍸
>
> While you can buy all the Jack Daniel's you want at the distillery, don't plan on popping any bottles while you're still in Lynchburg. Funnily enough, the town is situated within Moore County, which is completely dry.

🍽 Restaurants

Miss Mary Bobo's Boarding House and Restaurant

$$$ | **AMERICAN** | Diners flock to this two-story 1867 white-frame house (listed on the National Register of Historic Places) with a white picket fence to feast family-style at tables laden with Southern favorites like fried chicken, meat loaf, fried catfish, stuffed vegetables, and sliced tomatoes, along with corn on the cob, homemade biscuits, cornbread, pecan pie, lemon icebox pie, fruit cobblers, and strawberry shortcake. And, yes, the famous whiskey distilled nearby is used in some of the recipes. **Known for:** historic home; authentic Southern cuisine; Jack Daniel's–inspired recipes. ⑤ *Average main: $30* ⊠ *295 Main St., Lynchburg* ✛ *Half a block from Public Sq.* ☎ *931/759–7394* ⊕ *www.jackdaniels.com/ en-us/visit-us* ⊗ *No dinner.*

🛍 Shopping

Lynchburg Hardware & General Store

GENERAL STORE | More a souvenir shop than a hardware store, here you'll find lots of Jack Daniel's memorabilia and other local products. It's a good place to stop after visiting the distillery, as you won't find any souvenirs there. However, you won't find any booze here, so if you want to bring some home from the source, best to buy it at the distillery. ✉ *52 Mechanic St. S, Lynchburg* ☎ *888/221–5225* ⊕ *www.jackdaniels.com/en-us/visit-us.*

Arrington Vineyards

30 miles southeast of Nashville.

You can't miss the advertisements for Arrington Vineyards at the Nashville International Airport. Just 40 minutes south of Nashville, it's a great spot for a day trip or an afternoon outing if you need a break from the honky-tonk of Lower Broadway. Wine tastings are available in the tasting lodge, and, from April through October, there's live bluegrass and jazz music on the weekends.

For something more casual, you can buy a couple of bottles and grab snacks at the gift shop (or bring food from one of the great restaurants in town), and have a picnic on the lawn. Another picnic option is food delivered to you by Simply Living Life (⊕ *simply-living-life.com*), which has a special catering menu for vineyard guests.

GETTING HERE AND AROUND

Arrington Vineyards is 30 miles southeast of Nashville, so you'll either want to drive yourself or use a rideshare (though expect the latter option to be an expensive ride, given the distance). Depending on what time you leave, you may encounter rush-hour traffic, which could mean nearly an hour's drive. To avoid rush hour, try not to drive to or from Arrington between 3 and 6 pm.

Sights

Arrington Vineyards

WINERY | Beautiful views of the rolling hills of Middle Tennessee surround this 75-acre property co-owned by Kix Brooks of Brooks & Dunn. In addition to free tastings, Arrington Vineyards hosts live music on weekends (April to November), bonfires in chilly weather, and other seasonal events. Though there isn't a restaurant on the grounds, the gift shop stocks gourmet cheeses and truffles, and visitors are welcome to bring picnics and make use of the tables throughout the grounds. ✉ *6211 Patton Rd., Arrington* ☎ *615/395–0102* ⊕ *arringtonvineyards.com.*

Index

Photo Credits

Front Cover: Nikreates/Alamy Stock Photo [Descr.: Betty Boots store Lower Broadway Nashville]. **Back cover, from left to right:** FKevin Ruck/Shutterstock. 11photo/Shutterstock. Joshua Resnick/Shutterstock. **Spine:** Surpasspro/Dreamstime. **Interior, from left to right:** Joseph Hendrickson/Shutterstock (1). Schneidersimages/Dreamstime (2-3). **Chapter 1: Experience Nashville:** Susanne Pommer/Shutterstock (6-7). Jejim/Shutterstock (8-9). Nashville Convention & Visitors Corp (9). Patrick Green/Tennessee Tourism (9). Nashville Convention & Visitors Corp (10). Nashville Convention & Visitors Corp (10). Grace Boto/Nashville Convention & Visitors Corp (11). Lithian/Shutterstock (12). River Queen Voyages/Nashville Convention & Visitors Corp (12). Nashville Convention & Visitors Corp (12). Nashville Convention & Visitors Corp (13). Scott F Smith/Shutterstock (13). Lfistand47/Dreamstime (14). Steve Lowy/Nashville Convention and Visitors Corp (14). Nashville Convention & Visitors Corp (14). Nashville Convention & Visitors Corp (15). Steve Lowy/Nashville Convention & Visitors Corp (18). Nashville Convention & Visitors Corp (18). Grant Exline/CMA (18). Nashville Convention & Visitors Corp (18). Rolf52/Dreamstime (19). Nashville Convention & Visitors Corp (20). Nathan Zucker/Visit Franklin (20). Jejim/Shutterstock (20). Joshua Cox/TN State Museum (20). NMAAM/Nashville Convention & Visitors Corp (21). Nashville Convention & Visitors Corp (22). Nashville Convention & Visitors Corp (23). **Chapter 3: Downtown and SoBro:** Amy Cicconi/Alamy Stock Photo (51). Fotoluminate/Dreamstime (54). Fotoluminate LLC/Shutterstock (58). Mihai_Andritoiu/Shutterstock (60). Brenda Kean/Shutterstock (71). Jon Kraft/Shutterstock (75). **Chapter 4: The Gulch:** Travelpix/Alamy Stock Photo (83). Chad Robertson Media/Shutterstock (87). Pins Mechanical Co/Nashville CVC (100). **Chapter 5: Germantown and Marathon Village:** KennStilger47/Shutterstock (103). Nashville CVC (107). Courtesy of the Tennessee State Museum (110). **Chapter 6: Sylvan Park and The Nations:** Courtesy of Nashville Convention & Visitors Corp (121). Frothy Monkey/NashvilleCVC (124). Courtesy of Nashville Convention & Visitors Corp (135). **Chapter 7: Midtown, West End, Music Row, and Edgehill:** Fotoluminate LLC/Shutterstock (137). Bo Shen/Shutterstock (141). Courtesy of Nashville Convention & Visitors Corp (145). **Chapter 8: Hillsboro Village and Belmont:** Bluebird Cafe/NashvilleCVC (155). Jim Diamond/Alamy Stock Photo (158). Gallery of Iconic Guitars/NashvilleCVC (163). **Chapter 9: 12South:** Richard Ellis/Alamy Stock Photo (169). The Butter Milk Ranch/NashvilleCVC (175). ImogeneandWillie/NashvilleCVC (178). **Chapter 10: Melrose and Berry Hill:** J. Carlee Adams/Alamy Stock Photo (181). Courtesy of Paddywax Candle Bar (189). **Chapter 11: Wedgewood-Houston:** Courtesy of Nashville Convention & Visitors Corp (195). Courtesy of Nashville Convention & Visitors Corp (199). Anna Zeitlin/Zeitgeist (202). **Chapter 12: East Nashville:** Grimeys/NashvilleCVC (209). CPC Collection/Alamy Stock Photo (213). Nashville Convention & Visitors Corp (216). **Chapter 13: Opryland and Music Valley:** Courtesy Tennessee Tourism (227). Courtesy of Nashville Convention & Visitors Corp (233). Courtesy of Nashville Convention & Visitors Corp (236). **Chapter 14: Day Trips from Nashville:** Csfotoimages/iStockphoto (239). Marcus E Jones/Shutterstock (243). Images-USA/Alamy Stock Photo (245). Fotoluminate LLC/Shutterstock (254). Courtesy of Tennessee Tourism (257). **About Our Writers:** All photos are courtesy of the writers except for the following: Hilli Levin, courtesy of Jonathan Pfahl; Rachel Heatherly, courtesy of John Cole Photography.

*Every effort has been made to trace the copyright holders, and we apologize in advance for any accidental errors. We would be happy to apply the corrections in the following edition of this publication.

Notes